DREAMTIME

THE ABORIGINAL HERITAGE

Paintings by Ainslie Roberts

Text by Melva Jean Roberts

ETT IMPRINT

Exile Bay

First published by ETT Imprint, Exile Bay in 2024

All paintings and line drawings copyright Ainslie Roberts
Text by Melva Jean Roberts

First published by Rigby in 1981

First electronic edition ETT Imprint 2024

ETT IMPRINT
PO Box R1906
Royal Exchange NSW 1225 Australia

ISBN 978-1-923205-38-3 (pback)
ISBN 978-1-923205-39-0 (ebook)

CONTENTS

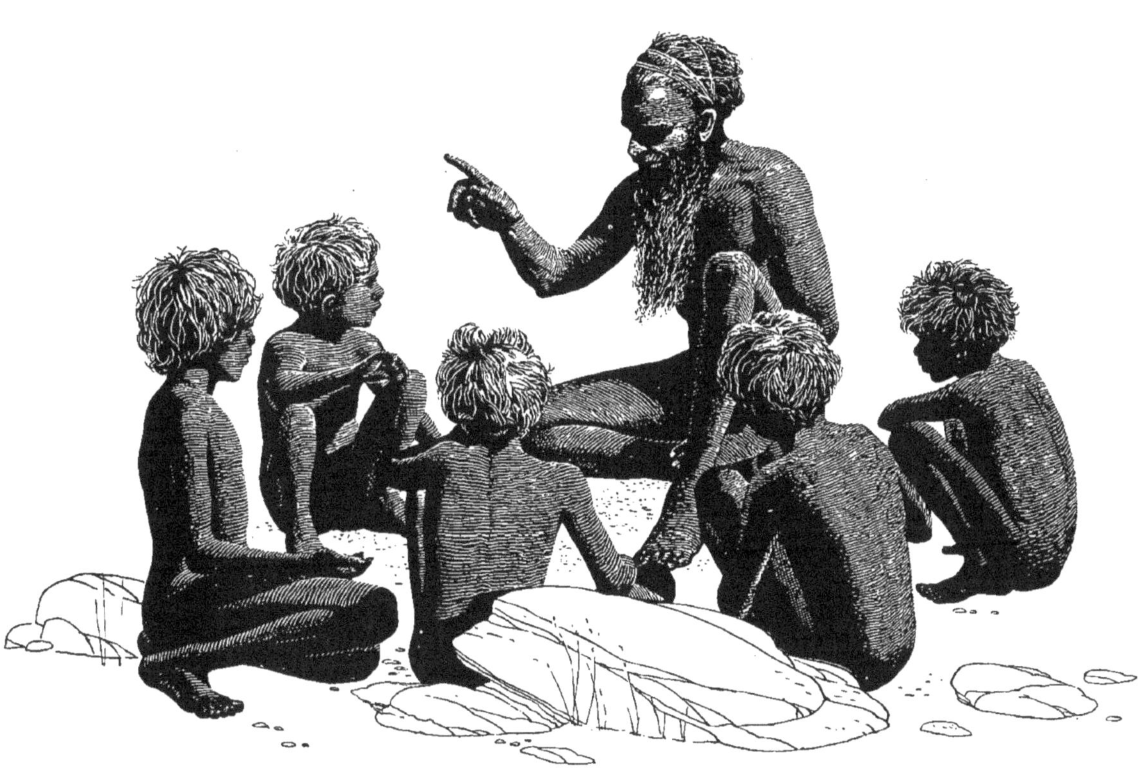

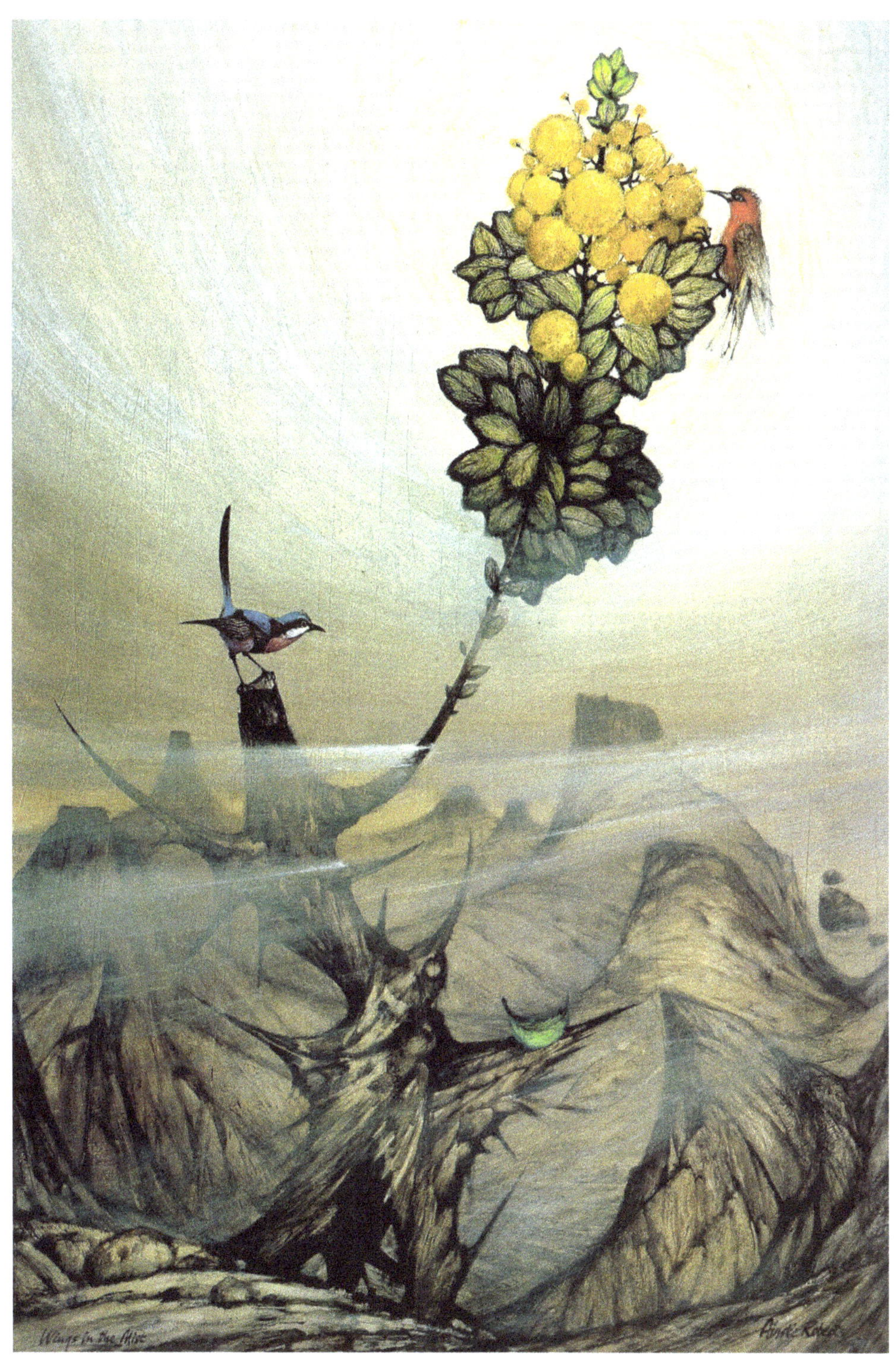

Dr D.C. McCarthy

INTRODUCTION: WINGS IN THE MIST

LIKE THE WINGS OF BRIGHT BIRDS which flutter momentarily out of enshrouding mists, and vanish again after giving us no more than a tantalising glimpse, the myths created by the Aboriginal people of Australia provide us with some of the rare clues to the manufactured culture of a unique lifestyle.

Charles Barrett, in his book *The Bunyip,* expressed the reason for our lack of knowledge when he wrote 'Today, we are gleaners in the field of Aboriginal folklore, which was ripe for harvesting a century ago; but the workers were so few that most of the rich harvest was wasted.'

That which has been recorded, although only a fraction of the whole, is all the more precious because of its rarity. This book presents a selection of interpretations of Aboriginal myths, in words and paintings, in the hope of aiding a closer understanding of the Dreamtime beliefs which are the basis of Aboriginal culture.

The mystical conditions known to Aborigines collectively as the Dreamtime, and to an individual as his Dreaming, defy rational explanation to people reared in a Western-style civilisation. Nevertheless it is possible for such people to understand with their hearts even if they reject the evidence presented by their minds.

Primitive instincts lie buried in even the most sophisticated adult, and in those blurred areas of the mind known as the unconscious there are powerful forces which most of us glimpse from time to time. The difference between ourselves and tribal Aborigines is that we have erected barriers of logic which prevent us from seeing clearly into our own Dreaming.

The Dreaming of each Aboriginal encompassed everything with which he had been associated since the dawn of consciousness. Before that, it extended into the Dreamtime. His Dreaming was a blend of many different factors and influences partaking of both spiritual and physical life, bound together so tightly that it became the core of his being.

His Dreaming included the laws of nature, of his totem, and of his tribe. It comprised his weapons and his skill in using them, his cunning as a hunter and courage as a warrior, and his obligations to people of every age group within his tribe. In the emotional sense it was confirmed by his initiation into. the age-old rites and ceremonies. It guided his hand as he worked with wood or stone, inspired him artistically in painting, carving, and body decoration, and leapt within his body as he performed the songs and dances to placate or worship the unseen powers.

Interwoven with all these factors was the feeling which every creature knows in greater or lesser degree; that which has been called the Spirit of Place. Biologists believe that birds are 'imprinted' with this feeling within an hour of being hatched, so that for the rest of their lives they are able to return unerringly to their birthplace. Other animals, and all people living in a state of nature, feel it with an instinctive strength. We who have surrendered our instincts to technology feel it only vaguely, though most people feel themselves to be more 'at home' in one specific place than any other in the world. This feeling pervaded the consciousness of the tribal Aborigines to such depths that it dictated their entire way of life.

A man's Dreaming merged with the Dreamtime.

Everything in life, whether tangible or intangible, had been influenced by the people of the Dreamtime: the creators of the world and those who lived in the beginning. Therefore, everything that he saw, did, felt, and experienced was to some degree sacred. The landscape in which an Aboriginal lived was shaped in the form he could observe because the Dreamtime people made it so. Countless features had a Dreamtime explanation: the exploits of Dreamtime heroes and villains had influenced the shape of rocks, the colours of the earth, the windings of a watercourse. Such features were tangible memorials of his tribe's creative ancestors and mainstays of its emotional life.

Together with these unchanging features there were those which showed a periodic change. The seasons of the year; the heavenly bodies; the light and shade which varied with each moment of the day; the ages of man; birth, life, and death. All of these had specific reasons for the ways in which they manifested themselves, and the reasons were enshrined in the stories of the Dreamtime.

The same applied to every living creature, whether bird, fish, mammal, insect, plant, or reptile. Many of them, in the Dreamtime, had been Aborigines or had acted under the impulse of human emotions. Their deeds or misdeeds during the creation era are reflected by their behaviour in non-human form. Each of them must forever conform to a pattern established in the Dreamtime, and these patterns could always be found in the body of Dreamtime lore handed down by the storytellers.

The emotional impact of this body of lore was immense. Its overall effect was one of complete security. A man knew, always and forever, his exact place in society and in his physical and spiritual world.

Together with these unchanging features there were those which showed a periodic change. The seasons of the year; the heavenly bodies; the light and shade which varied with each moment of the day; the ages of man; birth, life, and death. All of these had specific reasons for the ways in which they manifested themselves, and the reasons were enshrined in the stories of the Dreamtime.

The same applied to every living creature, whether bird, fish, mammal, insect, plant, or reptile. Many of them, in the Dreamtime, had been Aborigines or had acted under the impulse of human emotions. Their deeds or misdeeds during the creation era are reflected by their behaviour in non-human form. Each of them must forever conform to a pattern established in the Dreamtime, and these patterns could always be found in the body of Dreamtime lore handed down by the storytellers.

The emotional impact of this body of lore was immense. Its overall effect was one of complete security. A man knew, always and forever, his exact place in society and in his physical and spiritual world

As he grew from infancy into adolescence and passed through maturity into old age he knew that he would advance through the hierarchy of his tribe, with rights which no one questioned and obligations to be automatically fulfilled. He belonged to a totem which dictated the woman he could marry, the creatures he could hunt, and the ceremonies he should perform. He lived in a tribal area reserved to him and his people, with the secure knowledge that no one would ever challenge his right to be there. He would not leave it, or permit others to enter, without negotiations performed in accordance with ancient laws. And he knew that if he transgressed any of the laws of his community, punishment was inevitable.

In all these circumstances, he moved through life with the supreme confidence of a man who knows that he is surrounded by the spiritual beings who established his world. He was not called upon to believe in an unseen god: he could see proof positive of the beings in which he believed. He saw their marks on the earth. He observed them, in the form of plants and animals, obeying the patterns laid down for them in the Dreamtime. He felt them in the changes of the seasons and watched them as they moved through the skies in the form of sun, moon, stars, planets, and clouds. All life was one and he was a part of life, bound immutably within the great design worked out for him by his creation ancestors.

During the 'fatal impact' of Europeans on many other races, from Incas to Tahitians, a myriad age-old cultures were shattered or perverted. The tragedy of the Aborigines is that, during the period in which they broke under the impact, only a few Europeans had sufficient insight to discern the subtle depths of Aboriginal culture. The Aborigines were regarded as a kind of animal: the only dangerous animal on the continent, and predators upon the settlers' flocks and herds. They did not even have the romantic aura of Red Indians or South Sea islanders or the martial glamour of the Zulus and Maoris. Their art was weird and primitive to the sophisticated eye. Their crafts were limited to the simple use of natural materials. If they had any social organisation it was not easily apparent. They were Stone Age man.

As such, they were swept aside. They had nothing tangible to offer, they made poor servants, and they were of no use to Europeans intent upon making their fortunes. The tragedy is that when so many of the Aboriginal tribes were eliminated, they took with them one of mankind's last opportunities to study the very wellsprings of the human race.

It is now known that a thriving Aboriginal culture existed in Australia as much as 40,000 years ago, and possibly even earlier. This is not guesswork, but a fact proven by the carbon-dating process which enables scientists to fix an exact age upon bones and artefacts. But these remains cannot speak. They can act only as parts of a jigsaw puzzle, to be laboriously pieced together by anthropologists. But less than two centuries ago it would have been possible to talk directly to the inheritors of a culture reaching back through the mists of time, preserved almost intact within a continent which showed, by countless examples of its flora and fauna, that it was utterly different from the rest of the world.

That opportunity was lost. Nowadays, when white Australians have awoken to a dramatic awareness of the people who lived here before us, we must attempt to peer through the mists by interpreting the few remaining clues. Among the most colourful and revealing are the stories of the Dreamtime.

The most intriguing aspect of these stories is that so many of them, including some collected in this volume and others in its series, show a close relationship to the spiritual inheritance of other peoples of the world. The most obvious example is the recurrence of a Creator, or of what must be loosely termed the Creation Ancestors, in one after another of the Dreamtime tales. This being takes a variety of forms, and acts in a variety of ways. But there is always a basic resemblance between the Creator in the Dreamtime stories and the Creator who is a dominant figure in other religions or folklores.

Most of the great religions of the world, and some of the lesser ones, follow much the same theme. In the beginning there was nothing until a mysterious Creator formed heaven and earth, ocean, land, and all their creatures. The Aborigines had this belief and the story 'In the Beginning' gives explicit details of the Creator's activities. When he decided to create man he used clay, the very material used as a synonym for the transient nature of man in some Christian doctrine.

It may be argued that it is somewhat sacrilegious to compare the enshrined lore of the great religions of Europe and Asia with those of the primitive nomads of Australia. The idea that anyone could truly believe in the Rainbow Serpent, the great snake who ascended into the skies, may seem ridiculous. Yet hundreds of millions of Christians found no difficulty in believing implicitly that a snake spoke to Eve, that the sun stood still for Joshua and the Red Sea parted for Moses, that angels spoke from the sky and a child was born to a virgin. These and similar miracles are pillars of the Christian faith, and, even though modern thought may offer rational explanations, a belief in such miracles brought comfort to countless people over the centuries.

Perhaps the most important thing is that mankind should believe in something: that out of the struggling mystery of his life he should use the mysterious powers of imagination to create some guideposts whereby his spiritual life can find direction. This is exactly what the Aborigines did in their Dreamtime stories. The fascinating thing is that, in so many ways, they shimmer upon the edges of beliefs similar to those held by other religions. When the whole of mankind lived in the Stone Age, then perhaps these Dreamtime stories were the common currency of belief. If so, then the other races of the world followed them along different paths while the Aborigines, locked away from the world in their forgotten continent, preserved these beliefs intact.

A number of the stories, like those of the Old Testament, are moral parables which deal with the lusts of the flesh and the darker emotions of mankind. The Biblical story of Cain and Abel stresses the fact that brothers do not necessarily love one another: that of 'The Fighting Brothers' does the same. The basic principle of all religions is that life does not cease after death, but it is rarely described as beautifully as in the Aboriginal myth 'Birth of the Butterflies', which tells how reincarnation was deduced from the metamorphosis of caterpillars into butterflies. Primitive men in every land would have seen the same example of life returning, in a different form, to creatures apparently dead. Perhaps the story of the butterflies inspired some long-forgotten race to a belief in the theory of life after death, and thus to the foundation of a religion from which all others have stemmed. There is certainly a close link between religion and natural phenomena. The festival of Easter uses an egg as the symbol of rebirth.

The belief that people of all nations share the same mythical life is not new and has been explored exhaustively. And, despite the cold logic of science, mythical and mystical beliefs have an abiding appeal and spiritual comfort for much of mankind.

The fascination of Aboriginal mythology is that these 'Stone Age' men preserved a complex spiritual culture in which the Dreamtime myths, an integral part of this culture, may without any great stretch of the imagination be associated with the mystical life of peoples in other parts of the world. From this, one may play with the corollary that Aboriginal mythology derives not only from the Dreamtime of the Aborigines, but from the Dreamtime of the human race as a whole. It is not difficult to believe that the Aborigines, isolated on a continent which some scientists believe was once connected to the rest of the world, maintained a spiritual culture at one time common to all humanity but since diverted into many different channels.

If this is so, then the Dreamtime stories may demonstrate a deeper brotherhood than we are yet willing to concede. It is a brotherhood stretching back to the very dawn of time, when all men were of one race and all sought the keys to mysteries which still remain concealed.

THE RAIN-MAKERS

The mythology of the Australian Aborigines was the cornerstone on which their way of life was built. Their myths perpetuated the traditions and beliefs, the rituals and ceremonies, that sustained and guided them for tens of thousands of years.

One of these beliefs handed down from the Dreamtime days was a sturdy faith in the magical powers of the rain-makers. These powers were most important to Aboriginal welfare in central Australia; that harsh land of extremes where water is the essence of life.

The Aborigines of these desert regions displayed an uncanny instinct in their search for water, but in times of drought the rain-makers became awesome personalities. They were the experts whose gifts often meant the difference between life and death to the tribes.

The Arunta, Ilpirra, Kaitish, and Unmatjira tribes, who occupied the dry areas north and south of Alice Springs, had many Dreamtime ancestors. Among these mythical people, Irria, Inungamella and Ilpailurkna were potent rain-makers; men whose gifts could make the deserts bloom.

Irria's rain-making rituals centred around the black cockatoo, the bird appointed by the Dreamtime spirits to bring thunder and lightning down from the north. Only Irria could wear cockatoo feathers in his hair.

Irria taught Inungamella how to make rain, and gave him many gypsum stones which, when correctly sung over, produced the rain clouds which they resembled.

Ilpailurkna's magical power was associated with the yamstick. This was painted with red ochre and decorated with white feathers which, when blown off into the sky, were transformed into clouds.

And where these ancestors established totem rain-centres, their namesakes used the same magic to conjure up rain well into the present century. Even today these areas are lush and green and have a relatively high rainfall.

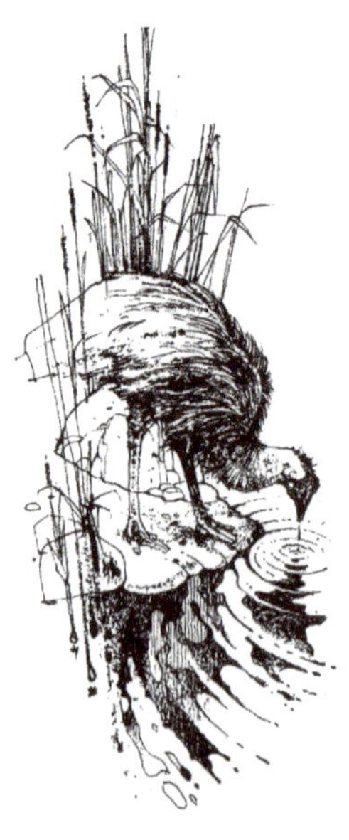

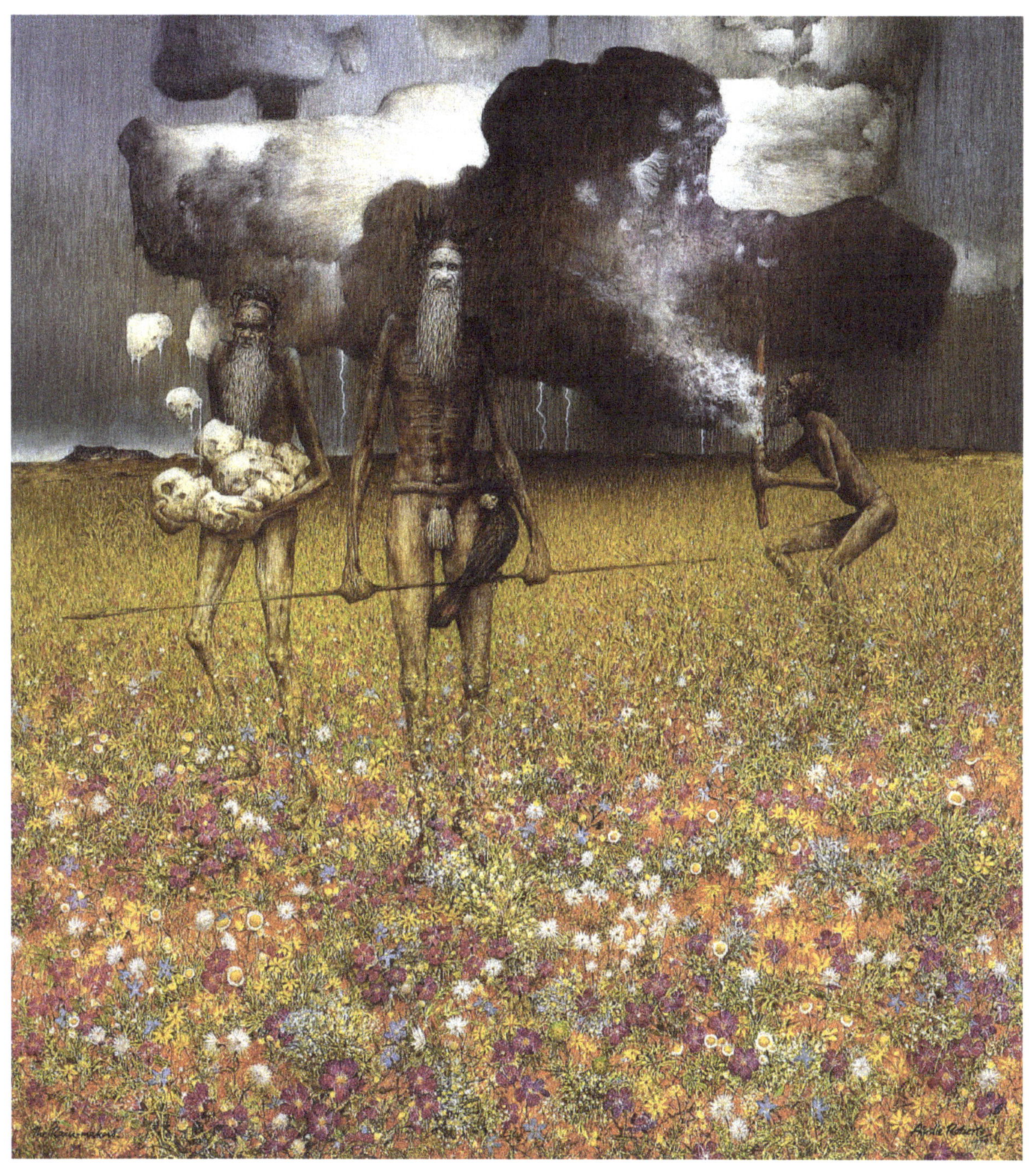

Mr and Mrs S. Olenick

LAUGHTER AT DAWN

When the world was young, everyone had to search for food in the dim light of the moon, for there was no sun. Then came the time when the emu and the brolga, both of whom were sitting on a nest of eggs, had a violent argument over the excellence of their chicks. Finally the angry brolga ran to the nest of her rival and, taking one of her eggs, hurled it into the sky, where it shattered against a pile of sticks gathered by the sky-people.

The yolk of the egg, bursting into flame, caused such a huge fire that its light revealed, for the first time, the beauty of the world beneath. When the people in the sky saw this beauty, they decided that the inhabitants below should have day and night.

So every night the sky-people collected a pile of dry wood, ready to be set alight as soon as the morning star appeared. But this scheme was not successful, for if the day was cloudy, the star could not be seen, and no-one lit the fire. So the sky-people asked the kookaburra, who had a strong voice, to call them every morning.

When this bird's rollicking laughter is first heard, the fire in the sky throws out but little heat or light. By noon, when the whole pile of wood is burning, the heat is intense. Later, the fire begins to die down until, at sunset, only a few embers remain to colour the western sky.

It is a strict rule of the tribes that nobody may imitate the kookaburra's call, for such an act might so offend the bird that he would remain silent. Then darkness would again descend upon the earth and its inhabitants.

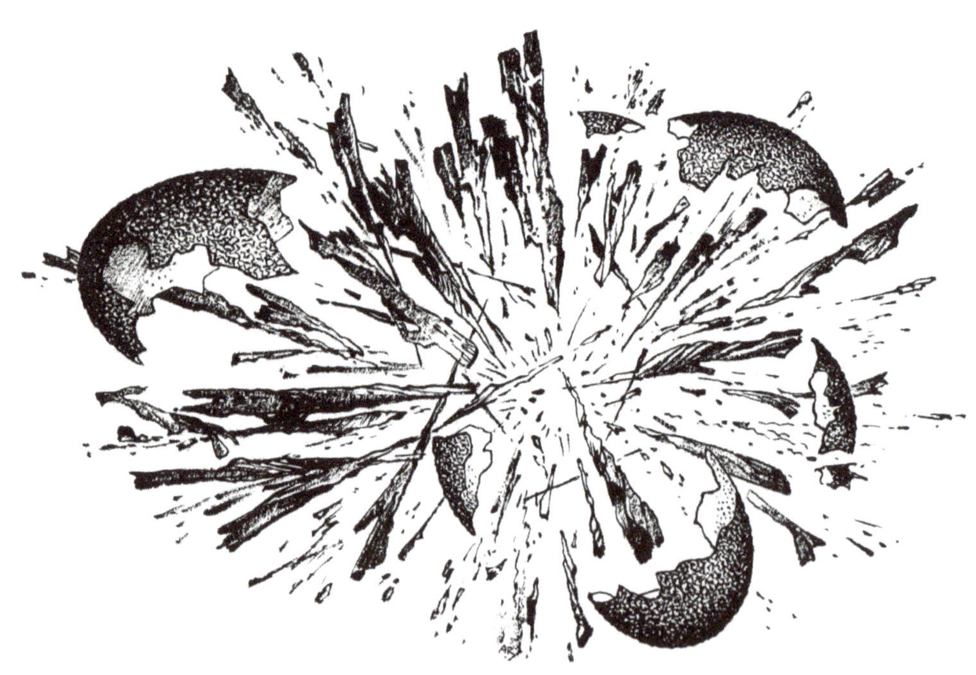

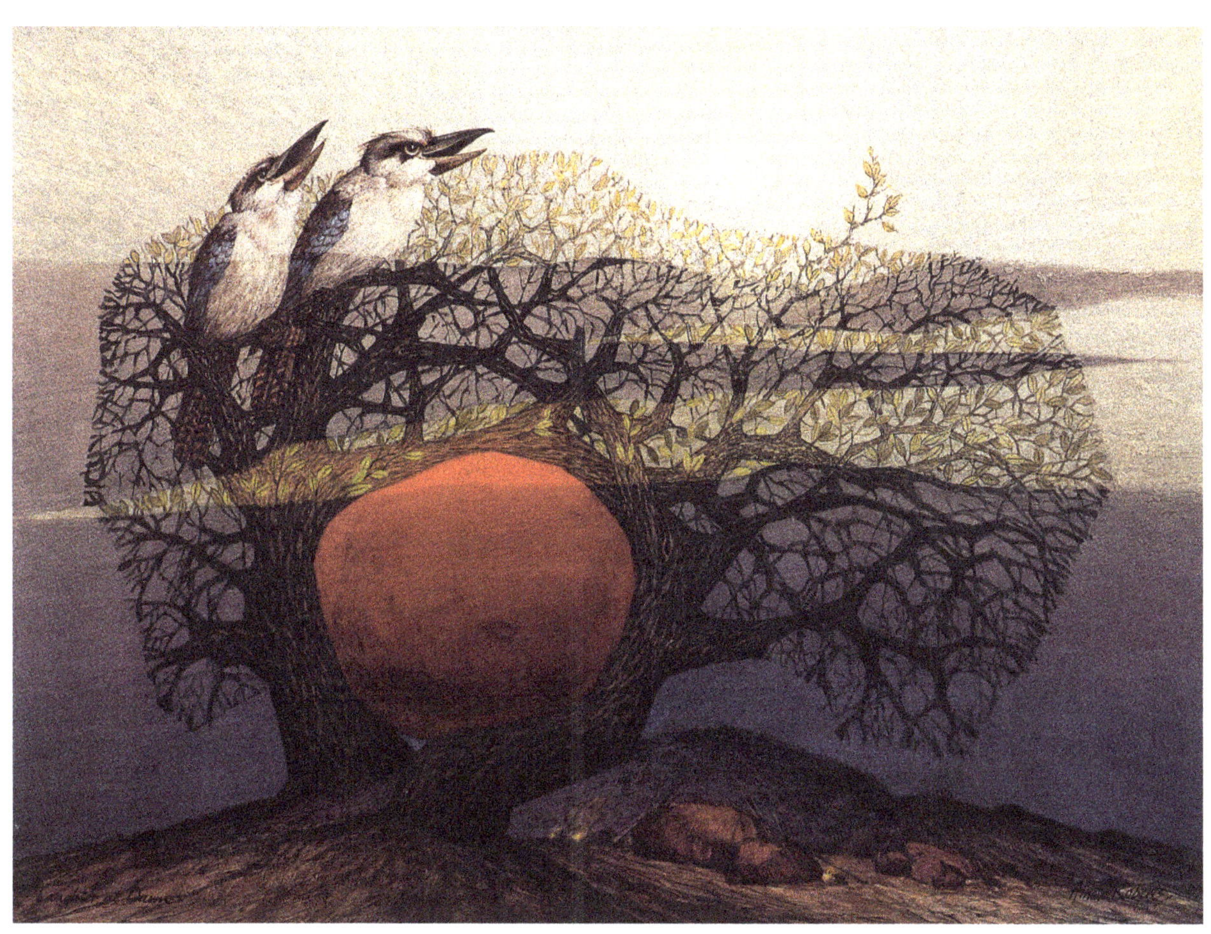

Mr Robert Nott

YULU'S CHARCOAL

The huge coal deposits of Leigh Creek in South Australia were first discovered by white men in 1888, when coal-bearing shale was found during the construction of a railway dam. But the old Aborigines of the Flinders Range area insisted that they knew about the coal deposits long before the coming of the white man. They called them Yulu's Charcoal, and Dreamtime mythology explains the origin of these deposits.

Yulu Yulura was a giant Aboriginal ancestor, who decided to attend an initiation ceremony to be held in the place we know today as Wilpena Pound. During his long journey eastwards to the Pound, Yulu lit many fires to announce his coming.

These fires were so extensive, and used up so many trees, that the charcoal left behind formed the present coal deposits and caused the vast treeless areas to the west of the Flinders Range.

The first open-cut mining in the 1940s disclosed that one of the coal basins was indeed burnt out, and the later discovery of the burnt shales of the Northern Basin was further confirmation of Yulu's spectacular journey of so long ago.

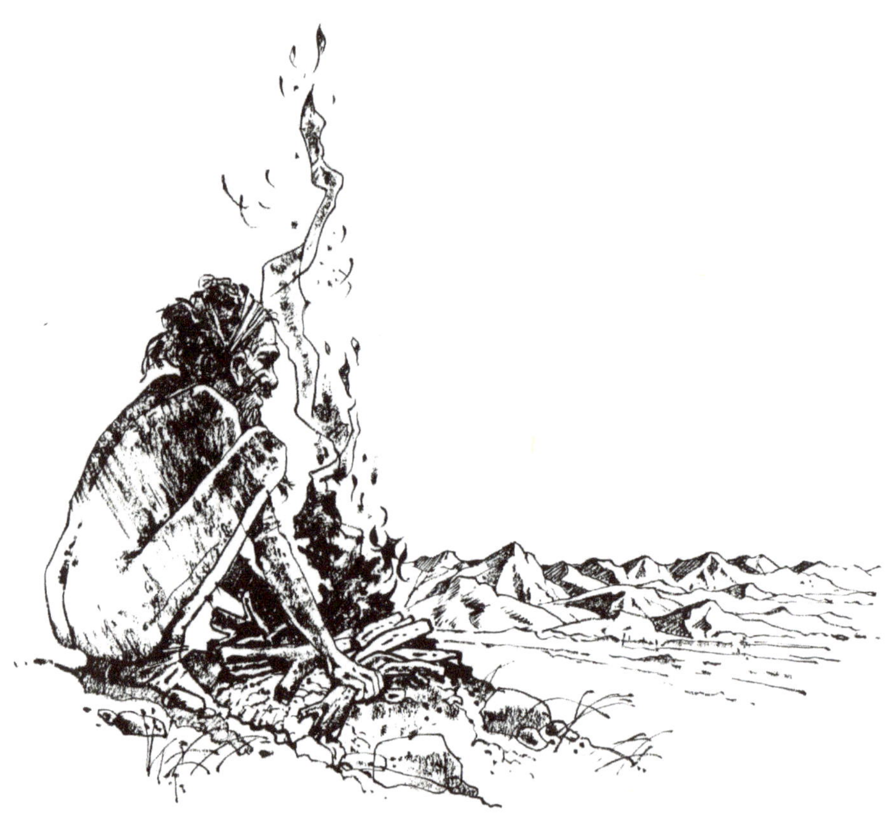

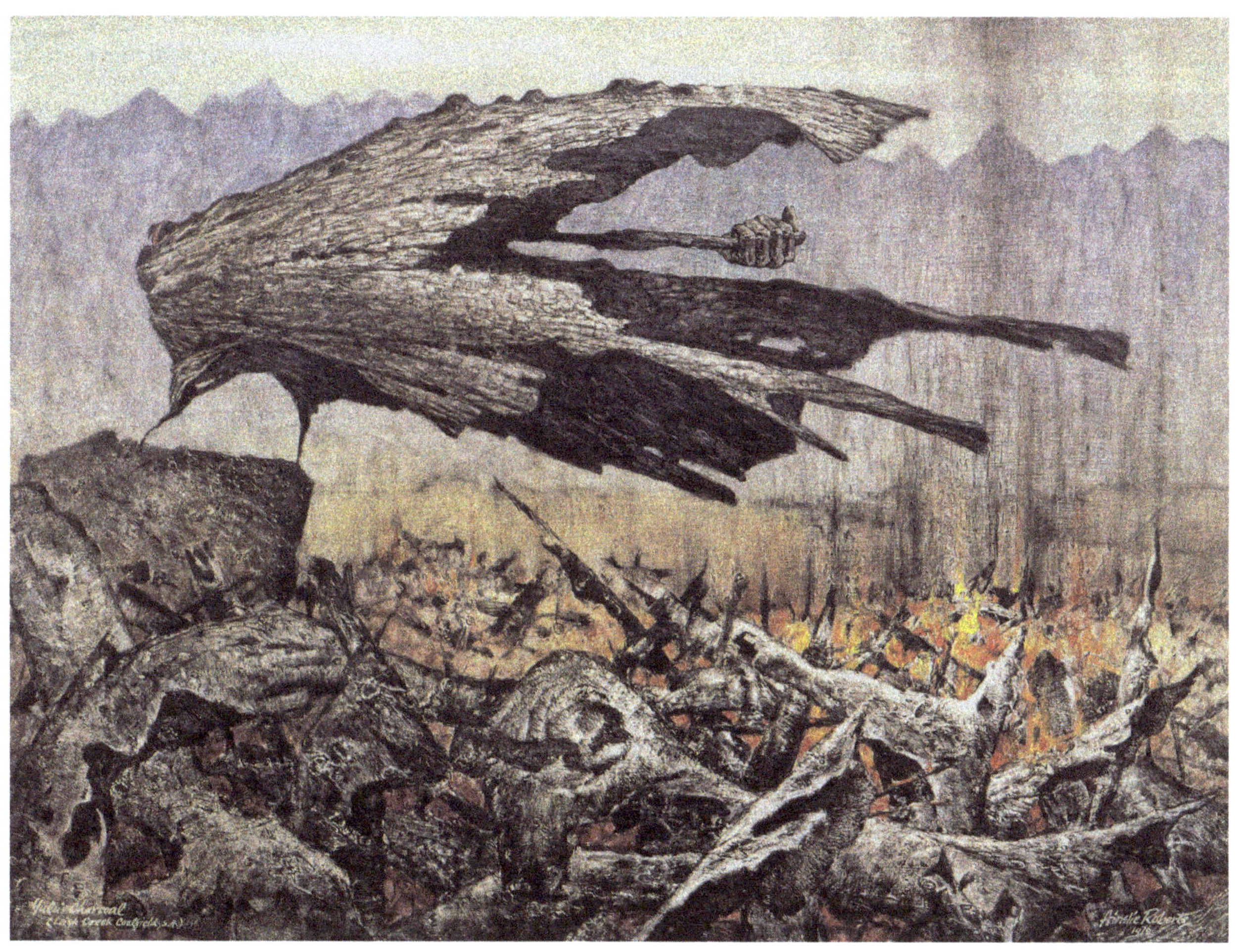

Mr and Mrs Charles E. Hulley

THE BONEFISH TREE

This myth from northern Australia relates how the hunters of the tribe are able to increase the supply of bonefish (bony bream), which, like all food that is taken from the rivers and the sea, varies in quantity from one season to another.

In the beginning, when all the creatures, birds, and plants of Australia had human form, Wilkalla the bonefish-man quarrelled violently with his sister. During the fight he threw a spear at her, and it sank so deeply into her head that she could not draw it out again. So she transformed herself into the mangrove, and Wilkalla's spear is the stalk which rises from the mud when a new mangrove plant is growing. Ever since then, the mangrove seeds have been an important item in the diet of the Aborigines.

But before Wilkalla's sister transformed herself into the mangrove, she struck Wilkalla a fatal blow across the back with her digging stick. As he was dying, he called to the other hunters of his tribe to carry him to a huge bloodwood tree standing on the banks of the river.

His spirit went deep into the earth, and into the roots of the tree which draw water from the river. It stayed there forever, to make sure that the tribe would always have enough fish in the river for their food supply.

And to this day, whenever the fishing is poor, the tribe knows that if they hit the bloodwood trees along the river then Wilkalla's spirit will send many fish out into the water for them to catch. And the bonefish still carries on his back the mark of his sister's digging stick.

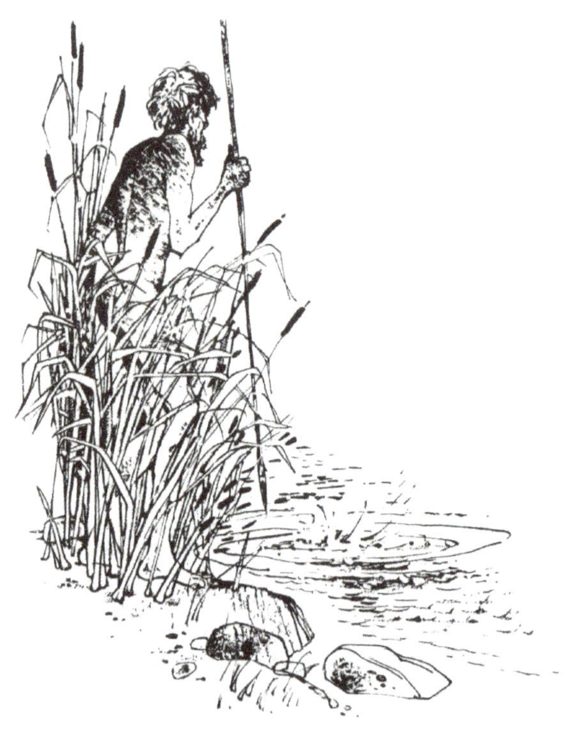

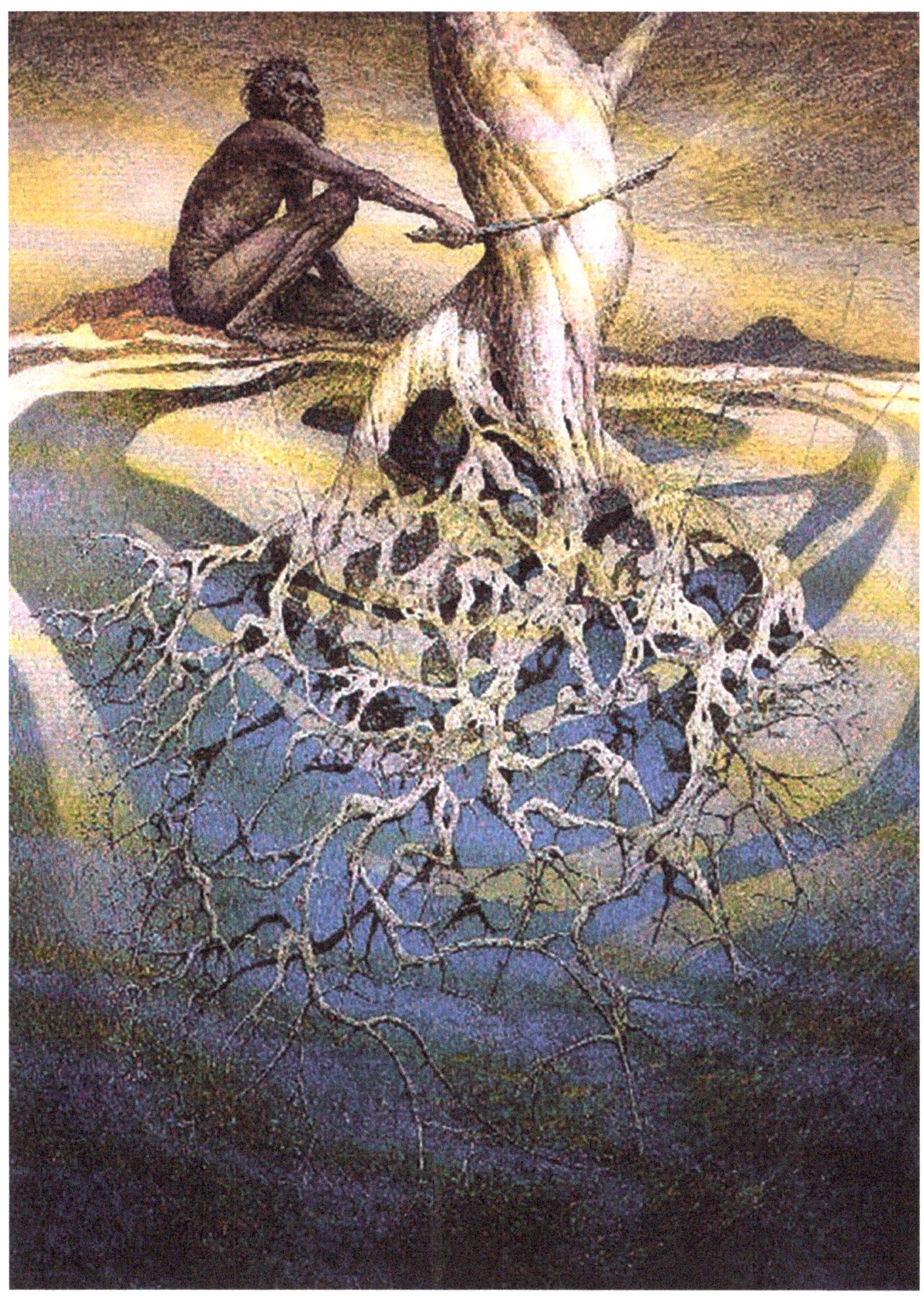

Mr Rhys Roberts.

THE WATERS OF WINDULKA

From the beginning of time the task of food-gathering has occupied the greater part of the life of Aboriginal men and women. This relentless, never-ending search has given rise to a number of myths which explain the topographical features of the countryside.

At one time during a severe drought, the bandicoot, Windulka, had to dig in so many places to get enough water to quench his thirst that the plain on which he lived was covered with burrows. During the same period, the dingo, Banguruk, unable to find game in the arid hills, was forced to hunt on the plains. Seeing the bandicoot, the dingo immediately gave chase, but he was so weak with hunger that Windulka was able to escape into the dense scrub. But Banguruk, urged on by his craving for food, was relentless in his pursuit, and every time the bandicoot paused to rest, the dingo again attacked.

Finally, Windulka dug a burrow under a pile of boulders, knowing that Banguruk could not capture him in so confined a space. But when the bandicoot heard his enemy tearing at the rocks that blocked his way, Windulka, in his terror, dug deeper and deeper until, without warning, he released such a large spring of water that it flooded the whole plain, completely filling the burrows dug by Windulka.

Today these burrows are springs of cool, clear water. The land is covered with grass, and trees provide shade for the creatures and nesting places for the birds.

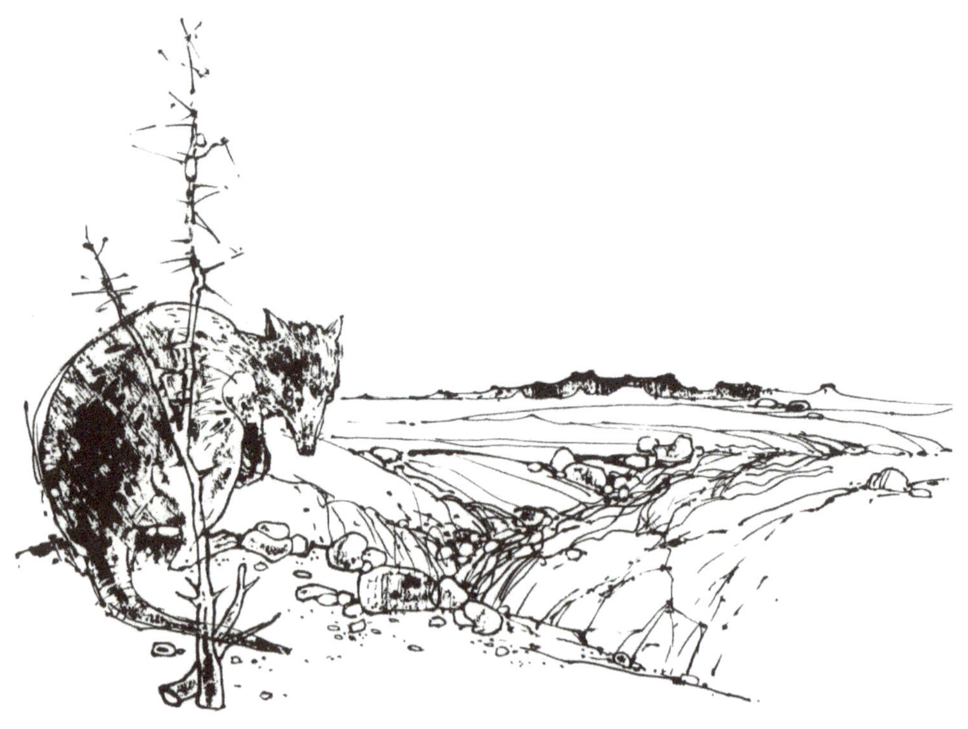

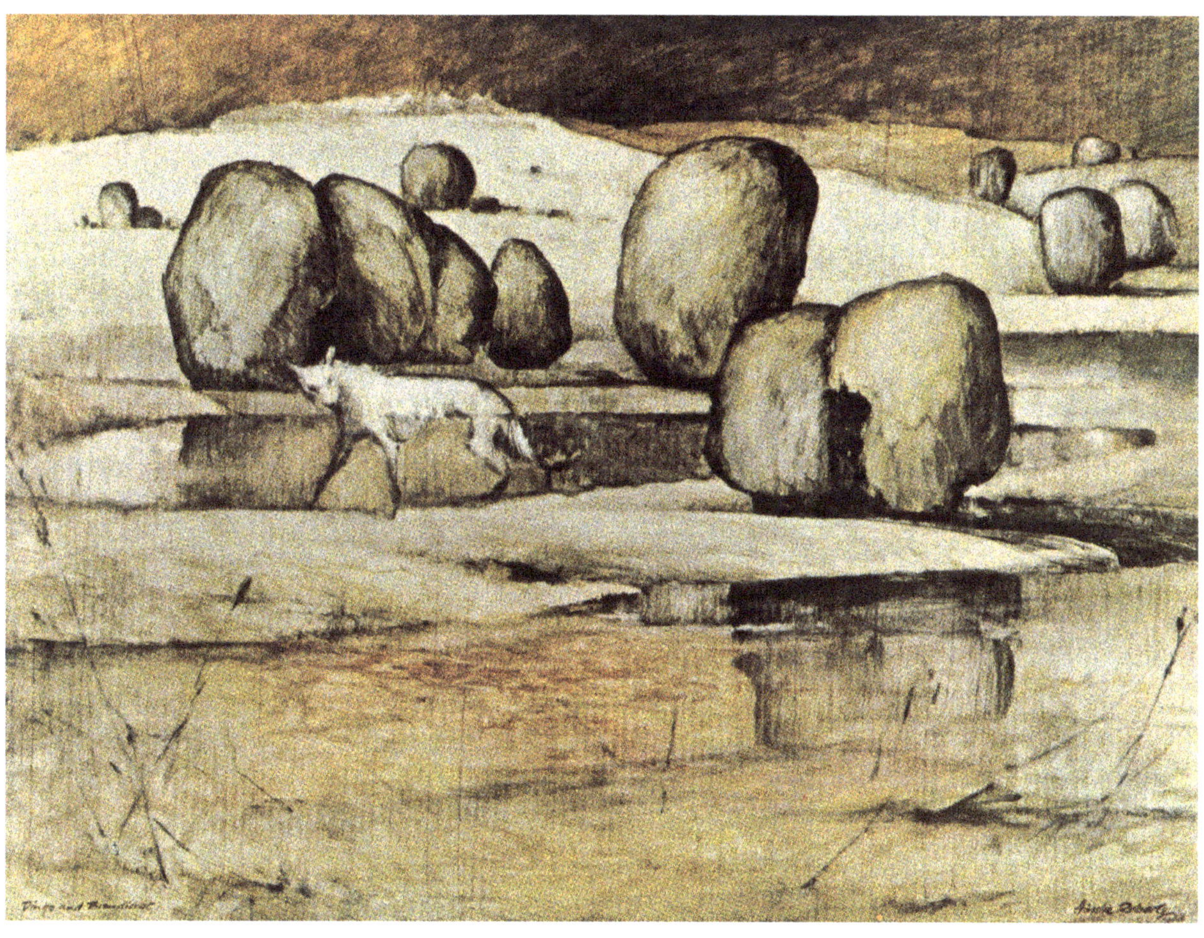

Private Collection.

THE ORIGIN OF THE PLATYPUS

Naruni, youngest and most beautiful woman in her tribe, had been promised in marriage to a tribal elder. But she was attracted to the younger and more attractive Kuralka, who persuaded her to run away with him to the hills country. After many months the pair became conscience-stricken and returned to the tribe in disgrace. Naruni was transformed into a duck, and Kuralka was punished by being changed into a giant water-rat. Both were banished to a far-distant river.

Rejected by the land and her people, Naruni in due course hatched two eggs. To her horror, she found that they did not contain ducklings, but strange creatures with bodies of fur, webbed feet, and duck bills.

So great was Naruni's disappointment, and so strong was her yearning for the solid ground and her lost tribal life, that she pined away and died. But her two children thrived in their watery home, and multiplied to establish the platypus family.

This is how the Aborigines explained the origin of the platypus to the early settlers of New South Wales, and they also described its habits and how it reproduced. When the first platypus skin was shown to European scientists it caused a sensation, and they were so astonished that they said the beak and feet of water birds had been sewn to the skin of some animal.

After that, controversy raged for eighty years over how the platypus produced its young, until it was proved that the creature laid eggs and suckled its offspring. This strange link in the biological chain is unique to Australia.

The myth in which Aborigines explained the origin of the platypus is characteristic of the way in which they used fantasy to account for phenomena which later were to baffle European scientists for many years.

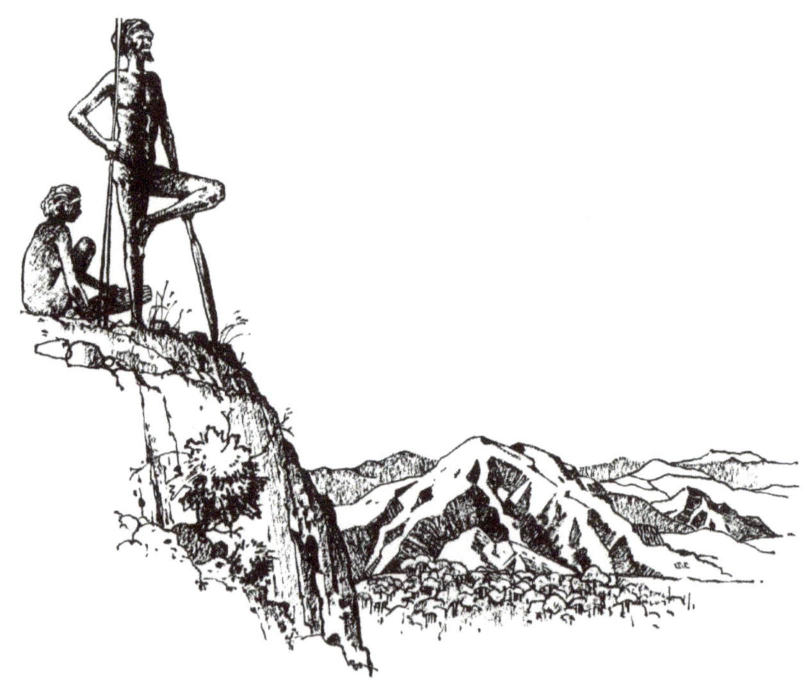

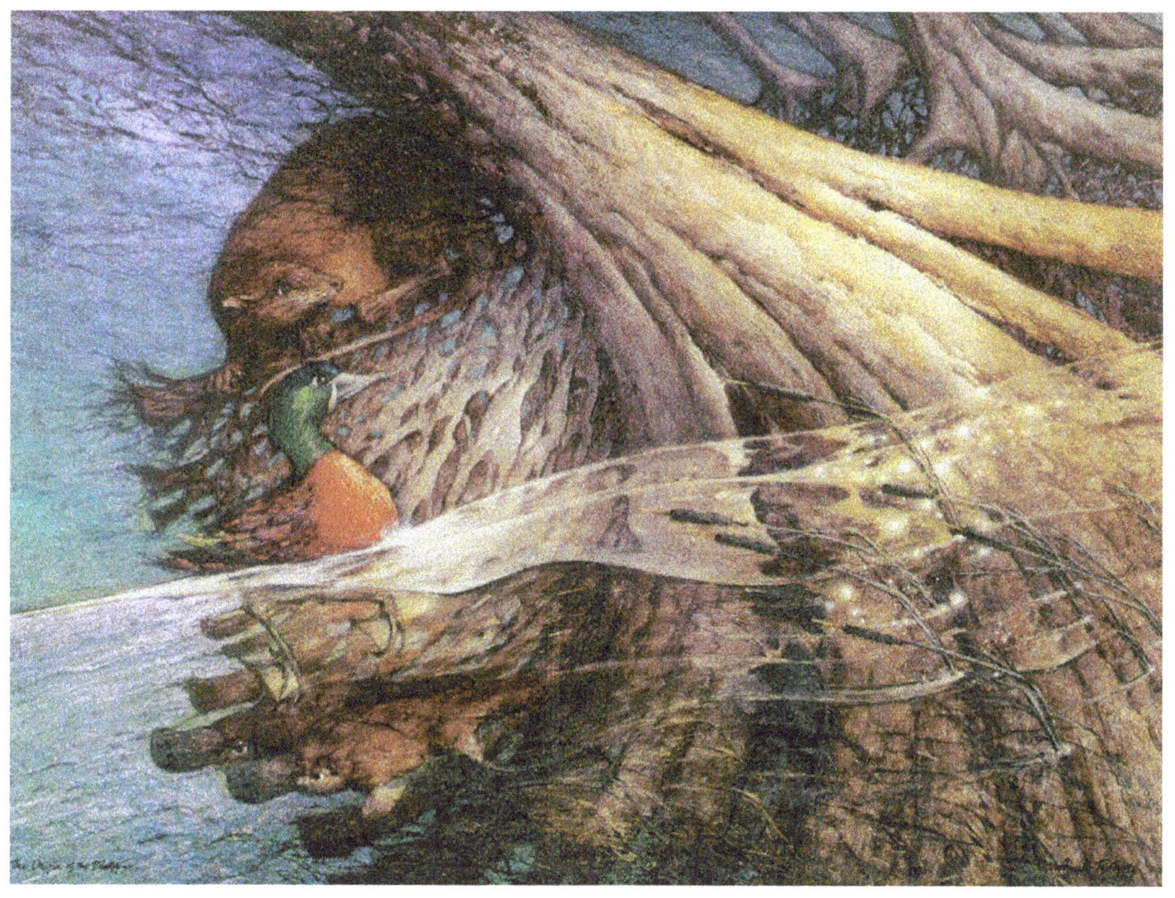

CSR Limited, Sugar Division, Glanville, S.A.

KALALA THE FIRE-TAILED FINCH

This Aboriginal myth tells of the time when the tribes had possessed fire for so long that they had forgotten how to make it. When two evil spirits, in the form of hideous old women, appeared on earth and stole every fire from the Aborigines, the people were cold and miserable.

The warriors made many brave attempts to storm the camp of the two women, but they had surrounded it by such a powerful spell that even the medicine men were powerless to break through. But Kalala, a small crippled man, succeeded where all the others had failed.

Kalala was crippled because he had rolled into a camp-fire when he was a little boy, and burnt himself severely. He grew up to be an object of mirth to the children, and was pitied by the adults. When he said he would try to recover the fire they laughed at him. But he had shrewdly reasoned that the two evil women would not consider a person so small and deformed as he was to be a threat to them.

And so it proved to be. After many months of patiently gathering wood, and doing other useful tasks around the women's camp, they allowed him inside the magic circle. Kalala, knowing that even one piece of wood taken from the camp-fire would deprive the women of all their magic powers, bided his time. And one night he snatched a burning stick from their fire and fled into the darkness.

Screaming with rage and frustration, the women set off after him, following the red pin-point of light that he could not hide. The chase continued until he was dying from exhaustion. Almost within reach of camp, he had to hide in the marsh reeds.

With the torch almost burnt away, he used the last of his strength and courage to cup his hands around the tell-tale flame and lay down on it. And as he died, he heard the evil ones blunder past him and on to the waiting spears of his tribesmen.

Where Kalala's body had been, his people found a small bird guarding the last live coals of his fire-stick. And from that time on the fire-tailed finch was held in reverence, for it held the spirit of Kalala, the cripple who brought fire back to the Aborigines.

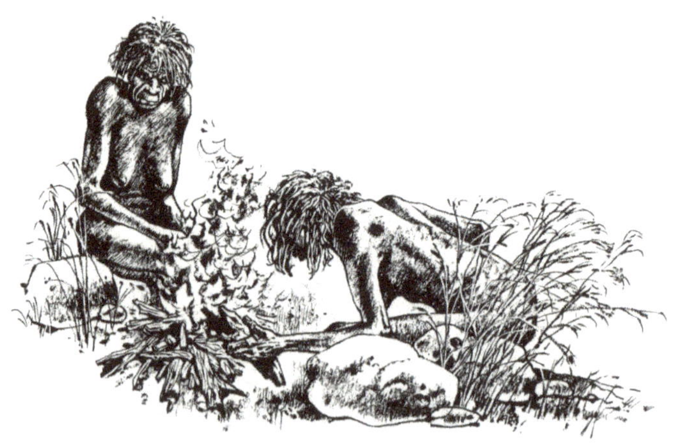

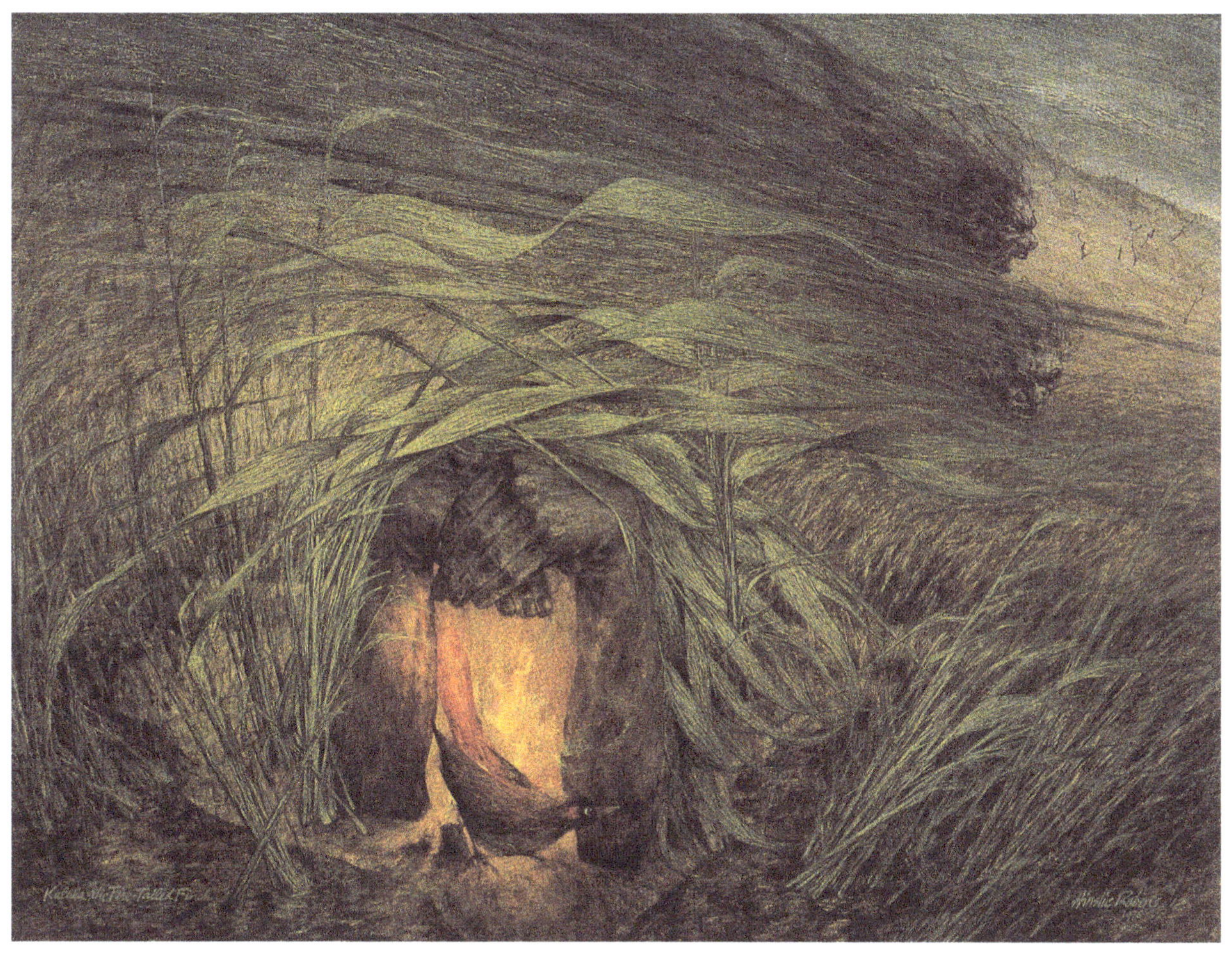

Mrs Melva Roberts.

THE BIRTH OF THE OPAL

In the Andamooka area, the Dreamtime Creator came down to earth on a great rainbow. He gathered his tribes together and instructed them on the laws they were to follow, and established their way of life.

He told them that one day he would return to them, when he judged they were wise enough to carry out his plan for unending peace on earth between men. They would know when that time had come by the rainbow which would appear in the sky. It would be so much bigger and brighter, and so different in shape from the usual rainbow, that they could not mistake it.

When the Creator had finished speaking to them, the rainbow gathered him up and bore him back into the sky. But where the rainbow had rested there was now a great area of rocks and pebbles that flashed and glittered in the sun, with all the colours of the rainbow that had given them birth-red, orange, green, blue, yellow, indigo, and violet. These were the first opals.

And from that time on, the Aborigines believed that their Creator would again appear at that spot, and regarded the area as sacred. Only the initiated men of the tribes were allowed there to hold their ceremonies.

In other opal-bearing areas of Australia, opals were looked upon merely as pretty stones, to be bartered with other tribes for decoration. But in the Andamooka region the opal was sacred, because of its mystical association with the Creator and the great rainbow in which he would one day re-appear.

Today, the opal is still a precious object, but only in the sense of commercial gain. Under the impact of European influence, the once-hallowed spot has become a market place for white men and the Aborigines alike.

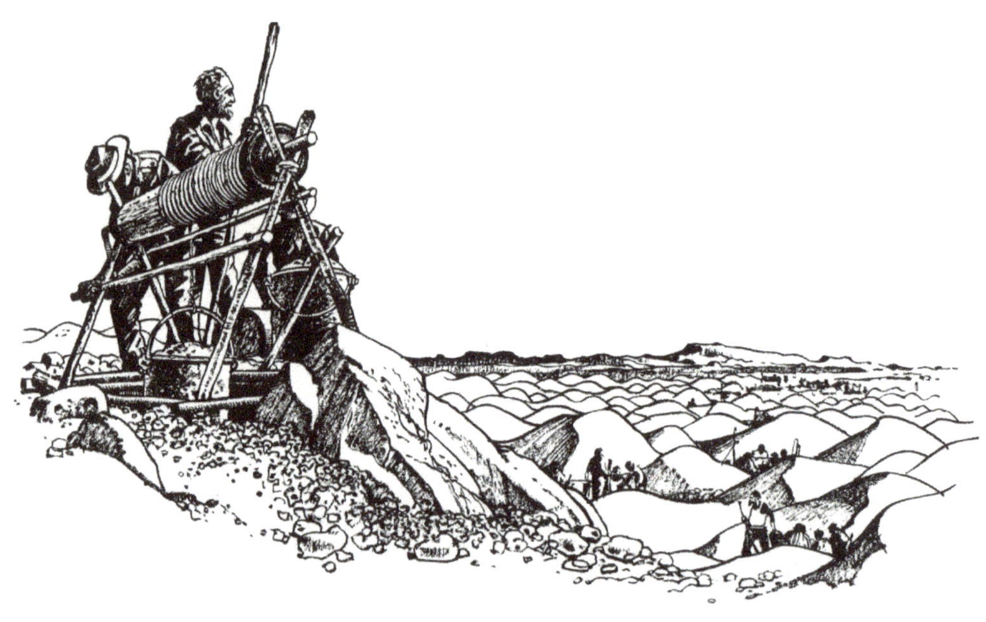

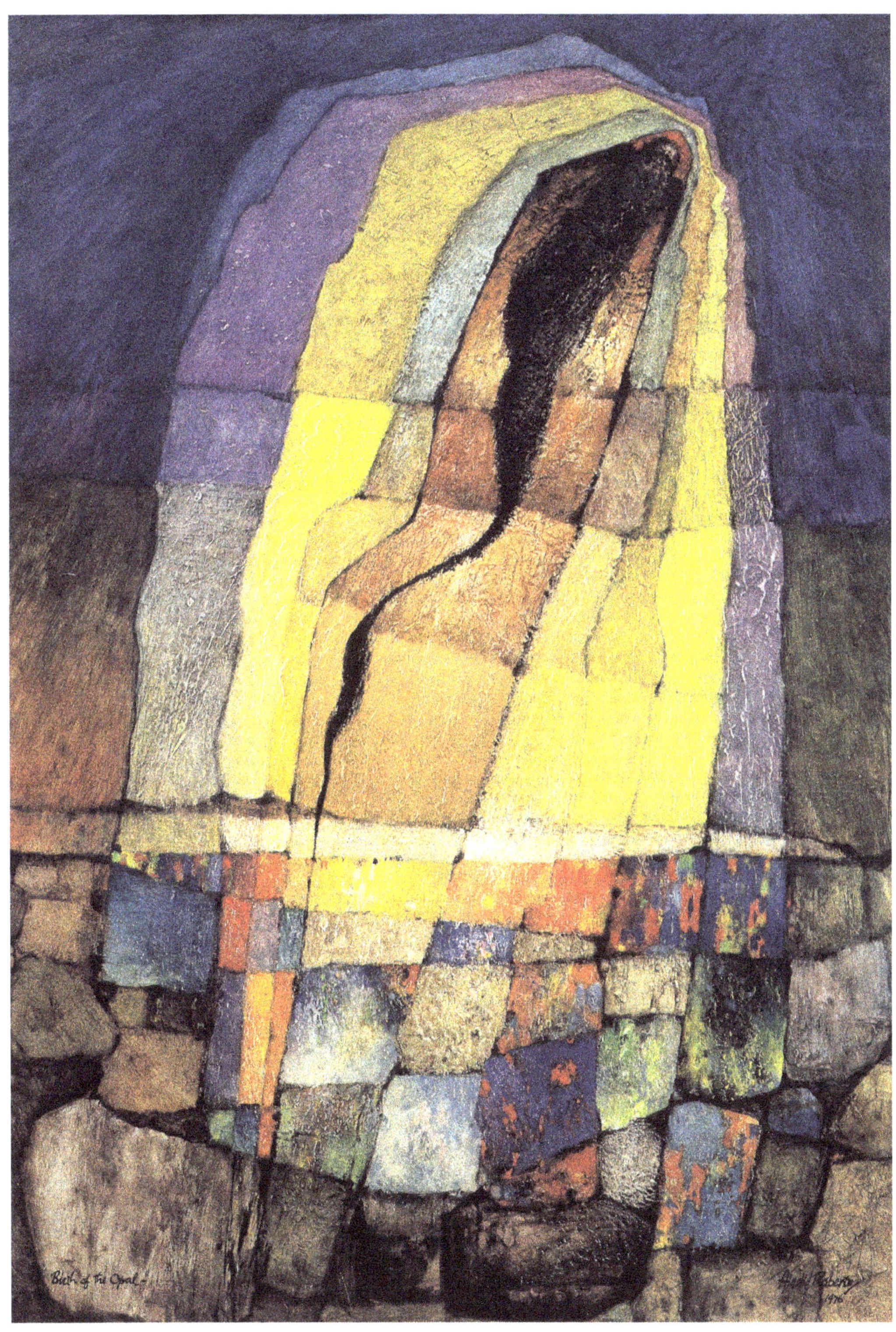

Private Collection.

THE DEATH OF THE MOON-WOMAN

According to Aboriginal Mythology, in most parts of Australia the sun is a woman and the moon is a man. But in the area of the Murray Mouth, on the great curved sweep of coastline known as Encounter Bay, the tribal myths described both the sun and moon as being female.

The earliest recording of this belief came from the Rev. H. E. A. Meyer. In a pamphlet published in 1846 he wrote, 'The sun is considered to be a female who, when she sets, passes the dwelling places of the dead. As she approaches, the men assemble and divide into two bodies, leaving a road to pass between them; they invite her to stay with them, which she can do for only a short time, as she must be ready for her journey the next day. For favours granted to some one among them she receives a present of a red kangaroo skin, and therefore, when she rises in the morning, appears in a red dress.'

In Meyer's view, the moon was 'not particularly chaste, either, being of very light character'.

The myth explains that the waxing and waning of the moon each month is brought about by the moon-woman eating rich, fattening foods from the time of her first appearance as a thin sickle, until the full of the moon.

Then the moon-woman, each time she sets, joins the tribes on earth. Her intense nightly association with the tribesmen causes her to become thinner and thinner, until she wastes away and dies. After three moonless nights, a new moon is born and the cycle begins all over again, with the new moon-woman searching for rich foods to build up her body.

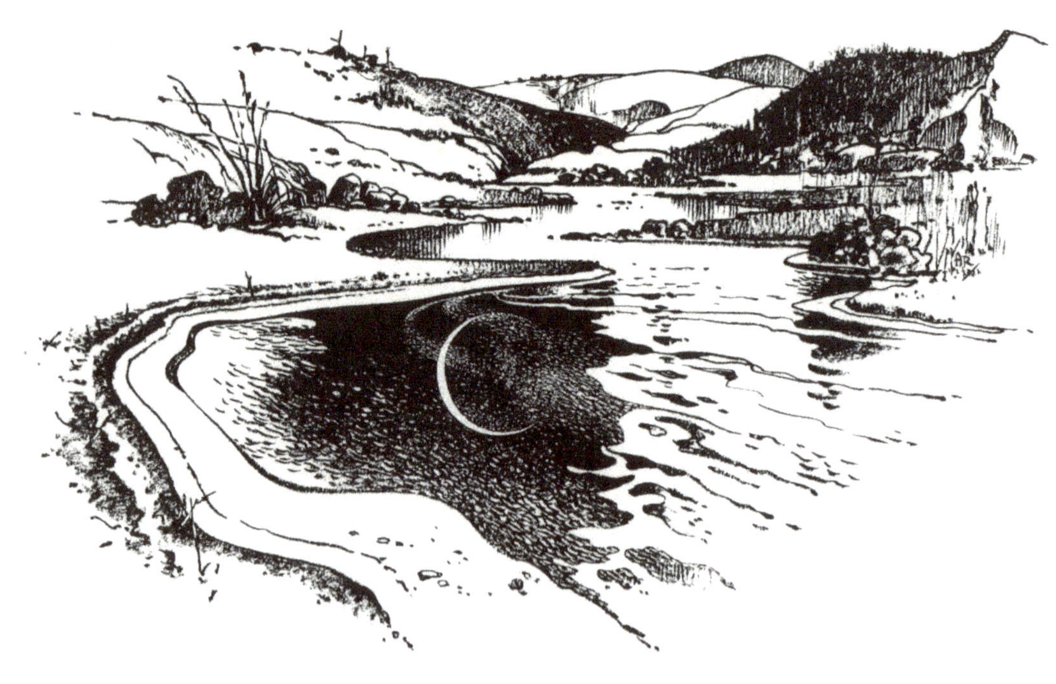

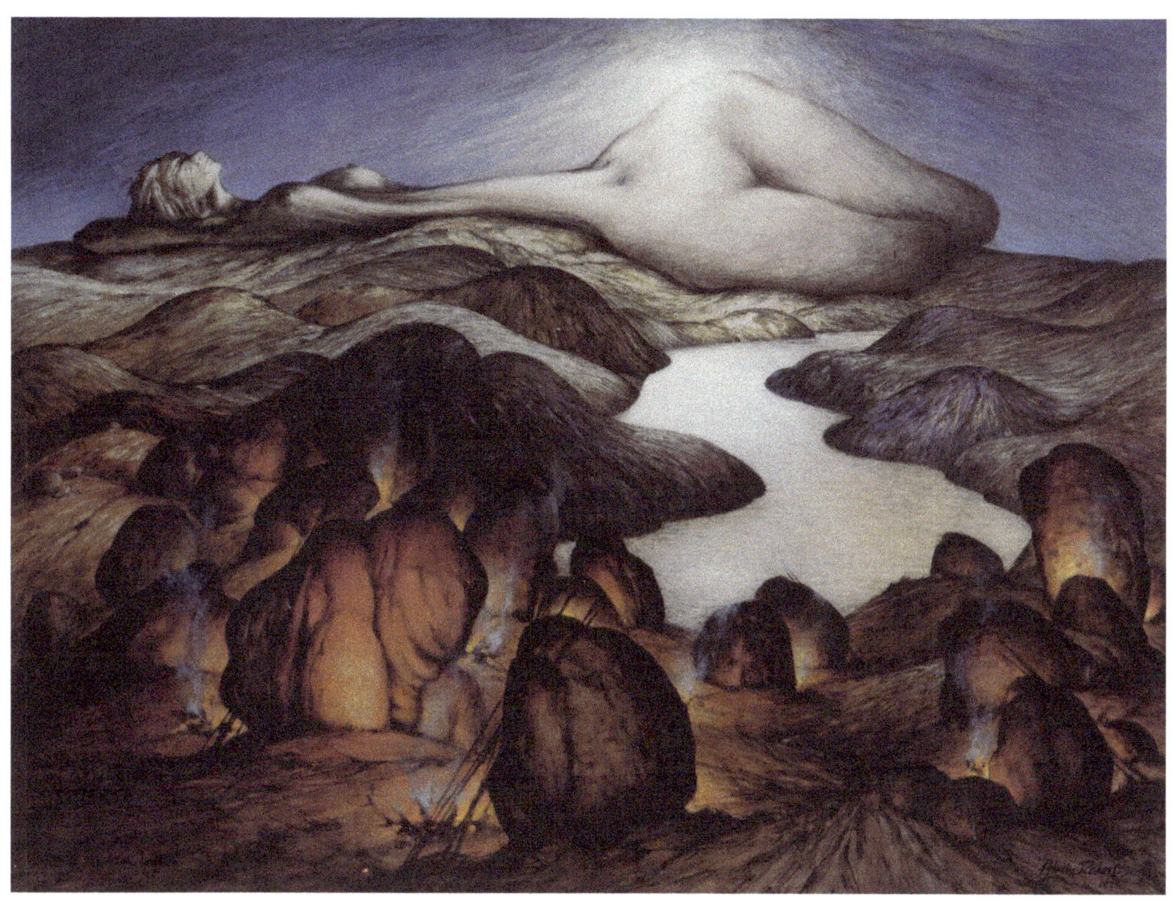

Mr and Mrs Charles E. Hulley.

KOOLULLA AND THE TWO SISTERS

The Aborigines of southern Australia had a belief that two sisters lived deep in the ocean in a vast forest of kelp. Sometimes they came up on the shore to search for crabs and shellfish among the rocks, and on one of these occasions they were so busy at their task that they did not see that Koolulla, who was a renowned hunter, was camped nearby.

Koolulla had been casting his net in the shallows, and had just finished cooking his catch when he saw the sisters. He was so impressed by their beauty that he resolved to capture them, and so he picked up his net and a large fires tick from the fire and crept close enough to the two women to throw his net over them. One wriggled out from under it and jumped back into the sea. Quickly, Koolulla secured the net around his one captive and leaped into the water in chase of her sister. As his firestick sank it created a burst of sparks which floated up into the sky.

Koolulla swam all that day in pursuit of the woman, but she finally led him into the kelp forest. There, exhausted and entangled in the great mass of seaweed, he sank to the bottom and was transformed into the shark, compelled always to hunt the deep waters in search of the woman he lost.

The sister on the shore, unable to free herself from Koolulla's net, eventually died and was changed into the evening star. The sparks from Koolulla's firestick may still be seen in the sky. They are the first stars to appear as night falls, and the brightest of them all is the evening star, keeping watch over her sister who still lives in the underwater forest.

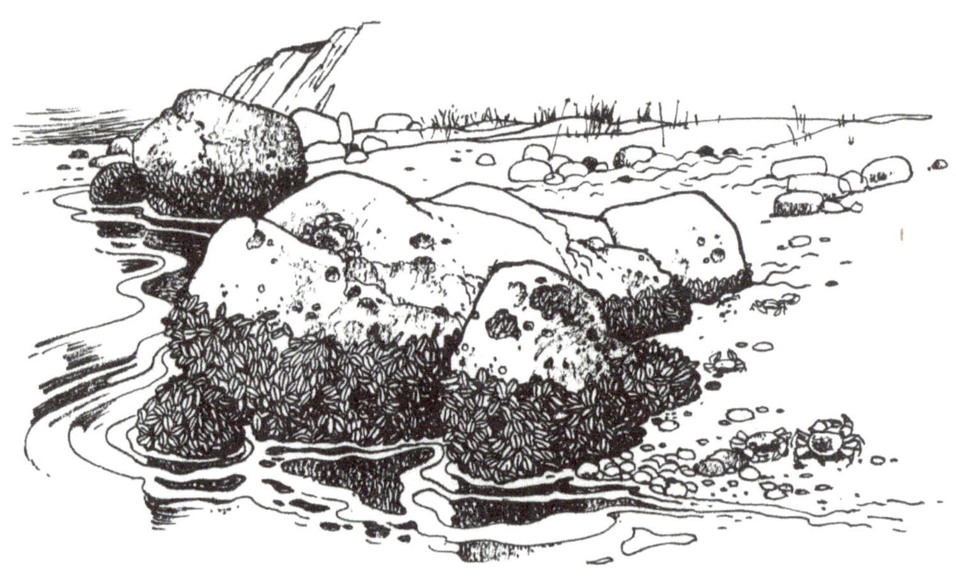

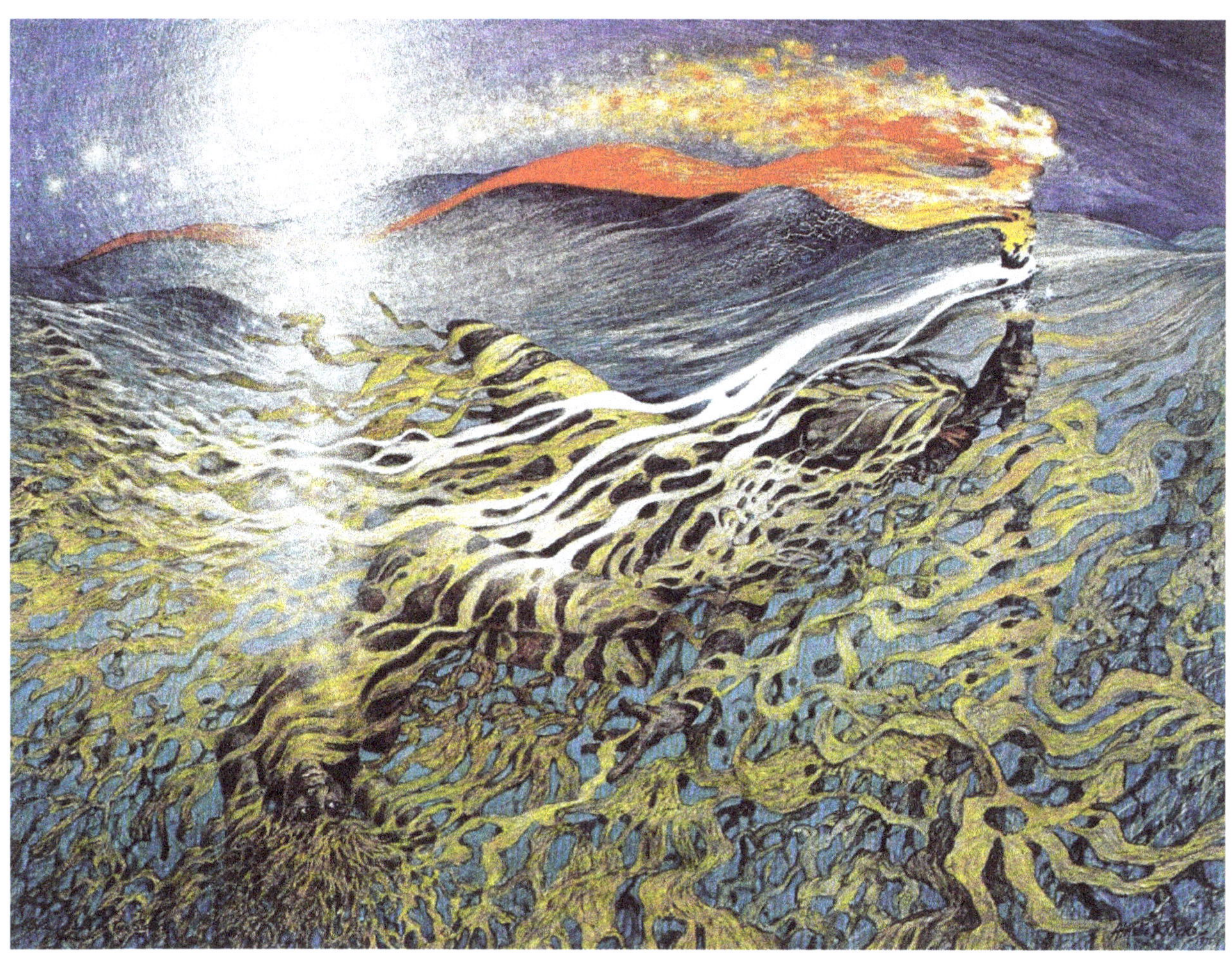

Private Collection.

THE GYMEA

One hot day in the long-ago Dreamtime, an Aboriginal tribe took refuge from a summer storm in one of the many huge caves in the mountains of New South Wales. The storm was so violent that it tore up every tree in the valley where they lived, and the great deluge of rain caused a landslide which blocked the narrow entrance to the cave.

The imprisoned tribe, terrified and in darkness, seemed to be doomed. But Bullana, the strongest and most courageous of the tribal warriors, found a narrow crevice which led up to the surface. With great difficulty he pulled and squeezed himself up until he emerged into the sunlight, but none of the others were strong enough to follow him.

Bullana determined to do all in his power to keep his people alive. For day after day he hunted, and speared fish in the river, and he made a long rope to lower food down into the cave. Many times each day he climbed up the mountain to let food down to the tribe which depended upon him.

At last this constant heavy work and responsibility had its effect even upon Bullana's strength. One day he slipped and fell into a ravine, breaking so many bones that he seemed unable to go on. But although he was so exhausted and in so much pain that he could only crawl he still tried to hunt and fish for his tribe. The effort was hopeless, and those in the cave began to die. The time came when Bullana knew he must abandon his struggle to save them, and he collapsed among the torn-up trees and tangled undergrowth of his beloved valley.

As he died, his hand grasped a small plant. As the spirit left him, this plant instantly grew into a mass of long broad leaves, and the great white flowers which burst from the centre became red with his blood. This is the plant which we know today as the gymea, or gigantic lily, and it gains its strength and endurance from the spirit of Bullan. The flower spike and the roots have been used as food.

Countless centuries after the sudden growth of the gymea, a group of white men discovered a way into the huge old cave and found that the floor was covered with the tangled skeletons of Bullana's tribe.

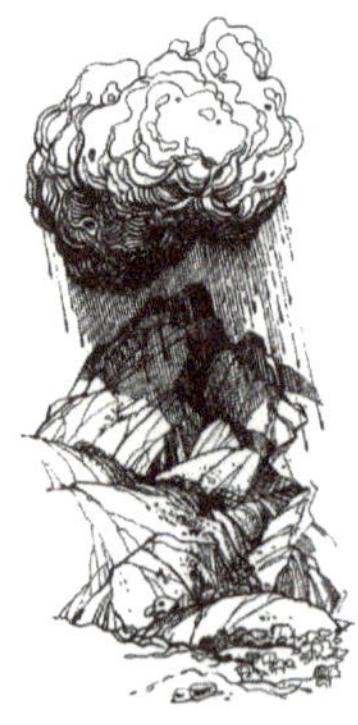

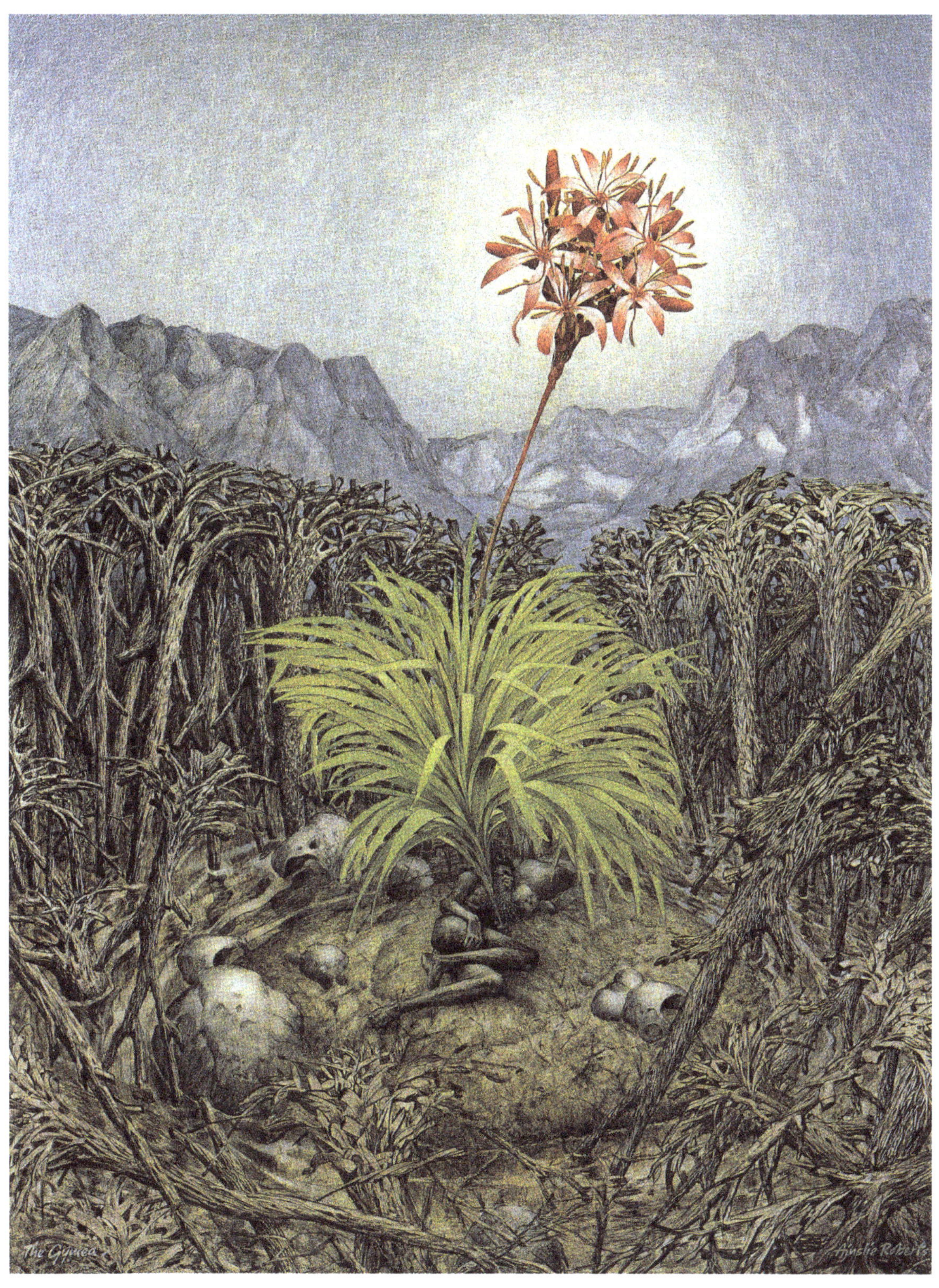

Mr Rhys Roberts.

NURUNDERI AND THE COD

The Aborigines who once lived on the shores of Lake Alexandrina, at the mouth of the Murray River, left behind a number of interesting stories about the exploits and adventures of the man Nurunderi, who created the fish in its waters and many of the natural features along its banks.

Nurunderi was a tall, powerful man, who once had a riverbank camp on the upper Murray. From this camp his wives deserted him, taking their children with them.

One day, when Nurunderi saw a huge cod swimming down stream, he followed it in his bark canoe. In those days the Murray River was only a small stream, but as the cod swam away from Nurunderi its great body burst through the land and enlarged the river to its present size.

By the time Nurunderi had followed the cod as far as Lake Alexandrina, he had almost given up hope of capturing so large a fish. Then he remembered that his brother-in-law, Nepele, lived further down the Lake, and might be able to spear it. So Nurunderi signalled Nepele that a large cod was swimming towards him, and Nepele managed to spear the fish as it passed his camp.

The two men then created all the fish in Lake Alexandrina and the Murray by cutting the cod into many pieces which they threw into the water. As they did so, they decreed that one piece would become the perch, another the callop, another the mulloway, and so on, until all the present day fish were named. A large part of the cod still remained, so Nurunderi threw that into the water, saying, 'You continue to be a Murray cod.'

Having completed his task of peopling Lake Alexandrina and the river with fish, and being unable to find his wives and children, Nurunderi made his camp with Nepele on the shores of Lake Alexandrina.

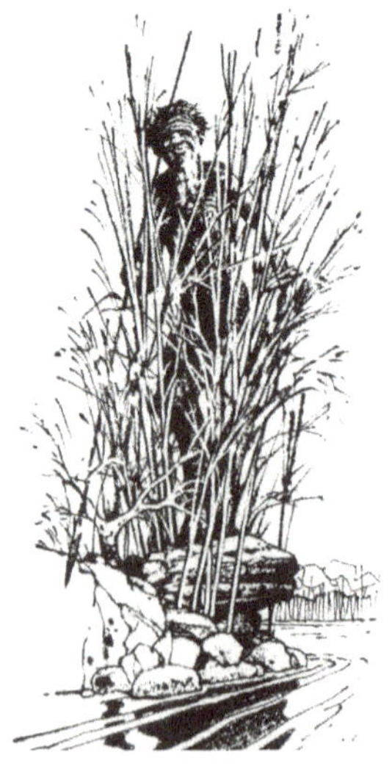

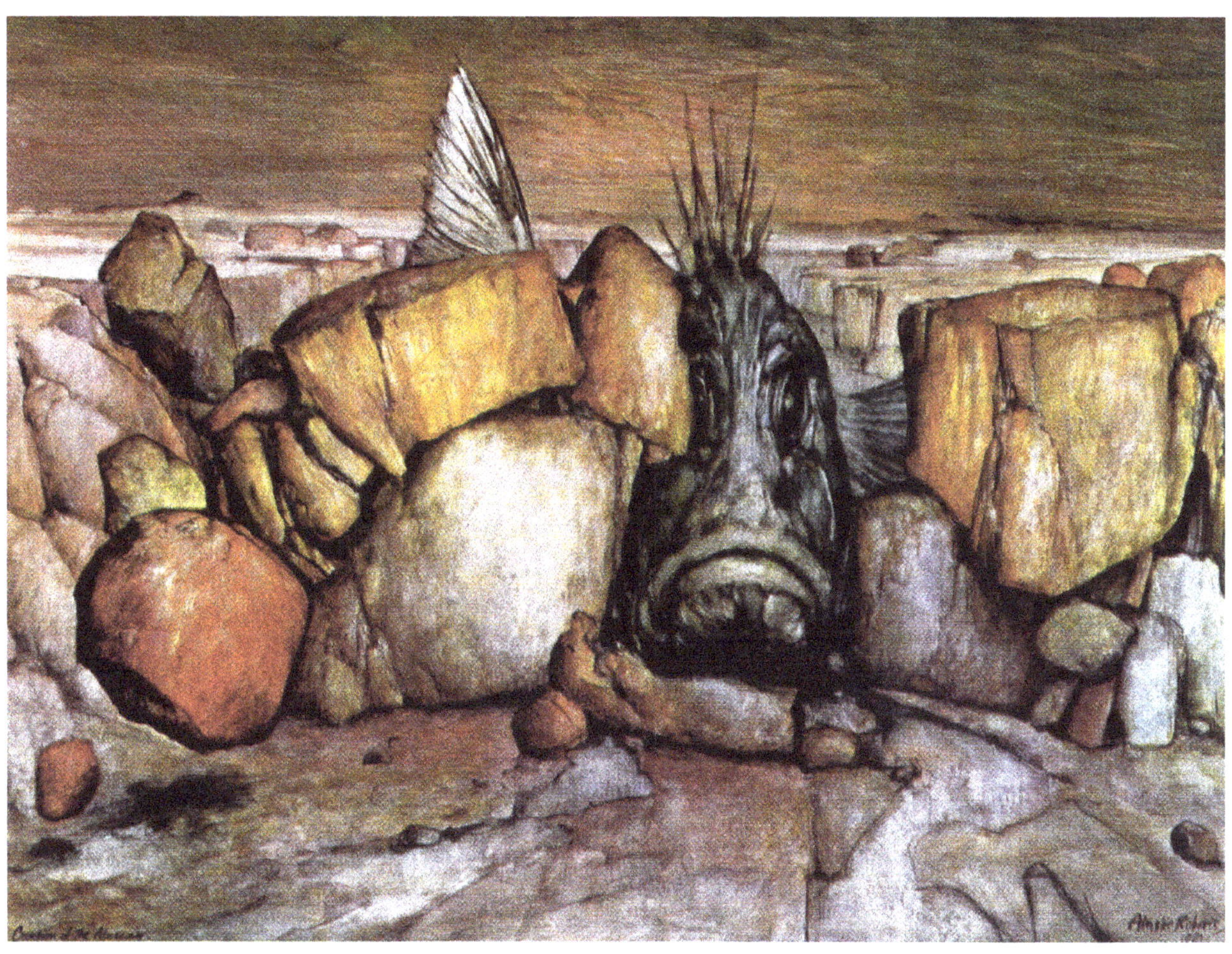

AMP Society.

THE CREATION OF THE MILKY WAY

Nurunderi, after spending some time with Nepele, his brother-in-law, became increasingly unhappy because his wives were not with him. As he had by then recovered from his exertions in capturing a huge cod, and creating a great river and all the fish in it, he decided to continue the search for his wives.

But as he prepared to move on he realised that his quest would be over land, and he would have no further use for the canoe which had carried him so great a distance. Not wishing to abandon so fine a possession, and noticing the many parts of the night sky where no stars shone, Nurunderi resolved 'to put his canoe to good use.

He selected the two highest sandhills in the area to stand on and lifted his canoe up into one of the dark spots in the sky, where it became the bright dusting of stars we call the Milky Way.

Nurunderi's two sandhills can still be seen at Mount Misery, close to the main road. In the language of the Jaralde tribe the word *juki* means canoe, and so they called the Milky Way *Ngurunderi Juki* or Nurunderi's Canoe.

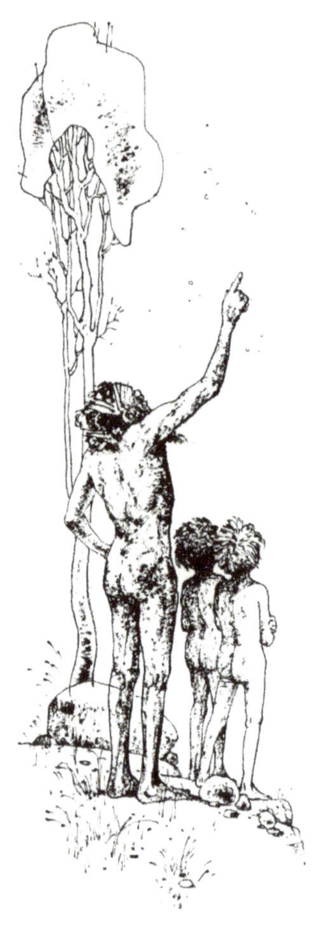

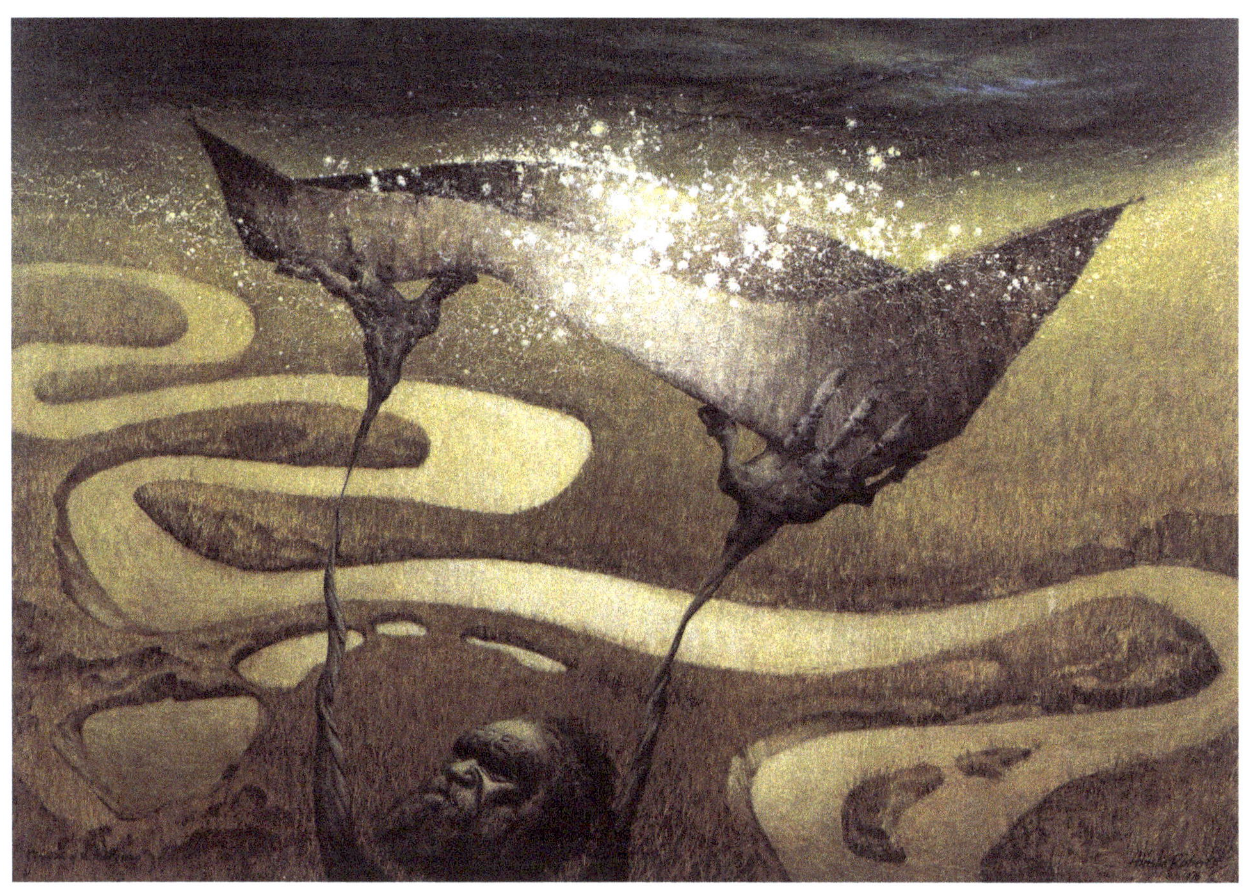

Mr Robert Nott.

THE BIRTH OF THE SEALS

After placing his canoe into the sky, where it became the Milky Way, Nurunderi set out on foot to recapture his wives. He created many of the natural features of the coastline as he did so, the most prominent of these being a rugged granite headland known today as Rosetta Head, or the Bluff.

From this high vantage point, Nurunderi located his errant wives far to the west. After resting for a while on this headland, which the Aborigines later regarded as his sleeping body, Nurunderi cast four of his spears into the ocean before resuming his chase. Where each spear pierced the water a rocky island arose.

One of these was Seal Rock, a small island surrounded by dangerous reefs and isolated submerged rocks. And with the creation of Seal Rock came the birth of the hordes of seals which gave the island its name.

For countless centuries, until the coming of the white man, Seal Rock was the birthplace and playground of generations of seals. The white man killed them for their hides, meat, and blubber, and rapidly reduced their numbers.

Today, there are no seals on Seal Rock, but the haunting cries of the sea-birds which nest on it remind us that long, long ago this was a place where nature was vital and unafraid.

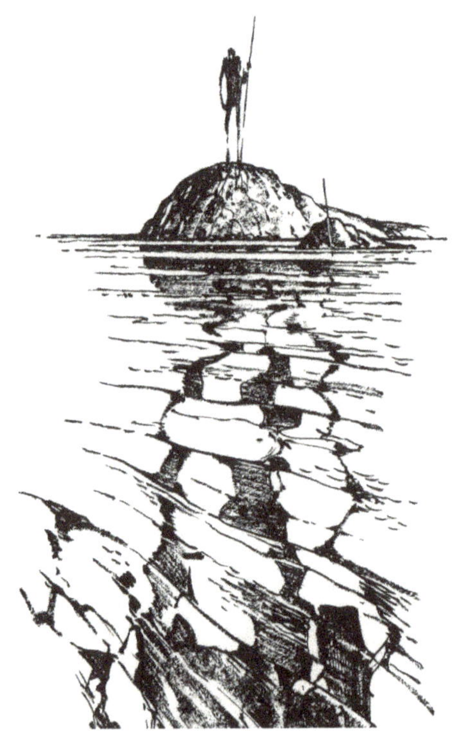

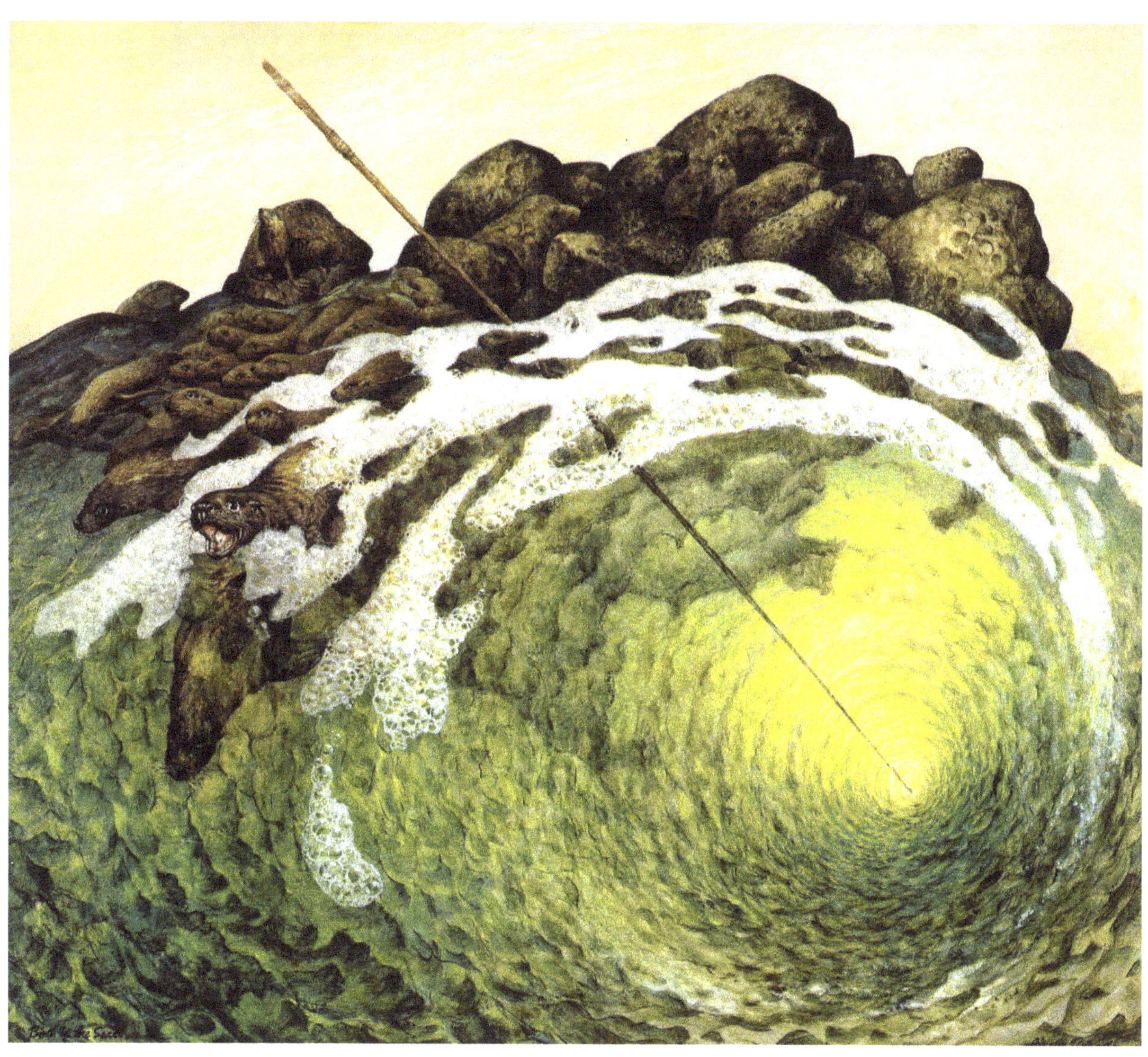

Mr and Mrs Charles E. Hulley.

THE CREATION OF KULPUNYA

The impact of the imposing beauty and vivid colouring of Ayers Rock on a modern traveller is an unforgettable experience. The relationship between Ayers Rock and the Aborigines of the surrounding desert adds a mystical significance to this massive geological feature.

The Pitjandjara tribe believed that Ayers Rock, their Uluru, rose miraculously out of a large red sandhill. The creation of all its natural features such as the great bays, the chasms in its steep sides, the waterholes, fretted surfaces, huge pot-holes, and caves, is explained in the rich store of myths handed down from generation to generation of the Pitjandjara.

One major myth relates that, in the Dreamtime, the Mala men of Uluru and the Windulka men of Kikingura became enemies. The Windulka had invited the Mala people to attend one of their ceremonies, but received such a rude refusal that they instructed their medicine-man to create Kulpunya, a huge and evil dingo.

The medicine-man laid out a framework consisting of a mulga branch for the backbone, sticks for the ears, moles' teeth at one end and a bandicoot's tail at the other, and women's hair along the back. For many days he sang his magic songs and lethal chants over the framework, until it stirred, rose upright, and came to horrid life as Kulpunya the spirit dingo. Full of hatred and malice, Kulpunya reached Uluru so swiftly that the Mala people were taken by surprise, and most of them were killed.

Today, the camps of the Mala men and initiates are the huge fretted areas on the Rock's northern face, the Naldawatta pole used in their ceremonies is an immense semi-detached slab of rock over five hundred feet high, the initiates are the boulders at its base, and dozens of minor features of the great monolith bear witness to Kulpunya's ferocity.

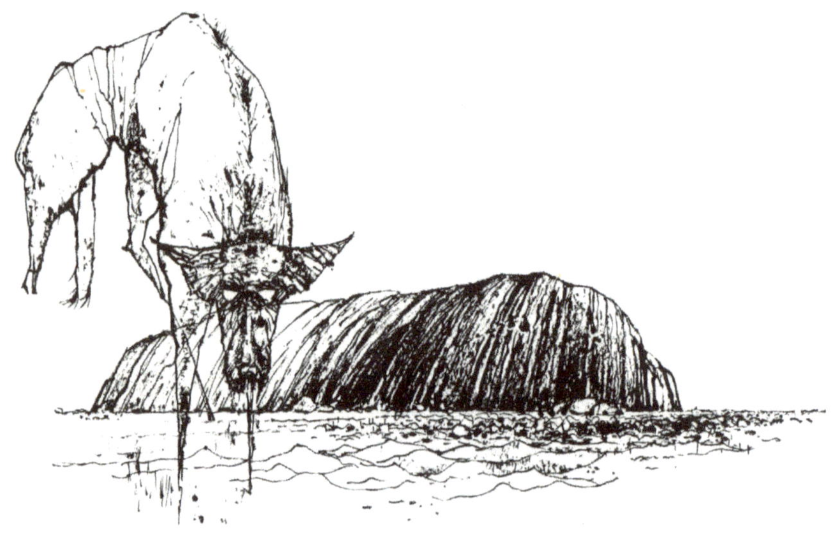

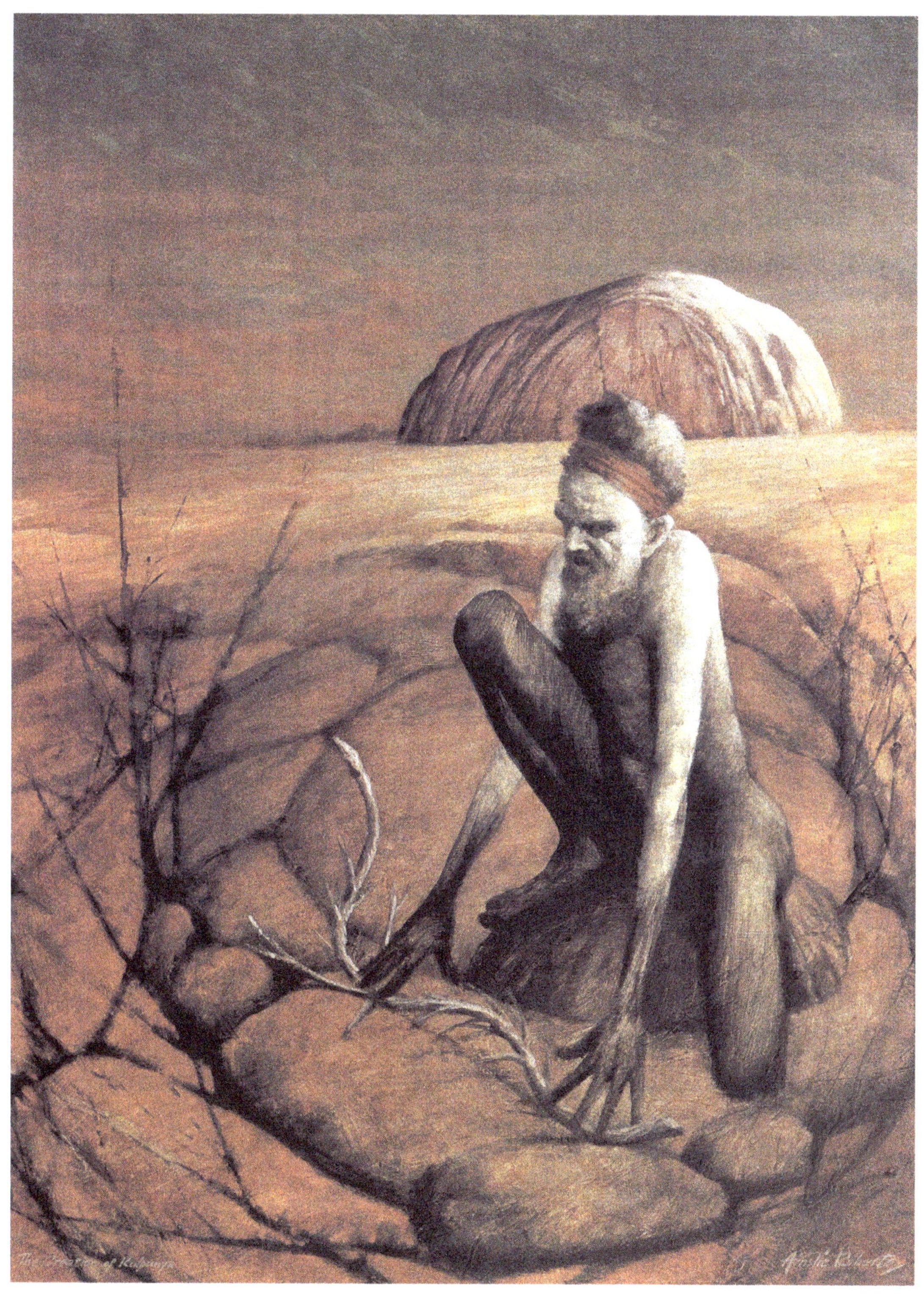

Mr and Mrs M. A. Klemich.

IN THE BEGINNING

The Storytellers, who handed down the beliefs from generation to generation, preserved the wealth of detail about the Aborigines' concepts of the creation of life. All their creation myths were based on an Ancestral Being, but the details and name of this creator varied between different tribes. A far-northern example relates how an old, blind woman rose miraculously out of the ground, bringing with her three infants-a boy and two girls. She was responsible for all the natural features, the vegetation and the animals of that area.

But in the desert areas in the west of South Australia, the Aborigines' creator was Bunjil, who made the world and all things on it. First he made the sun, the moon, and the stars. Then he made the hills, the valleys, the great plains, and all the trees and plants. Next he created all the creatures to inhabit the land.

Having done all this, Bunjil became lonely. He felt the need for companions with whom to sing and dance, and so he decided to make a man. He searched for the finest clay, fashioned a man to his own likeness, and added some finely-shredded tree-bark for the hair. Bunjil was so pleased with his creation that he immediately made another.

When both figures were finished he breathed on them to give them life. His breath was a wind of great violence that blew for many days and swept every growing thing from that area. When the land grew still again the two figures came to life, and the clay that was left over became the oddly-shaped rocks that are in the region today.

Bunjil stayed with the two men for a long time. He taught them to sing and dance, and under his guidance they gradually became wise in all things. Eventually they, in their turn, could pass on Bunjil's wisdom to all the Aborigines who followed them.

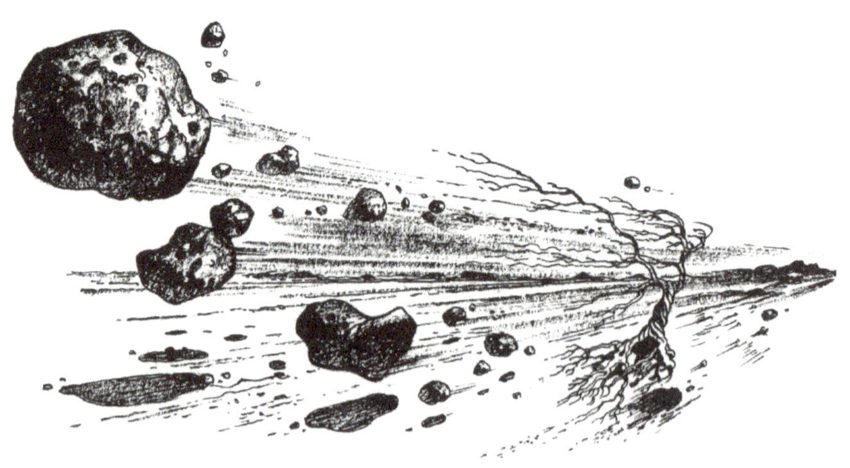

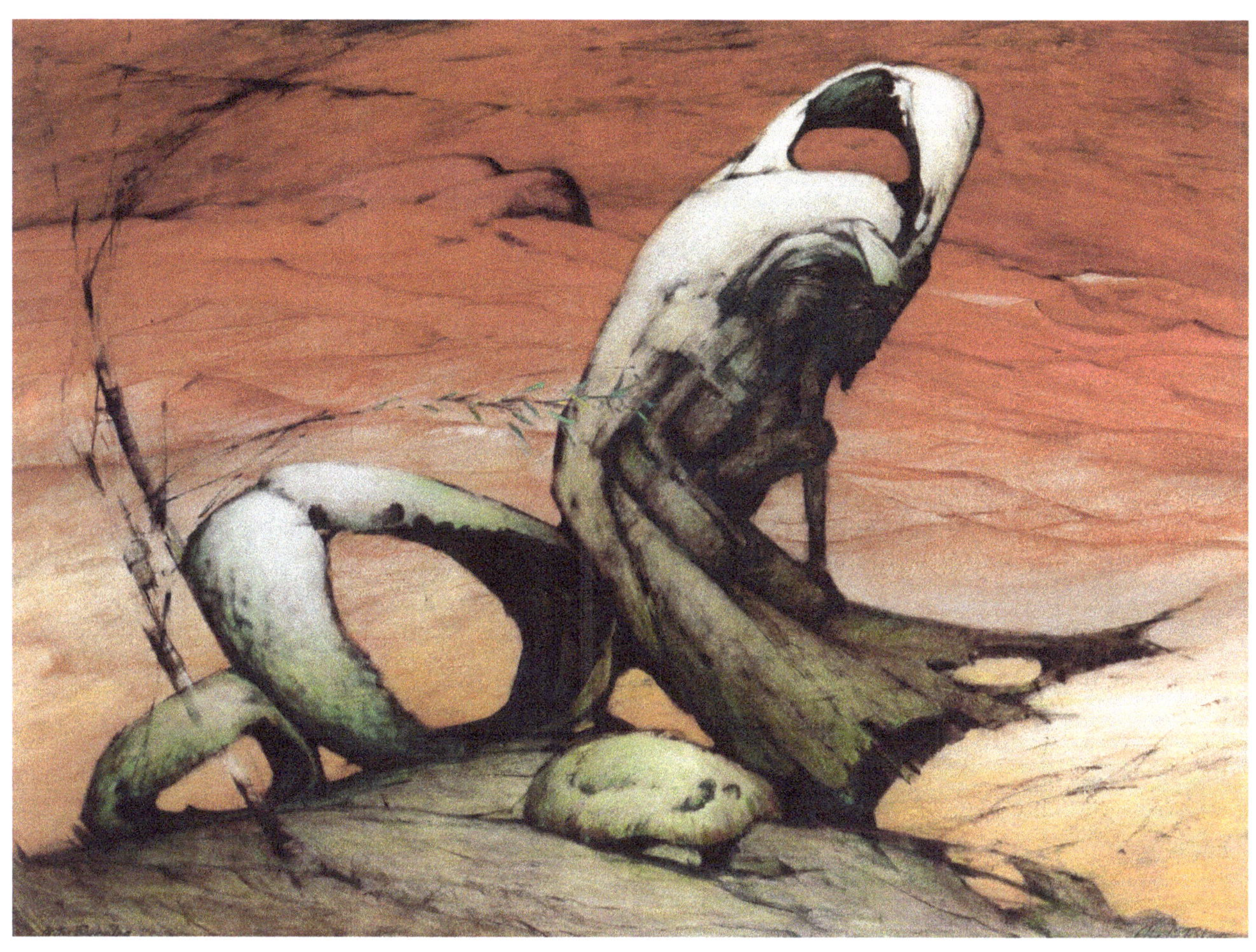

Mr Robert F. Carney.

JARAPA AND THE MAN OF WOOD

Jarapa, a man of the Waddaman tribe in the long-distant past, fancied himself as a magician and tried to create a human being. He cut a piece of wood from a tree, shaped it to look like the body of a man, and added sticks for the arms and legs, and rounded stones for the knee and arm-joints. All day and night Jarapa beat his tap sticks and sang a secret song over the image until his voice became hoarse, but it did not respond. At last Jarapa gave up in disgust and walked away.

But he had not gone far when he heard the crashing of trees behind him, and he saw that the man of wood, grown hugely, had come to life and was following him. A white cockatoo clung to the monster and screeched warnings to all creatures in its path.

Terrified, Jarapa could not escape the man of wood until he realised that it was pursuing him by sight only. It became confused when Jarapa was out of sight. So he hid behind a large rock, and his creation blundered past and at last disappeared over the horizon.

For countless generations of Aborigines, the spirit of Jarapa's man of wood was known as the Wulgaru, the self-appointed judge of the dead. Some believe that it still wanders around northern Australia in search of its creator.

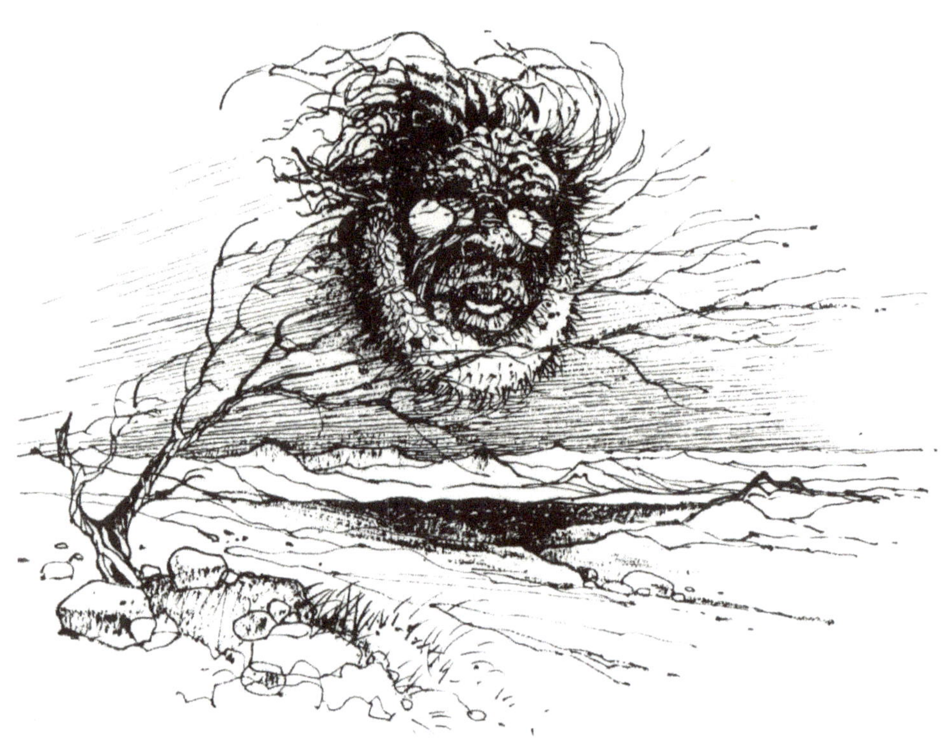

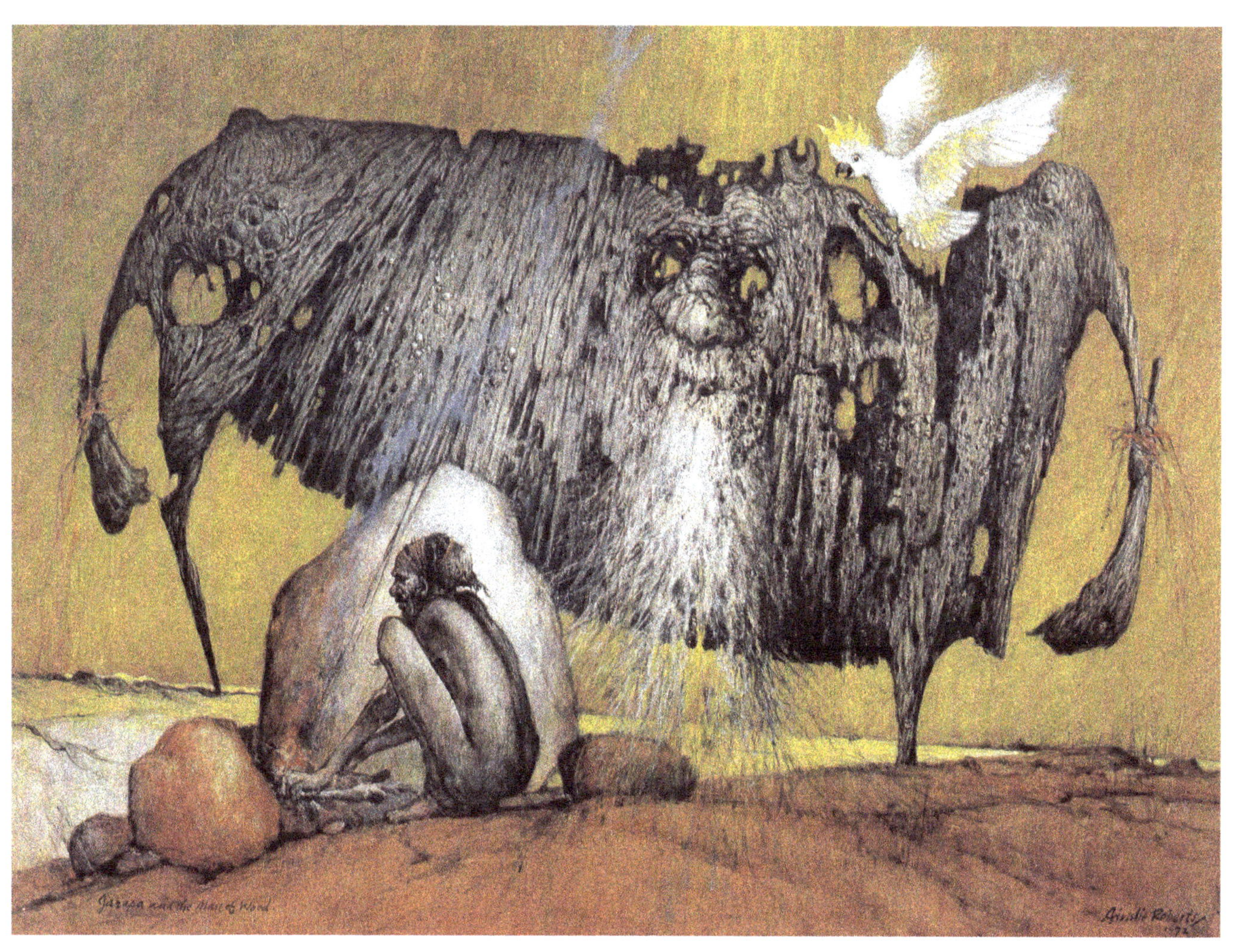

B. Consiglio.

THE BURNING ANT-HILL

In this myth from Melville Island two women, caught in a heavy thunderstorm, were near a tree which was shattered by a flash of lightning. After the storm, one of them picked up a piece of wood, which glowed in a manner she had never seen before. But she dropped it immediately, and called out, 'Yakai! That thing bit me! It's not a snake, what can it be?'

They saw the glowing wood burst into flames, and found its heat warmed their bodies and that their meat and seed cakes tasted much better when thrown on the hot coals. The two women decided to keep their discovery to themselves. They hid the fire in a huge termite mound well away from the camp, took it out to cook their food, and hid it again afterwards.

Their two sons soon discovered this secret, and were so angry at their mothers' selfishness in not sharing this good fortune that they changed themselves into crocodiles. When the women were gathering waterlily bulbs in the lagoon, they pulled them under and drowned them.

The sons, like their selfish mothers, planned to keep the fire for themselves, but when they hurried back to the great ant-hill they found that the fire was growing larger and larger. It burst from its hiding place, and the flames leapt and danced in all directions until they hid themselves in every piece of dry wood.

Since then, the Aborigines have only had to rub two dry sticks together to bring out the hidden fire, but the sons were changed back into their crocodile forms, to live in cold and gloom and never to enjoy their mothers' discovery.

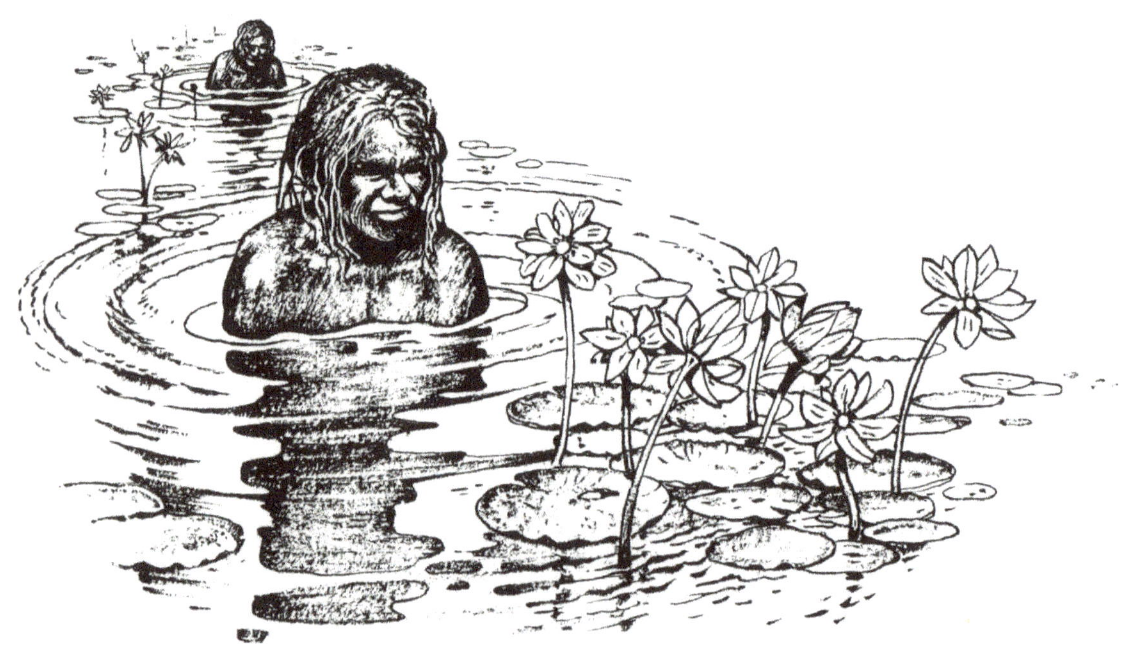

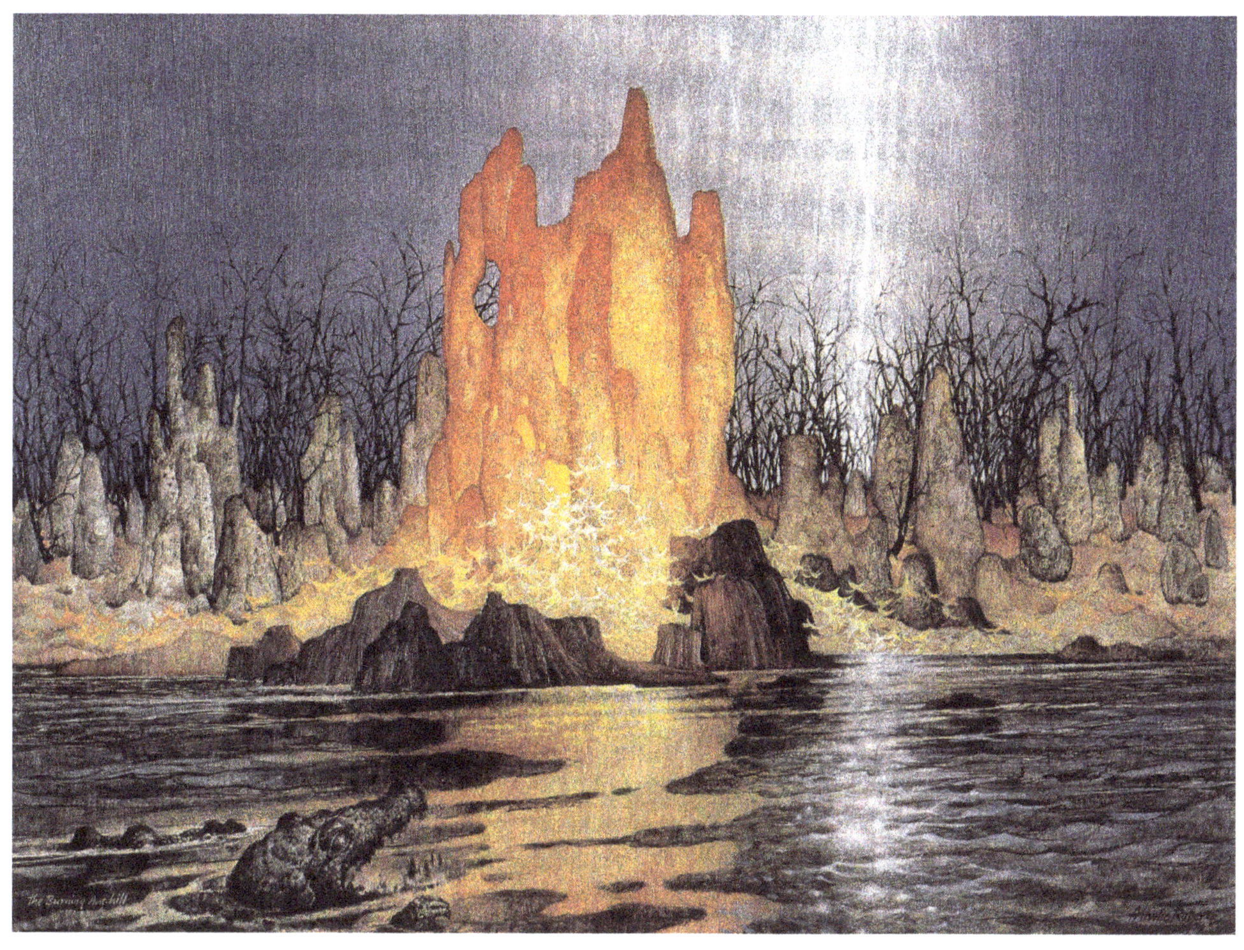

Mr Lance M. Lee.

THE EAGLE AND THE DINGO

The Australian Aborigines who lived on Melville Island, north of Darwin, collected their best ochres from Arunumpi, on the island's southern shores. At this place there are two large ochre deposits, one of yellow and another of white, which were used in their ceremonies for body decoration and for painting their unique burial poles.

But the locality also has a special significance. The tribal mythology relates how, during the great Creation period, Mudati and his wife Kirijuna were camped at this spot when Mudati saw his wife's brother, Jurumu, coming towards them.

Mudati warned his wife not to speak nor even look at her brother, for so it had been decreed by the spirits. But the woman, who had not seen her brother since they were children, took a quick look just to see how much he had grown.

Instantly, she dropped dead at her husband's feet. But even as he watched, he saw the body slowly transformed into the first dingo, rise to its feet and slink away. The brother, Jurumu, was changed into the eagle.

Ever since then the dingo, ashamed of its disobedient action in those far-off times, keeps out of sight, and has developed the ability to merge with its surroundings to an uncanny degree.

The dingo slinking through the bush, and the eagle soaring high above her, remind Aborigines of Melville Island of the ancient spirit law: that once brothers and sisters have grown to be adults, they may no longer look at or speak to each other.

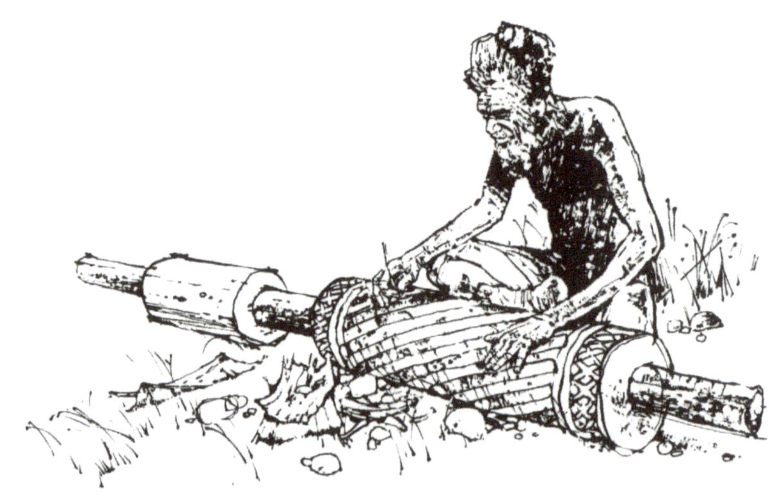

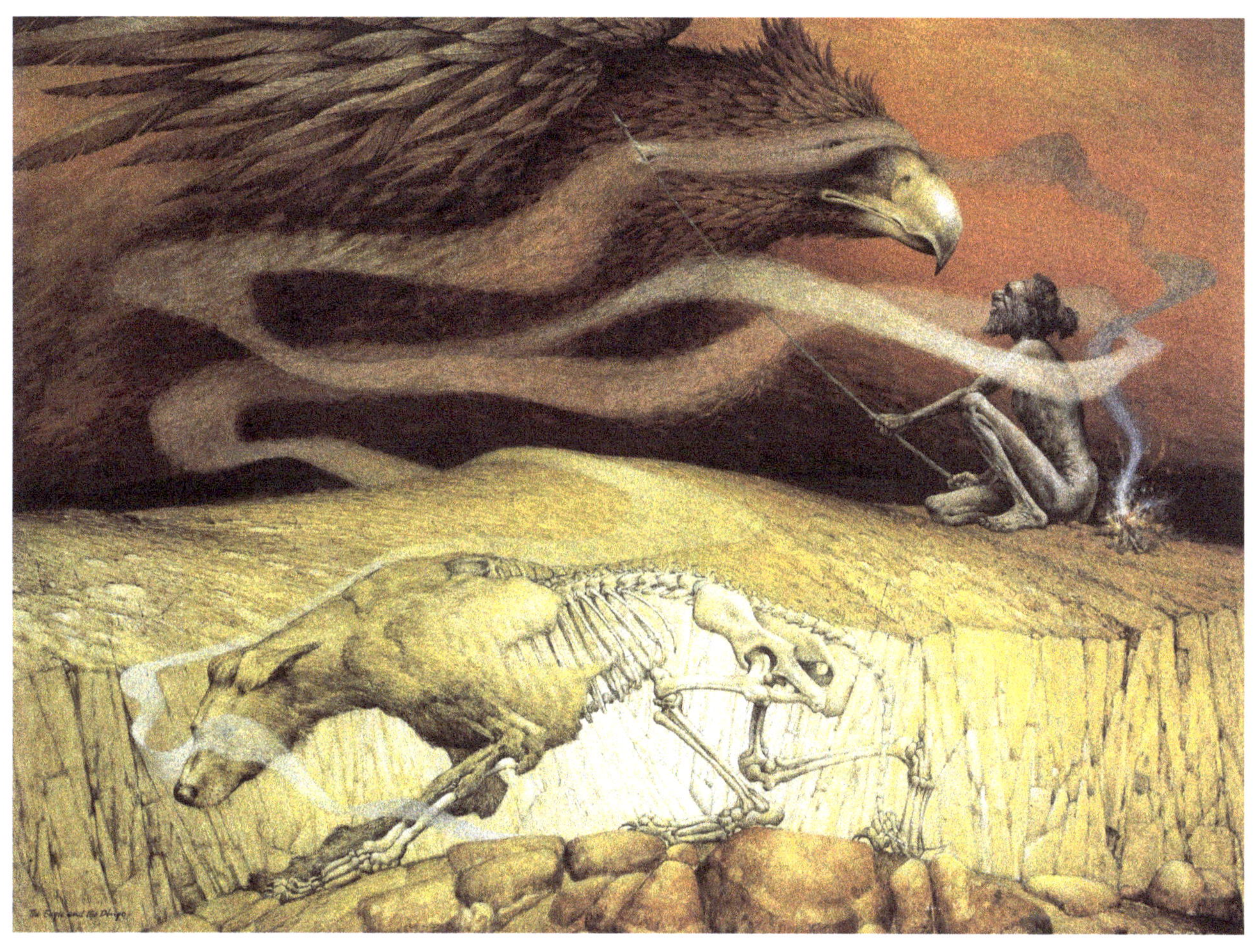

Dr and Mrs Brian Ancell.

PURUKUPALI'S WHIRLPOOL

Purukupali, one of the great creators of the Tiwi tribe of Melville Island, had an infant son, Jinini, whom he loved very much. But one day Jinini died. His mother, Bima, had neglected him while she was with her lover, Japara.

On hearing of the child's death, Purukupali became so enraged that he beat his wife over the head with a throwing-stick, and hunted her into the jungle; he then attacked her lover and covered his face with deep wounds.

Despite this, Japara wanted to help the anguished father to restore his son to life within three days. But Purukupali angrily refused the offer. He picked up the dead body of his son and walked into the sea, calling loudly as the waters closed over his head, 'As I die, so all must die and never again come to life', a decree that brought death to all the world.

The place where Purukupali drowned himself is now a large and dangerous whirlpool in Dundas Strait, between Melville Island and the mainland. In this place the current is so swift and strong that any Aboriginal attempting to cross the maelstrom in a canoe would be drowned.

When Japara saw what had happened he changed himself into the moon and rose into the sky, with his face still bearing the scars of his wounds. But, although Japara cannot entirely escape the decree of Purukupali, and has to die for three days each month, he is eternally re-incarnated.

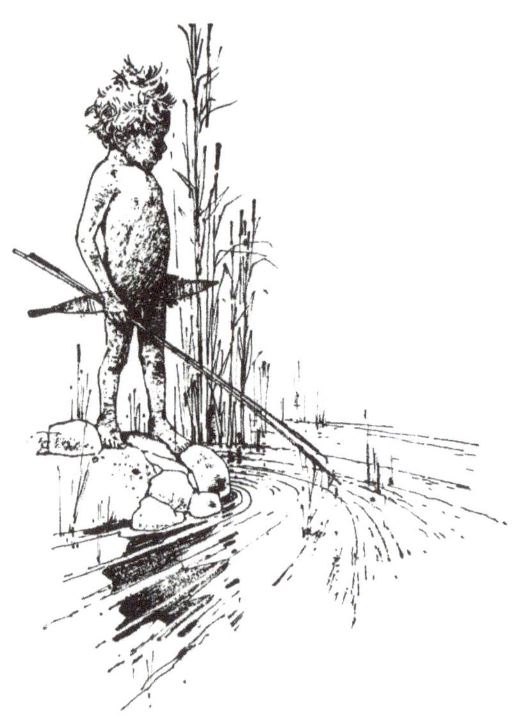

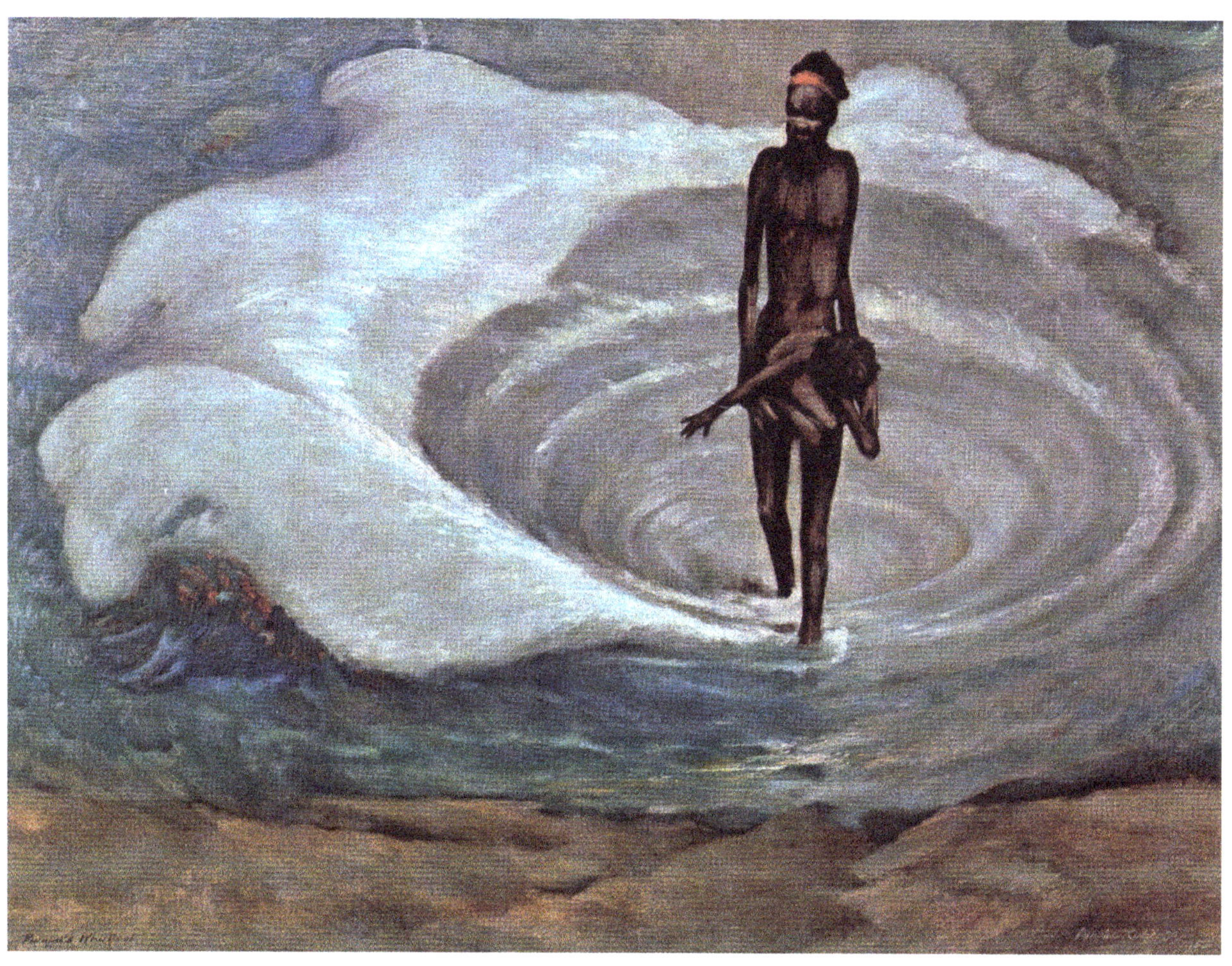

Mr and Mrs R. W. Griffiths.

BIMA THE CURLEW

When Purukupali heard that the death of his son was caused by the conduct of his wife Bima and her lover Japara, the rage of the father was unbounded.

After striking his wife over the head with a club, and hunting her into the jungle, he attacked Japara. The two men, locked in a deadly struggle, fought for hours, each wounding the other so severely that they finally fell to the ground exhausted.

When Purukupali, recovering slightly, walked into the sea with his dead son and drowned himself a great change came over the world.

Japara became the moon-man and rose into the sky, the wounds made by Purukupali still visible on his face. Bima, mother of the dead Jinini, was changed into a curlew who even now roams the forest at night, wailing with sorrow over the loss of her son and the calamity she brought to the world.

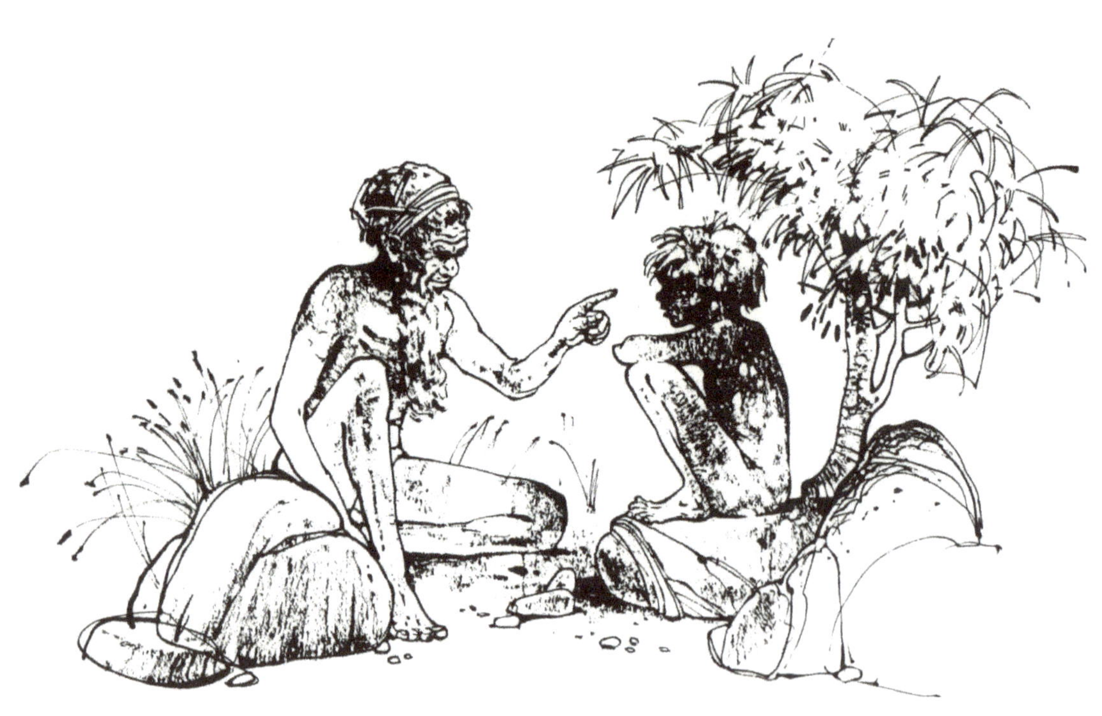

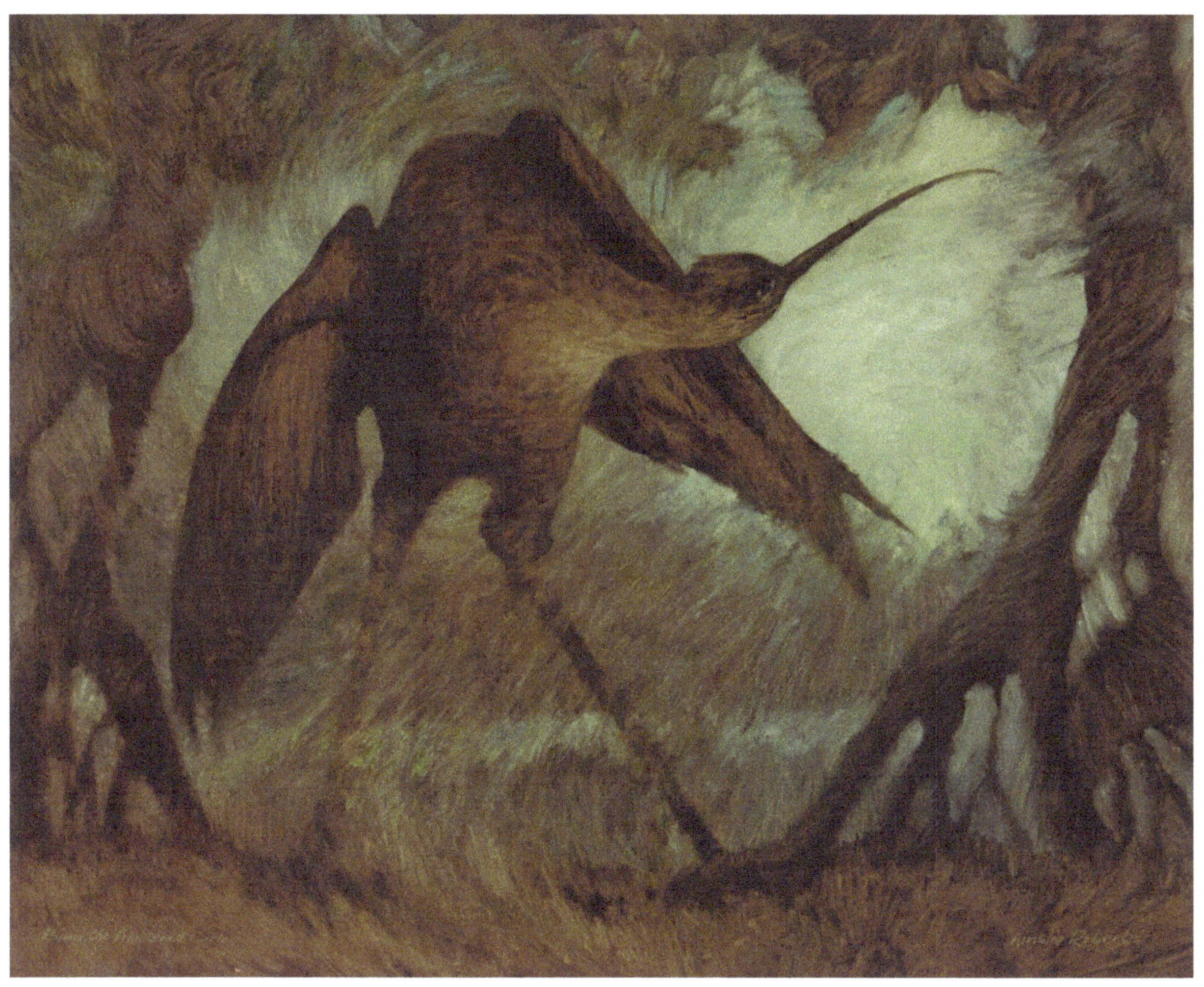

Mr M. Anders.

THE TREES BORN OF FIRE

Wapanga, although a noted warrior, was not a popular man. His preoccupation with his good looks, and his arrogant attitude, made the people of his tribe avoid him. Feeling an outcast, he took to roaming far from camp on his hunting trips, until one day he saw a young woman, Tilpana, in a neighbouring camp.

Wapanga was so captivated by her beauty that he returned to the place many times, until at last he found her alone. He asked her to go away with him, but Tilpana, liking him no better than did the women of his own tribe, made her feelings plain and ran back to her people.

Furious and humiliated, Wapanga determined to have his revenge, not only on Tilpana, but on the whole of her small tribe. So on a day of fierce heat and high winds he set light to the dense scrub near her camp. The small flames quickly became a roaring bushfire, which swept down on the camp with such speed that few escaped alive.

Tilpana was one of the few who outran the fire, and when she saw Wapanga standing in the ashes gloating over the dreadful carnage, she showed herself in the open and Wapanga gave chase. Tilpana lured him into a patch of thick scrub, and waited.

Now Tilpana had many times concealed herself to watch the secret ceremonies of her elders, and this had given her much forbidden knowledge. Although too fearful to use it before, she now called on the spirits to help her and, when Wapanga was almost upon her, surrounded him with a ring of flame and smoke.

As Wapanga tried to escape from his fiery prison, he saw with horror that the seeds dropping from the trees burst into life as soon as they fell in the flames. They grew with such speed that he was instantly enclosed with a wall of growth so thick that he could not escape.

Exhausted, Wapanga fell into the flames and died. Tilpana, who had not managed her magic quickly enough to escape the fire of her own making, was badly burnt and, as punishment for using forbidden secrets, was transformed into the crow.

Ever since that time, the crow has been black, and the strongest seed germination in the Australian bush always follows a bushfire.

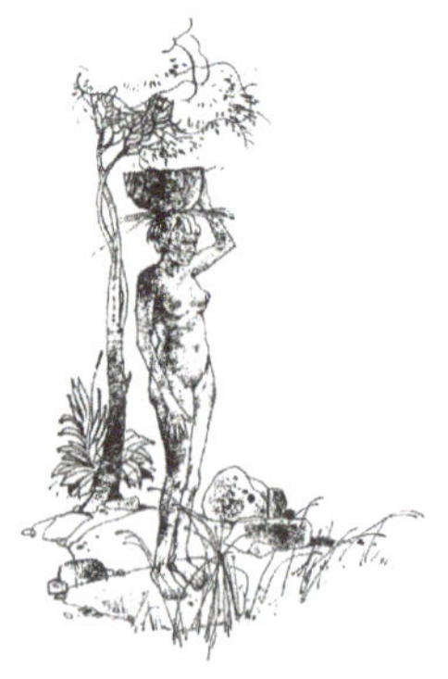

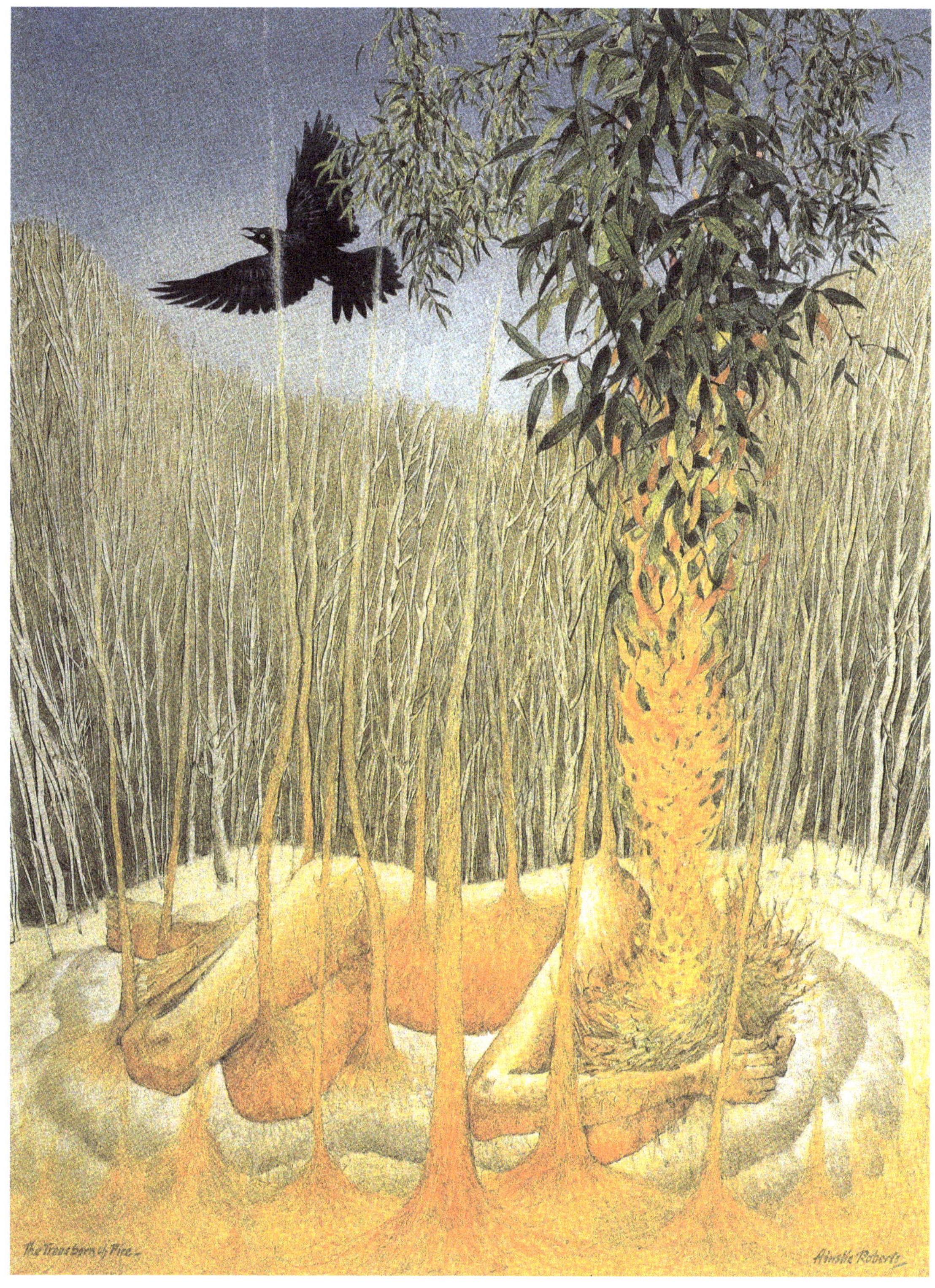

Private Collection.

BARACUMA'S FISHING NET

In a myth from South Australia, Baracuma owned the only fishing net in the world. It was so good that when he cast it into the water the net immediately filled with fish. Wandi, a friend from a neighbouring tribe, heard the story of the wonderful net and begged Baracuma to allow him to use it.

Baracuma refused to lend the net, because he knew that if it was out of his possession for any length of time he would die. Wandi pleaded with Baracuma, assuring him that he would return the net promptly. Baracuma, persuaded against his better judgement, at last allowed Wandi to take the net a way.

However, the fish were so plentiful that Wandi forgot his promise until darkness forced him to return the net. To his dismay, he found that Baracuma was dead. He tried all night to bring his friend back to life, but without success. Wandi was so ashamed over the result of his selfishness that he changed himself into a hawk and flew to the top of a high tree.

An old kangaroo-man heard that Baracuma had died for his generosity, and used magical powers to restore him to life in the form of a native cat.

The Aborigines believed that this is why Wandi the hawk lives and nests high in the treetops, and hunts for his food during the day, while Baracuma the native cat avoids the selfish Wandi by making his home underground and catching lizards and other small creatures during the hours of darkness.

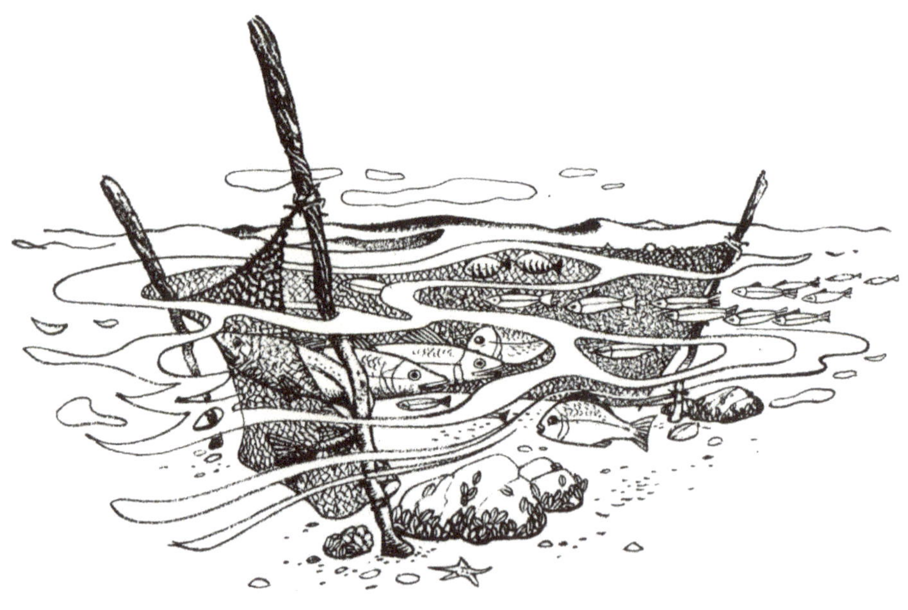

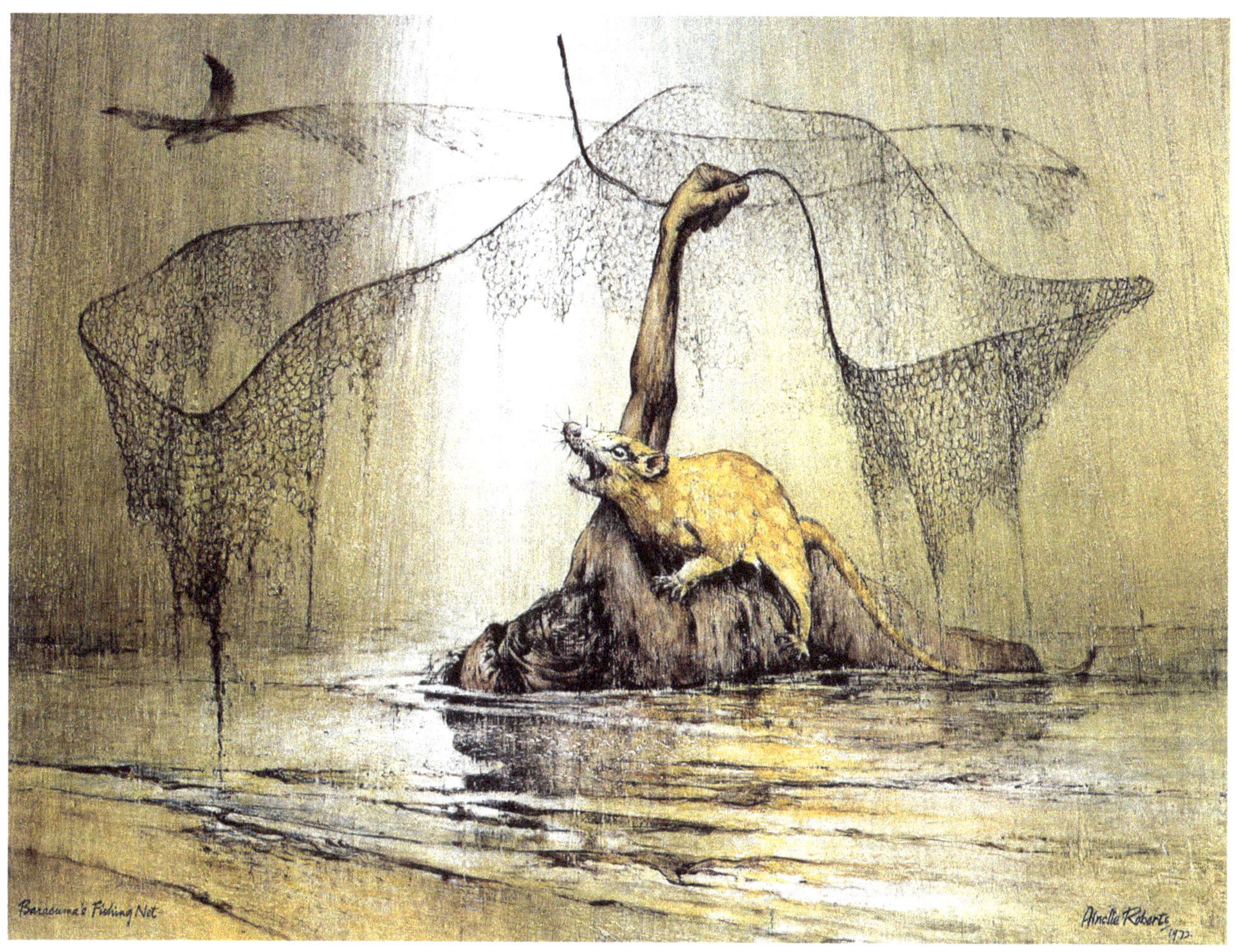

Mr and Mrs Norman Parrar.

THE WONGA PIGEON AND THE WHITE WARATAH

This story was told by an old Aboriginal who lived in the Blue Mountains, and it explains why an occasional white waratah may be found although such flowers are usually red.

The old man said that, long ago, all waratahs were white. In those days, the first wonga pigeon camped in the forest with her mate, and they grew fat on the rich food on the ground. They never flew above the trees, because they were afraid of their enemy, the hawk.

One day the wonga pigeon's mate went hunting for food, but did not return to their camp. She became anxious and set out to search for him, but without success.

After she had been searching for a long time, she plucked up her courage and decided to fly above the treetops in an attempt to see him from a height.

She had just left the shelter of the trees when she heard the call of her mate down in the forest. With her heart full of gladness she turned to fly down to him.

But she was too late. The circling hawk had seen her. Swooping down, he clasped her in his sharp claws, tearing her breast open as he carried her upwards. Her blood rained down on the forest, but she tore herself free and hid among the blossoms of the waratahs.

The hawk had just flown away when she again heard her mate calling to her. Although she was weak from loss of blood, and could fly only short distances, she endeavoured to reach him. Every time that she rested on a white waratah, to recover her strength, her blood stained its bloom. In a final struggle she reached yet another waratah, and there she died as the last blood ebbed from her wounded body.

Today, the old man explained, it is possible, though it is rare, to find a waratah that has not been stained by the blood of the lonely wonga pigeon who lost her life while searching for her mate.

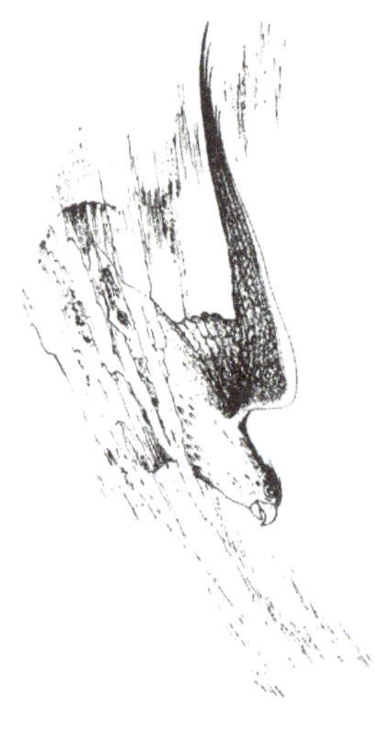

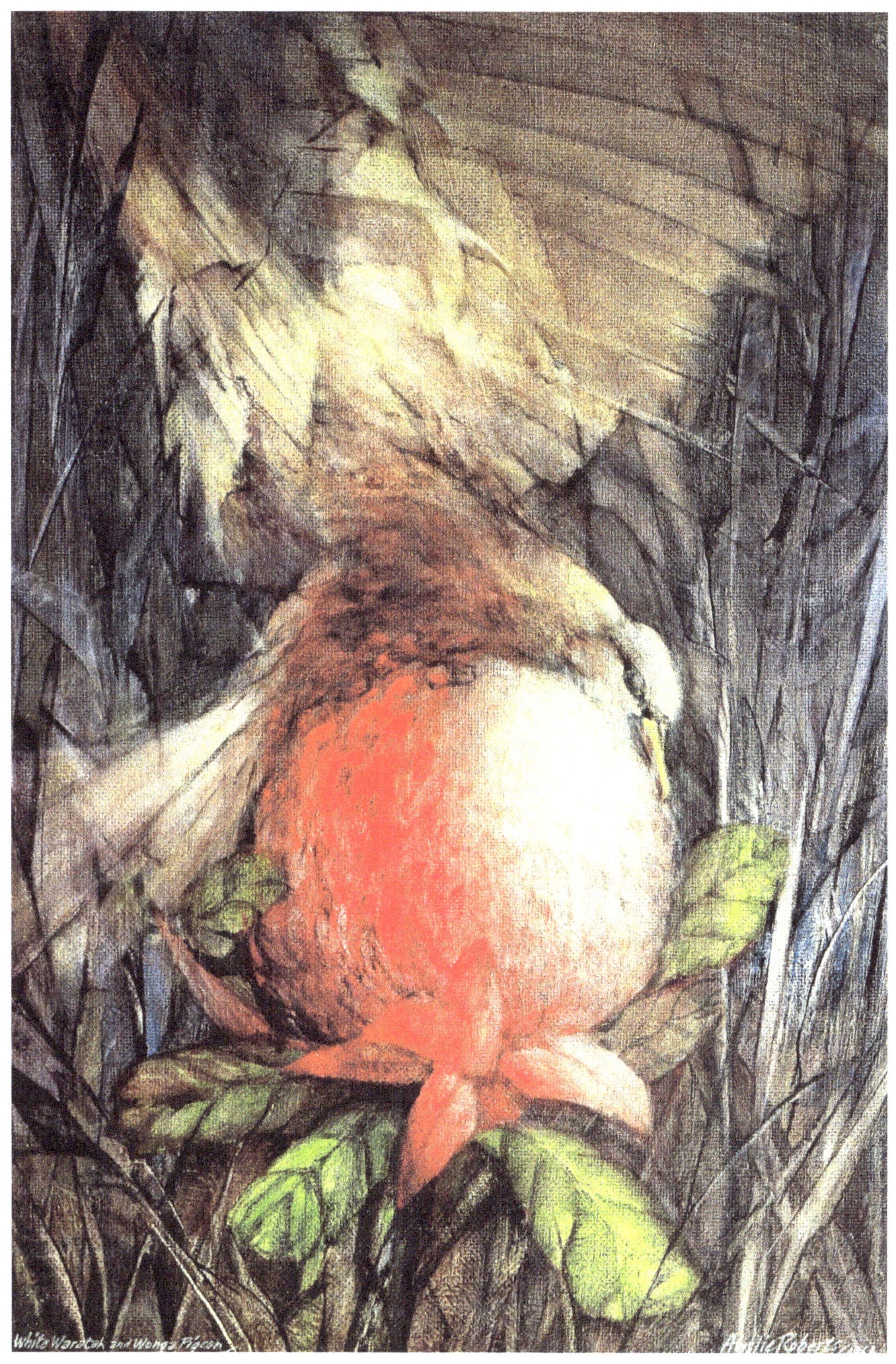

Dr Graham Welch.

THE TRANSFORMATION OF BURNBA

The hawk-man, Wabula, was without a wife. One day he visited a neighboring tribe and was attracted to an unmarried girl, Burnba. Wabula went to the near-by beach, caught some lobsters, and cooked them. Then he returned to the camp and offered them to the girl who, much to his disgust, would have nothing to do with him.

Wabula was determined to capture her. He retired to a spot out of sight and hearing of the camp, and there he built a bark hut. That night he returned to the sleeping camp and carried Burnba away by force, placed her in the hut, and blocked up all the openings so that she could not escape.

Afraid and lonely, Burnba cried all night for her father to help her. He was a skilled magician and had a spear-thrower with which he had performed many wonders. The first time he rubbed it, a heavy wind sprang up and grew stronger and stronger. It blew violently upon the bark hut, which shook so much that cracks appeared in it everywhere. The magician rubbed the spear-thrower a second time, and transformed his daughter into a butterfly. In this form she was able to escape through one of the cracks.

At last the wind lifted the bark hut off the ground and Wabula discovered that Burnba had gone. Still yearning for the girl, he changed himself into a hawk, so that he and Burnba could always live in the same element.

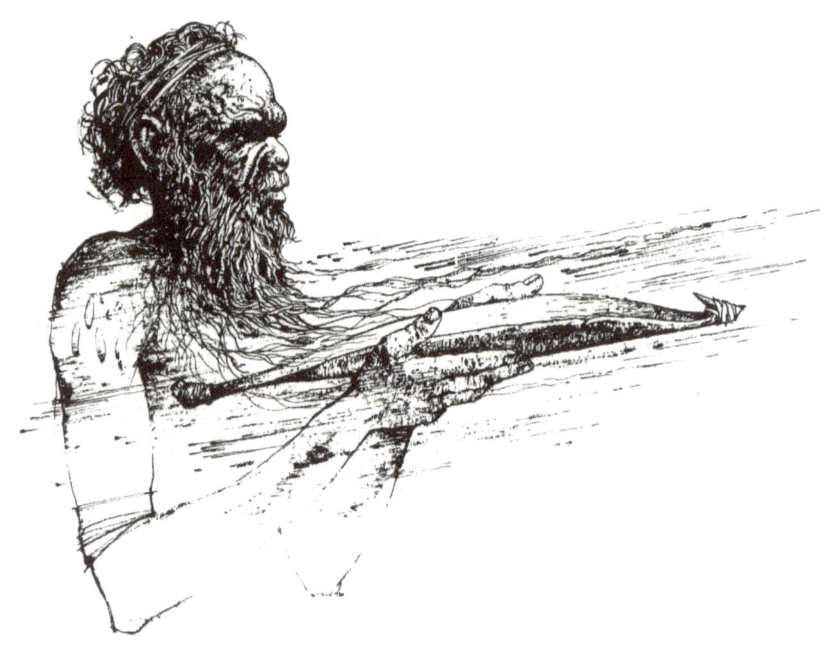

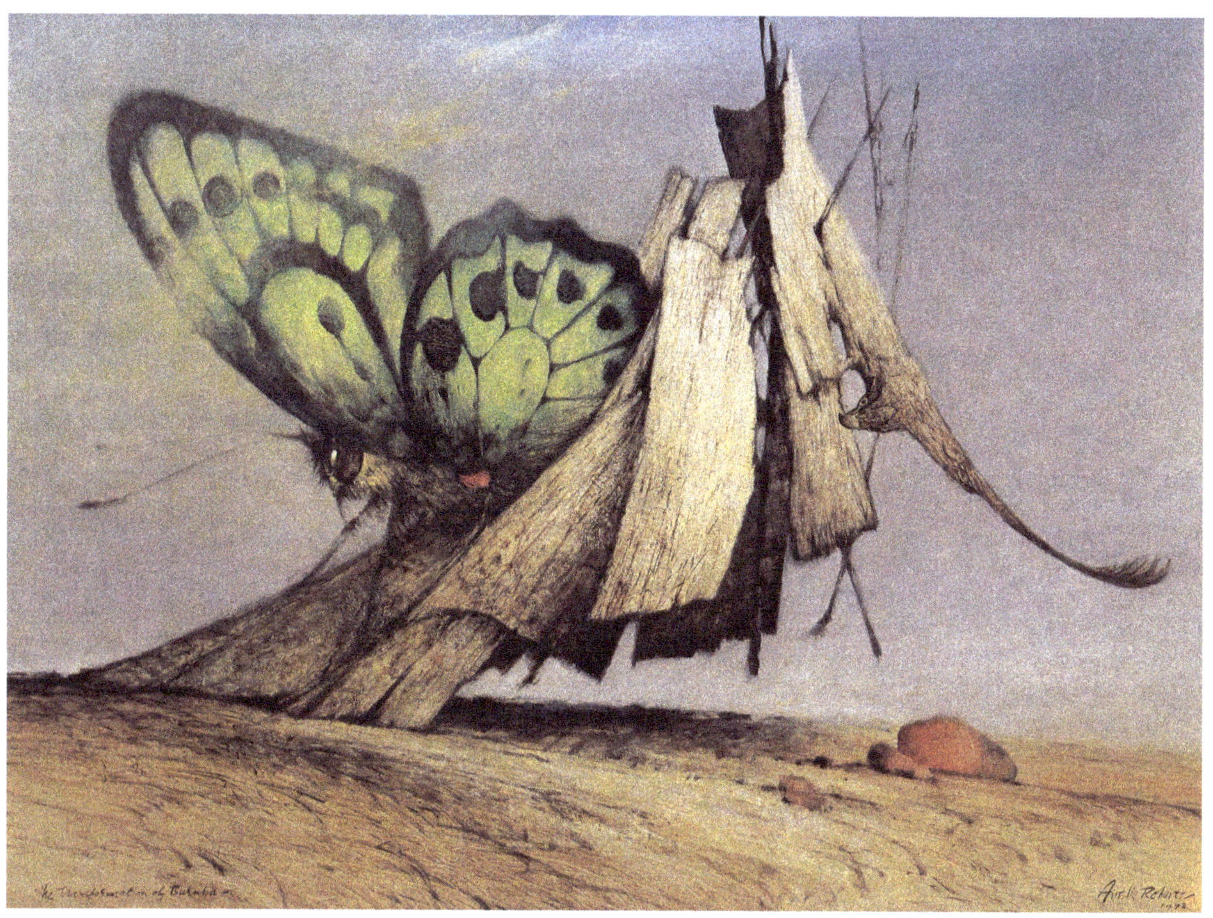

Mrs Melva Roberts.

THE LIGHTNING-MAN WALA-UNDAYUA

The Aborigines of northern Arnhem Land are afraid of the mythical lightning-man, Wala-undayua. During the dry season he spends most of his time in a deep waterhole in the Liverpool River, though sometimes he hunts for wallabies among the cabbage palms along its banks.

Wala-undayua looks on these palms as his personal property, and should anyone so much as touch their trunks, he would kill them with a lightning flash. But should an Aboriginal throw a stone into his waterhole, an even greater misfortune would happen, for then the lightning-man, furious over this indignity, would rise into the air and create thunderstorms of such violence that everyone would be destroyed.

But it is when the monsoon rains begin that the lightning-man becomes most belligerent.

Leaving his waterhole, he travels in the clouds, roars with the voice of thunder, and with his long arms and legs (which are the lightning flashes) savagely strikes the ground, leaving the burnt-out forest and shattered trees of the devastated landscape as evidence of his wrath.

At the end of the wet-season, Wala-undayua returns to his waterhole, where he lives peacefully until the monsoon clouds again form in the sky to renew his violence.

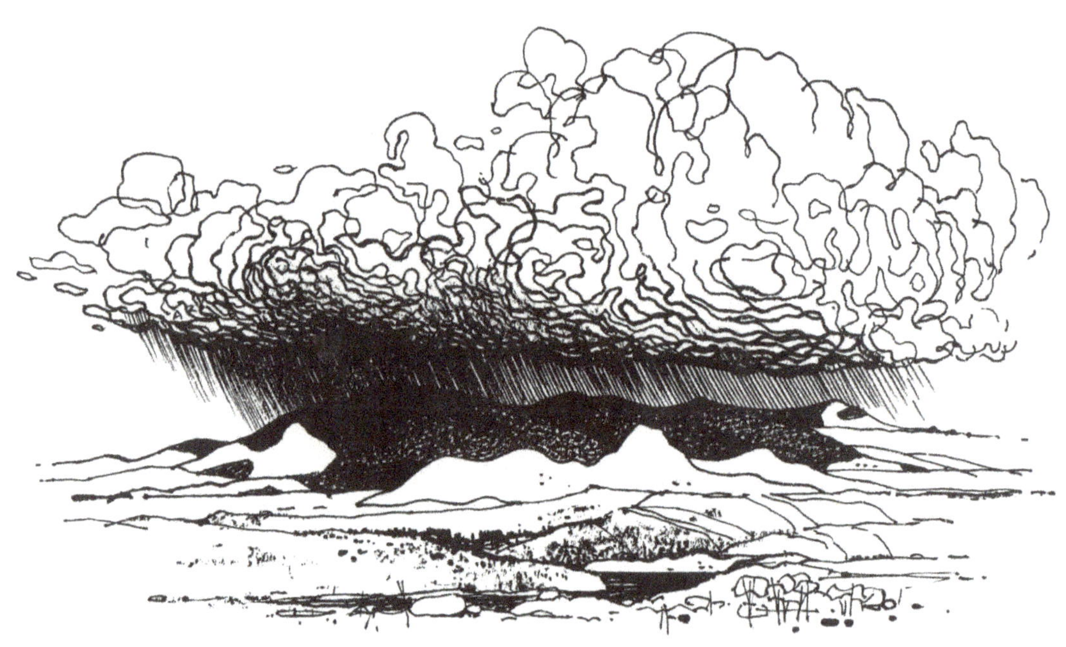

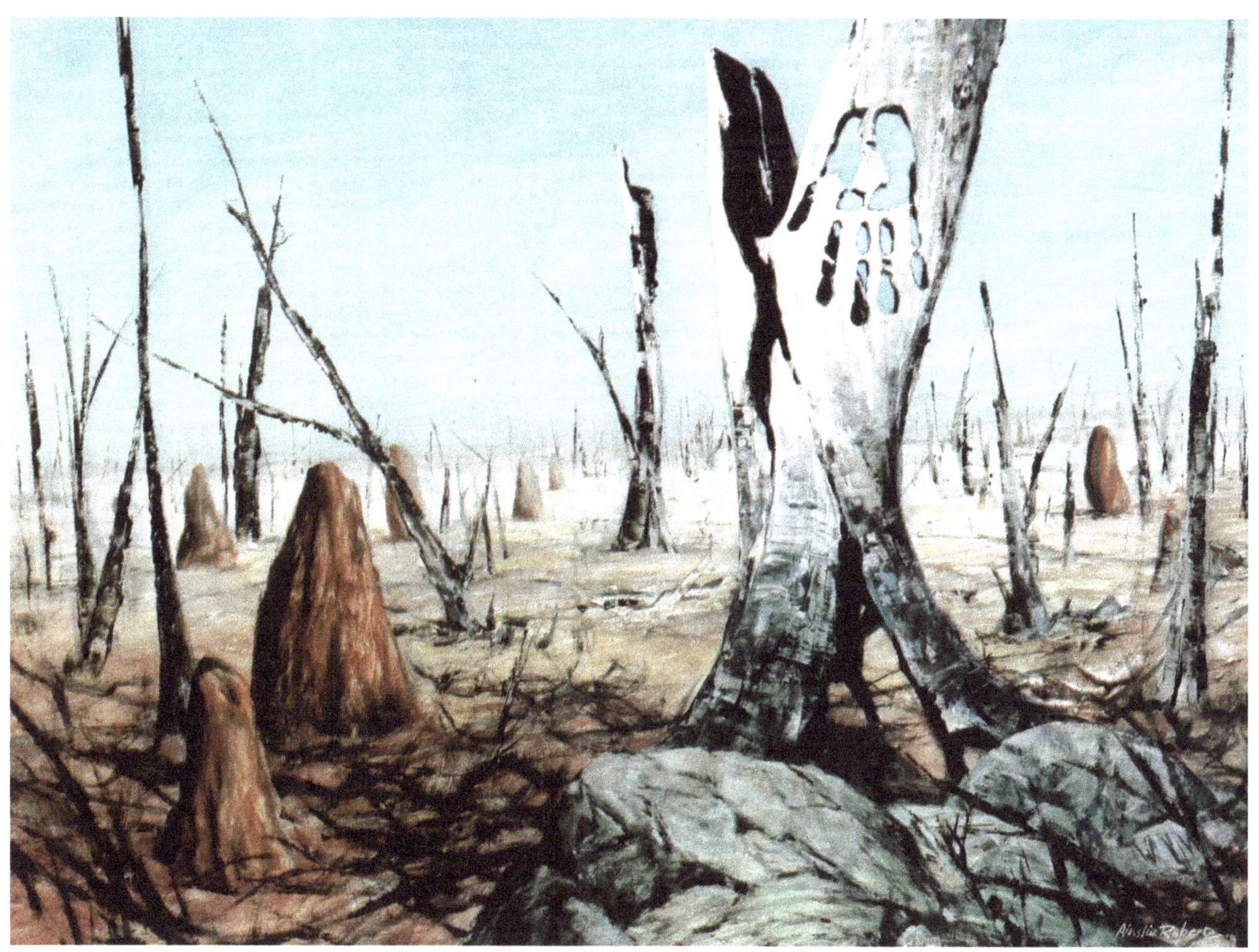

Mrs Lindsay C. Mills.

THE BURNING CORMORANT

The Aborigines of Yorke Peninsula in South Australia believed that the origin of the cormorant, or shag, happened in this way, long ago in the Dreamtime.

Buthera, a powerful tribal chief, was on a journey to visit a distant southern tribe when he encountered an old enemy, Madjitju, chief of the Bat-tribe. Buthera accused Madjitju of trespassing and, after exchanging many insults, they resorted to violence. They fought for many hours until finally Madjitju suffered so many injuries that he died.

Exhausted, and in pain, Buthera slowly continued his journey, and at last reached his destination. But he was angry to find that the willy-wagtail, always the first with any news, and always the first to gossip about it, had spread stories of the fight far and wide. Not only did the whole tribe know about the fight and Madjitju's death, but some of the many variations of the story were plainly damaging to Buthera's prestige.

Now Buthera was a renowned man of magic, as well as a great chief, and he used his magical powers to punish the tribe for spreading malicious gossip about him. He pointed his spear to the east, to the south, to the west, and finally to the north.

Fires sprang up everywhere and a great wind came down from the north. Soon the whole country was blazing, and the tribe crowded into the deep water holes to escape the flames. Having burnt out their country, Buthera finally took pity on them, and transformed all of them into cormorants.

To this day, the cormorant only has white underneath. The rest of him is jet-black where he was scorched by Buthera's fire.

And the willy-wagtail, who was also caught in the fire, is marked in the same way. But he is still an inquisitive gossiper.

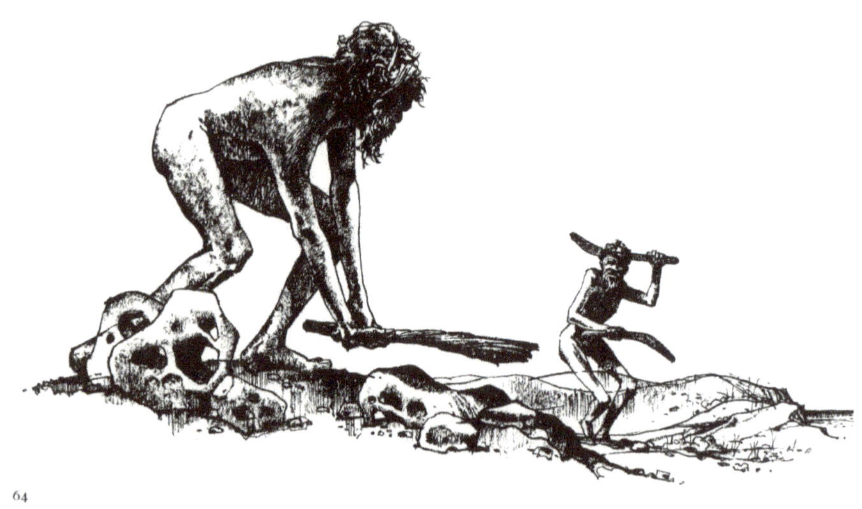

64

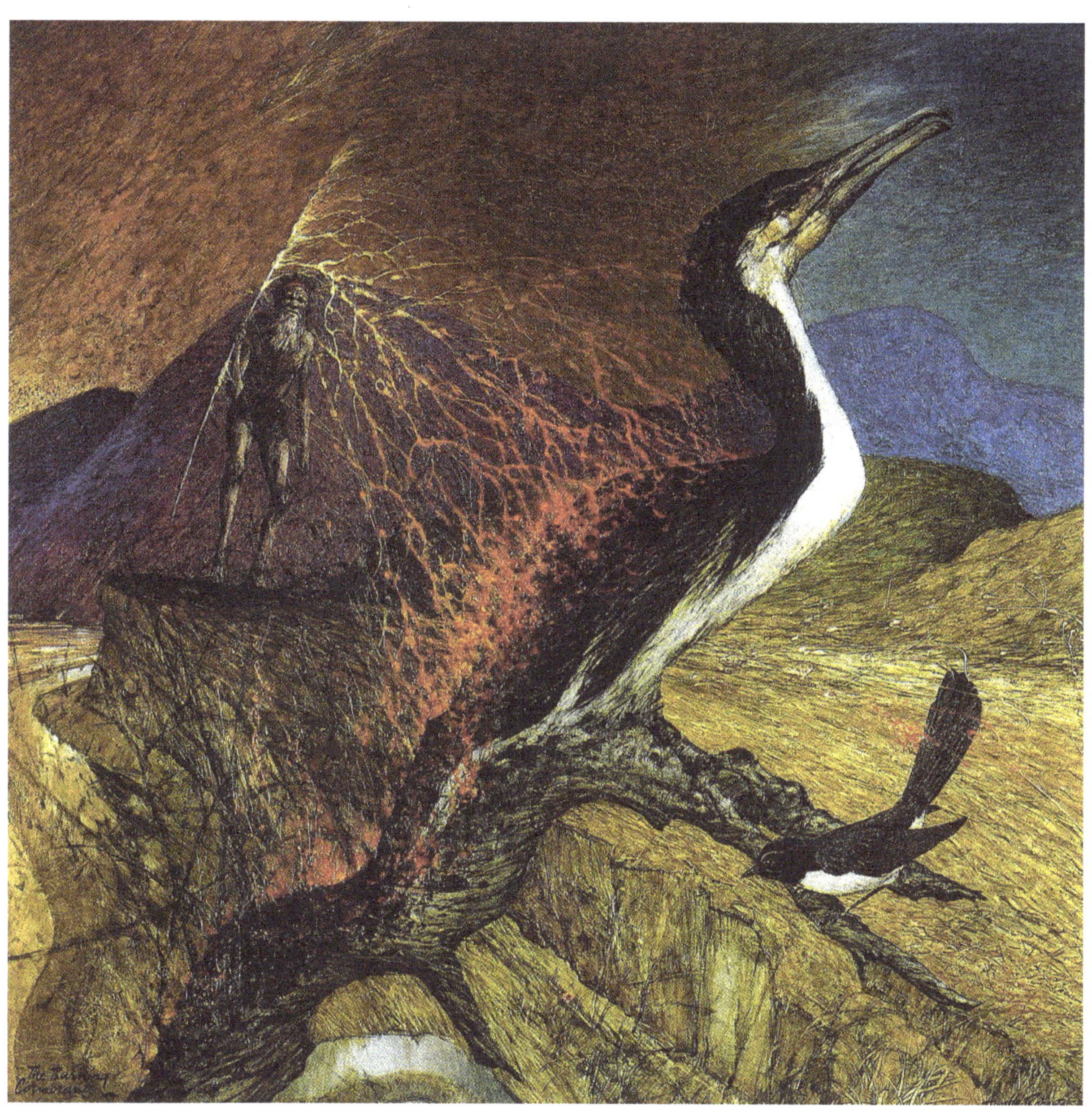

Private Collection.

THE MIMICS

In the great creation period of the Australian Aborigines, the animals and the birds enjoyed a common language. In their communal life there were no sorrows and no antagonism, and always there was an abundance of food. Each year they held many corroborees and feasts.

But at one of these gatherings the frog, who in those days was a wonderful mimic, started imitating the voices of his companions. He was so pleased with his efforts, and at the perfection of his gift, that he could not stop. He went on and on, making ruder and ruder remarks until many quarrels and fights broke out.

The eagle, the native cat, the kangaroo, the platypus, the goanna, and the crow all seemed to be hurling insults at each other, until the frog, in the voice of the wombat, called out 'To battle, to battle', and in the resultant fight many creatures were killed or hurt. Only the lyrebird took no part in the uproar, and tried in vain to stop it.

This fighting annoyed the spirits so much that they took away the common language and made each creature adopt a language of its own. But as a reward for the lyrebird's part in the affair, the spirits gave it the power to imitate all the animals, birds, reptiles, and insects.

And so the lyrebird became the greatest mimic of all, and the Aborigines took care not to annoy it. They knew, through their mythology, that what had happened because of the frog might well happen again if the lyrebird was not kept in a happy frame of mind.

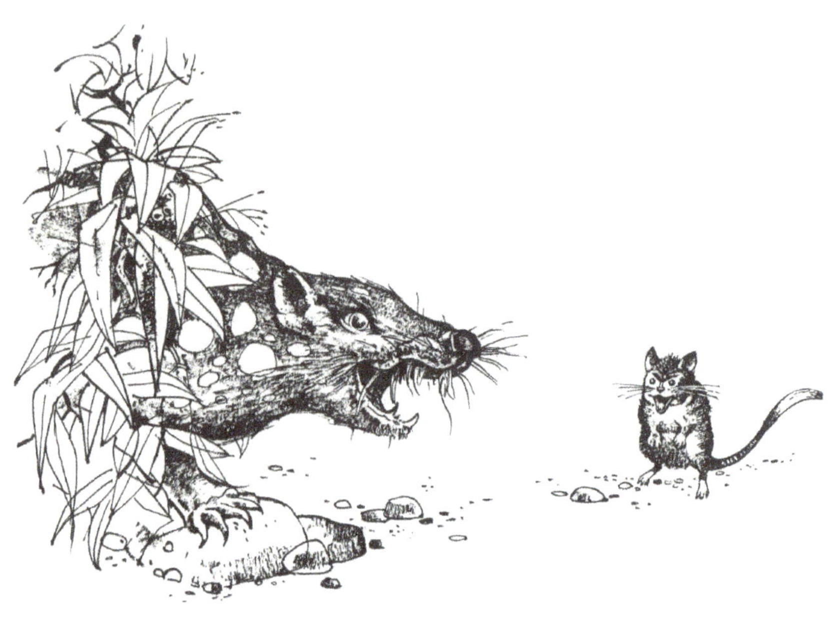

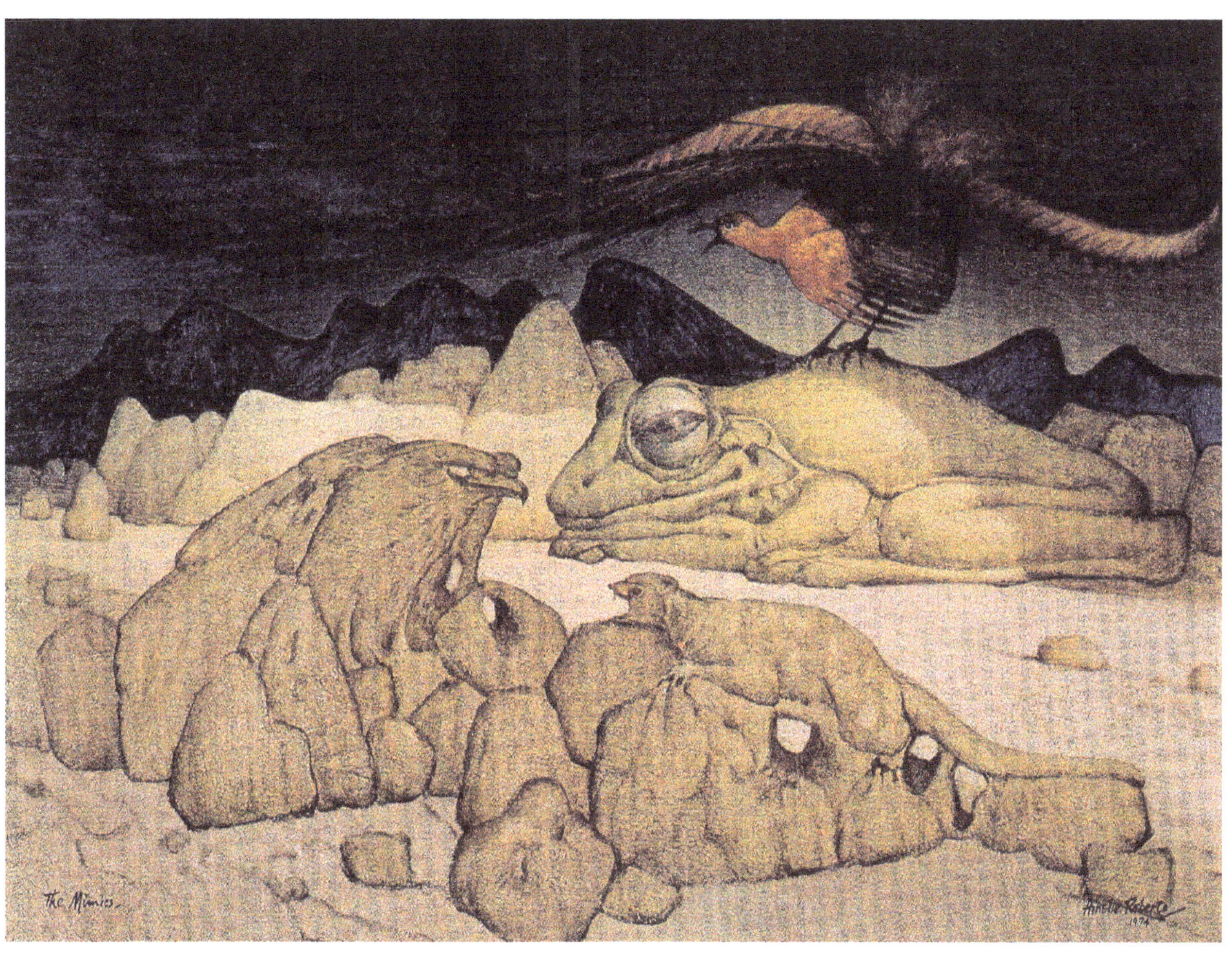

Sir Robert Helpmann.

THE ISLAND OF SPEARS

The Murrumbidgee River was once the dividing boundary between two tribes. Each group respected the laws of the other, but there came a day when Gobba-gumbalin, a young warrior from the southern tribe, spoke to Pomin-galana, a young woman of the neighbouring tribe who was swimming by the bank.

After this they took every opportunity to meet, even though the woman was promised to a warrior of her own tribe. Their desire for each other became so strong that they planned to run away to the near-by hills, where they hoped they would be safe from the certain vengeance of both tribes.

Their love was so strong that they became incautious, and both tribes came to know of their nightly meetings. The elders decided that, for the sake of tribal peace, the lovers should be destroyed. So on the night when they swam to meet each other in the centre of the river, intending to escape by swimming downstream, many spearmen from both tribes were hidden in the reeds lining each bank. Just as the lovers reached each other they were pierced by a hail of spears and sank to the river bottom.

Today, a reed-covered island in mid-river marks the spot where they died. The Aborigines say that the reeds are the spears that killed the lovers; that the red cliffs further downstream were stained by their blood; and that the frogs on either side of the river still mourn their fate, because those on one side call 'Gobba-gumbalin', and the frogs on the opposite bank reply with the sound of 'Pom in-gal ana'.

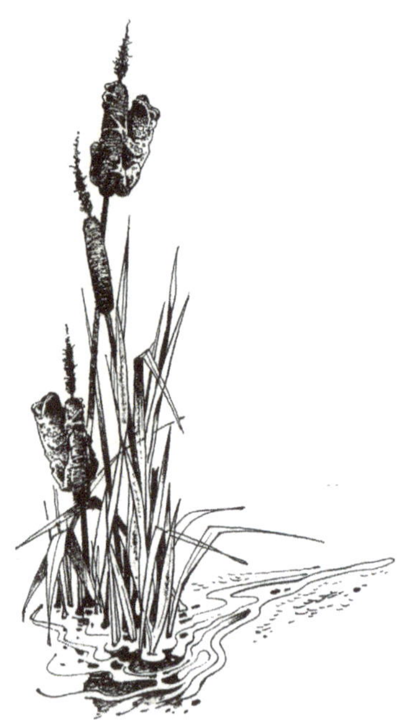

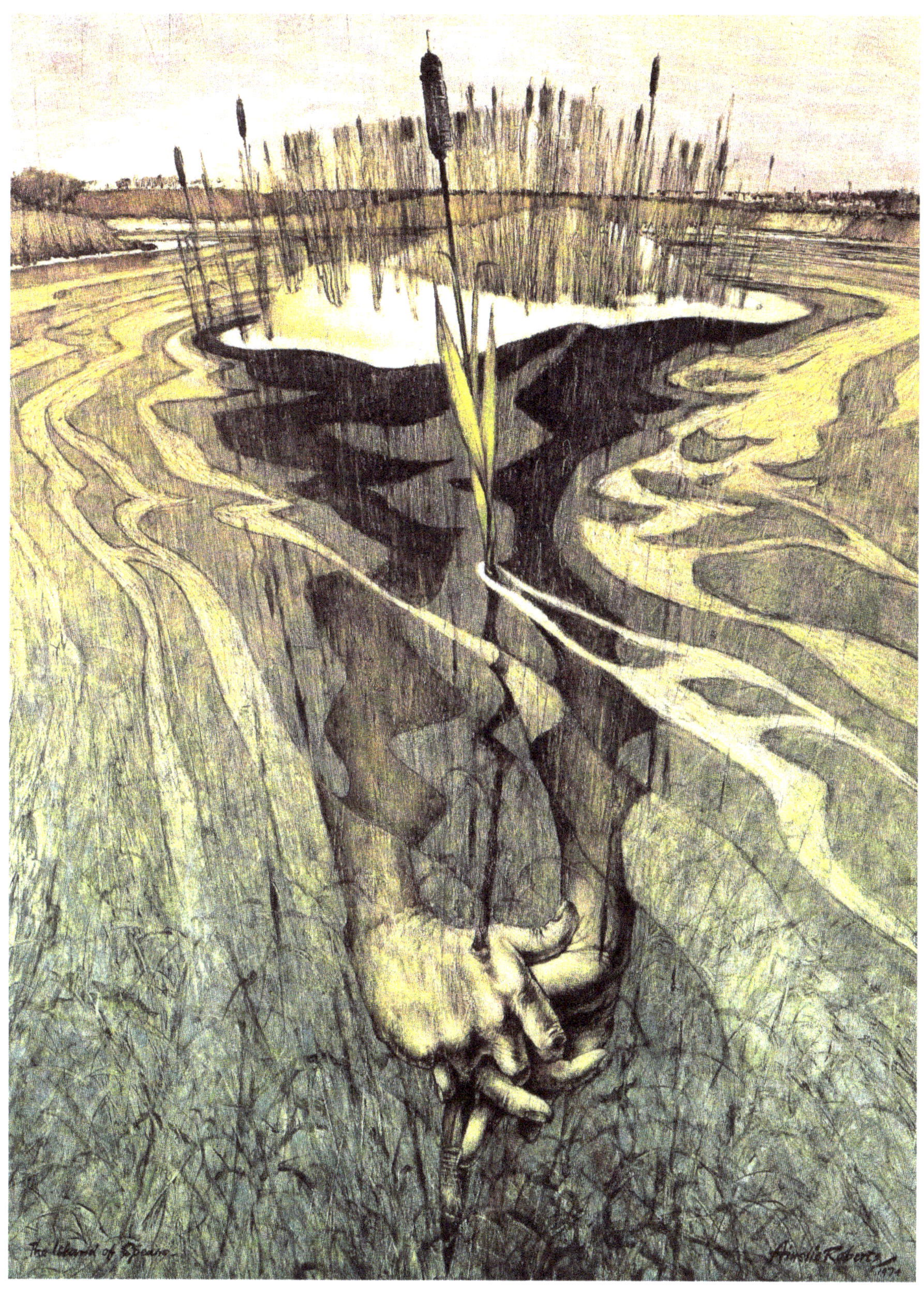

Commander and Mrs R. Brasch.

THE CREATION OF BLACK MOUNTAIN

The Aborigines of the Cooktown area related how, long ago in the Dreamtime, there lived two brothers, Tajalruji and Kalruji. Since childhood they had been close companions, and in manhood they became mighty hunters. They supplied their tribe with food gained almost daily from their journeys to the tribal hunting grounds. The country in this region was flat and covered with shining black boulders.

One day, when the brothers were hunting on the farthest edge of their land, they saw a beautiful girl digging for yams. She was of the rock python totem, and would have been an acceptable mate for either of the men, who were of the wallaby totem.

In that moment, when each wanted the girl for himself, the previously inseparable brothers became enemies. They decided to fight for her, but this decision was hard to carry out. They both knew that their tribal laws forbade them to use hunting weapons against another member of the tribe. Eventually they decided that each should make a mound of the great black stones so that he who built the highest could cast a boulder down to destroy his rival.

Watched by the girl, the men toiled day after day until two huge piles rose from the plain.

First one and then the other would be just a little taller, but not enough for either brother to cast the final boulder. So preoccupied were they with the deadly task that neither of them saw the first shreds of cloud that Kakahinka, the cyclone, flew as a warning that he was near.

The cyclone struck, and in its devastation the two brothers died on their mounds of stones. The girl was blown away by the wind and lost in the tangle of boulders and vegetation left in the wake of the cyclone.

Today, the great mass of stones still remains and is known as Black Mountain, or the Mountain of Death. The story explains why the only living creatures to be found there are the huge rock pythons and the black wallabies.

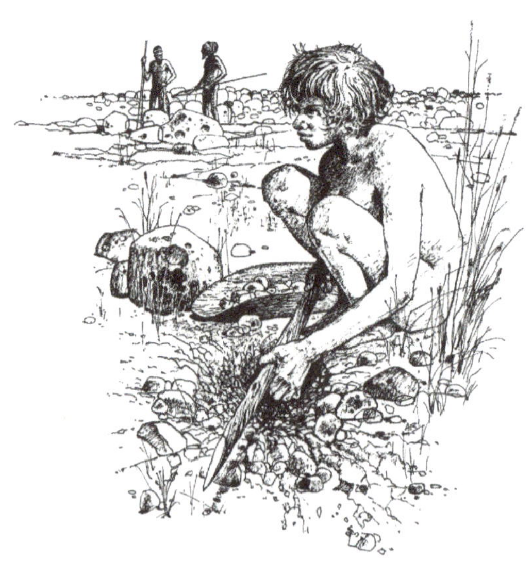

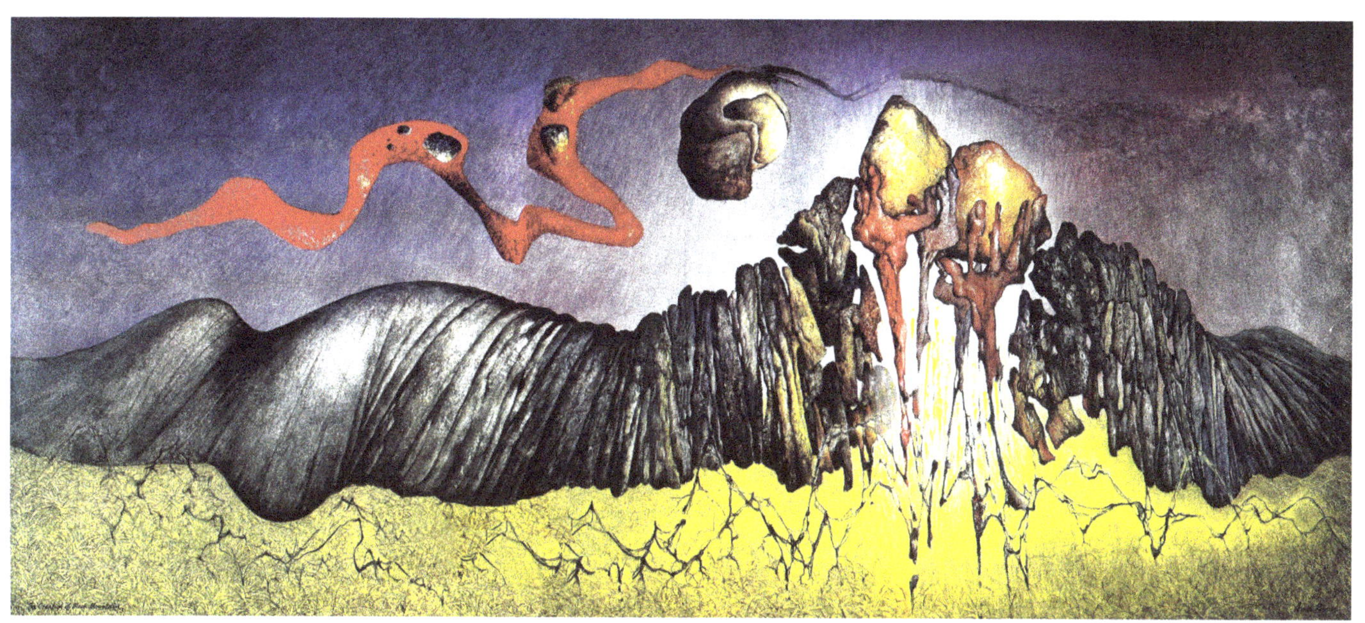

Hans Looser of Cooktown, who recorded this myth, describes Black Mountain as 'the most evil place in Australia'. The mountain of black boulders rises bare and sinister out of the tropical rainforests a few miles south of the old gold-mining port. Honeycombed with caves and tunnels, it has always been a place of tragedy. A man was first recorded as having disappeared there in r877, and since then eleven men are known to have ventured on to Black Mountain and vanished without trace. Straying cattle and horses have also disappeared. No vegetation grows on the slopes of the mountain, birds and animals shun the area, and the Aborigines would never approve.

Mr Dale Roberts.

THE SEVEN EMU SISTERS

Wanjin, the men of the dingo totem, desired as their wives the seven emu sisters, the Makara. But the unwilling women evaded their suitors by flying to another locality, for in those times emus had full-sized wings.

To escape the advances of the Wanjin, the Makara sisters made their home under the tumbled boulders of a rocky outcrop, but the dingo-men, with their keen sense of smell, soon found their hiding places.

Realizing that they could not lure the women from their home, the dingo-men lit a bushfire that quickly surrounded the whole outcrop. The men knew that the smoke would drive the Makara into the open, and that the blazing fire would so scorch the wings of the Makara that they could be easily captured.

The plans of the Wanjin were only partly successful; the flames from the bushfire did deprive the emu-women of the power of flight, but the strenuous efforts of the Makara to step over the burning grass and bushes made their legs grow so long that even to this day the emu can outdistance almost every other creature.

Escaping from the fire, the Makara ran to the ends of the earth, but still the Wanjin followed them. Finally, the desperate women rose up into the sky to become the group of stars known today as the Seven Sisters. The Wanjin men, so that they could still pursue the Seven Sisters, also went into the sky, changing themselves to the constellation of Orion. But the emu-women are always the first to reach the western horizon, where, for a time, they are safe from the unwelcome attentions of the dingo-men.

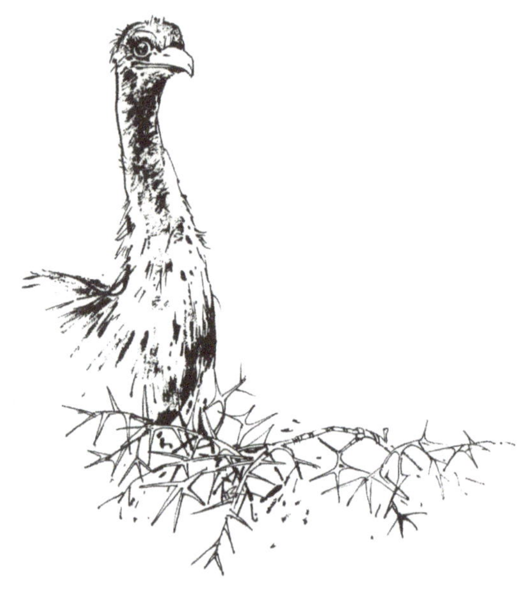

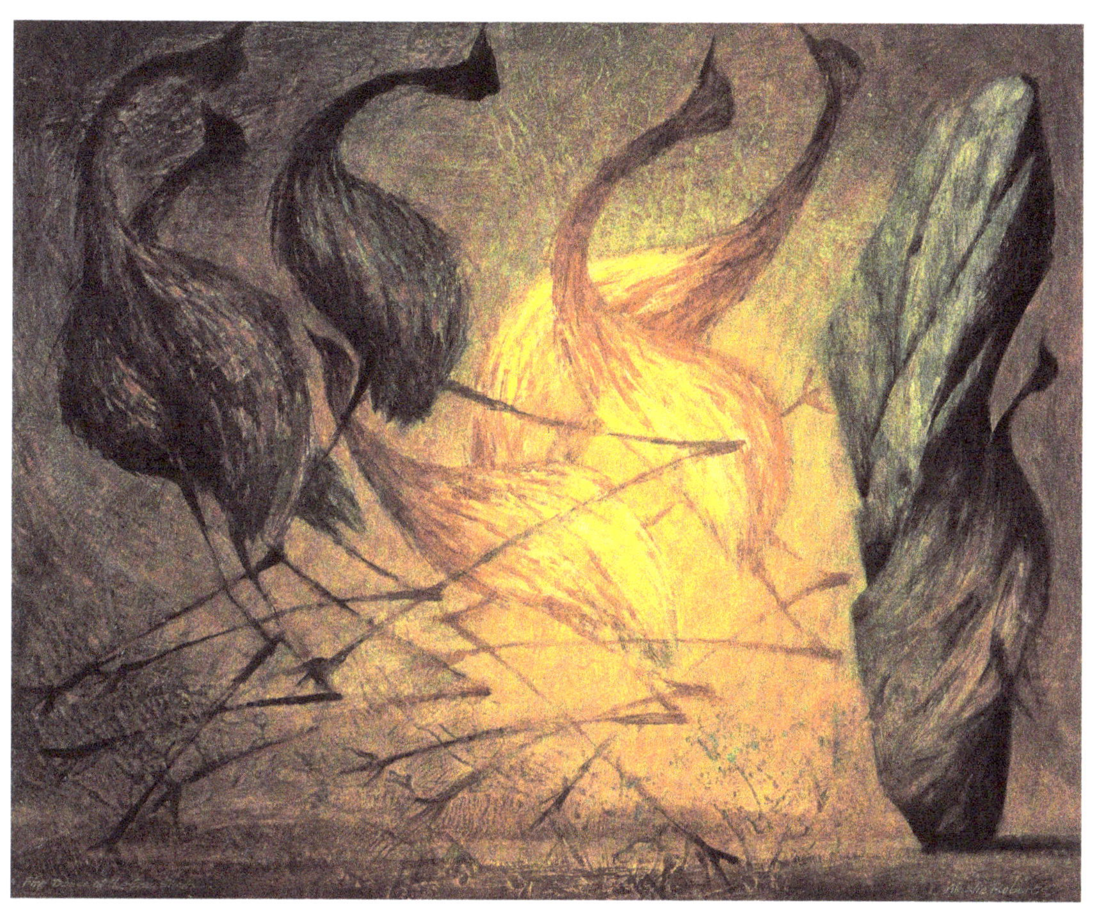

Mrs T. B. Simpson.

THE VOICE OF NATURE

The Australian Aborigines' complete identification with their environment was not only their solution to the problem of survival but also a rich and rewarding spiritual experience. The great Ancestral Being of the creation period - the Dreamtime - made their world and all forms of life, and dictated the laws and patterns of behaviour that governed their tribal life. They felt secure in a belief that the voice of their creative Ancestor spoke to them in everything.

But they were not always faithful to this belief. An Aboriginal myth from southern Australia relates how, in the beginning, the voice of the Ancestor spoke each day from a great gum tree, and the tribe gathered around to listen. But as time went by the people grew weary of hearing his words of wisdom. One by one they turned their backs on the voice to pursue their own pleasures, and a vast silence settled over the whole of the land and the sea. There was no wind and the tides were still, no birds sang, and the earth seemed to be dying.

The tribe soon wearied of the pleasures of their own making and began to be afraid and lonely. They returned to the great tree again and again, hoping to hear the words that would ease their misery. And one day the voice of their Ancestor spoke again.

He told them it was the last time his voice would be heard, but that he would give them a sign. The great tree split open, a huge tongue of light came down into it, and then it closed up again.

Since that time the Aborigines have known that the voice of their Ancestor exists in all things, and speaks to them through every part of nature.

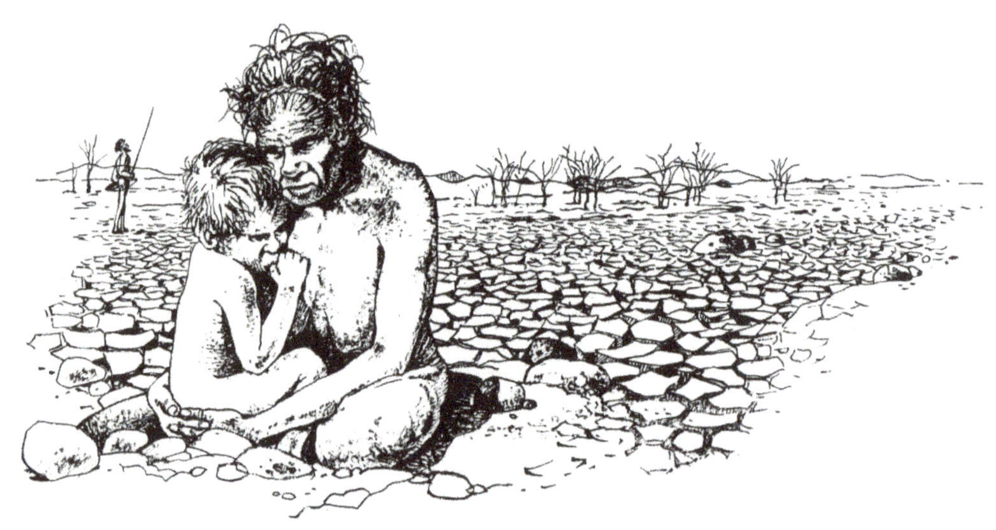

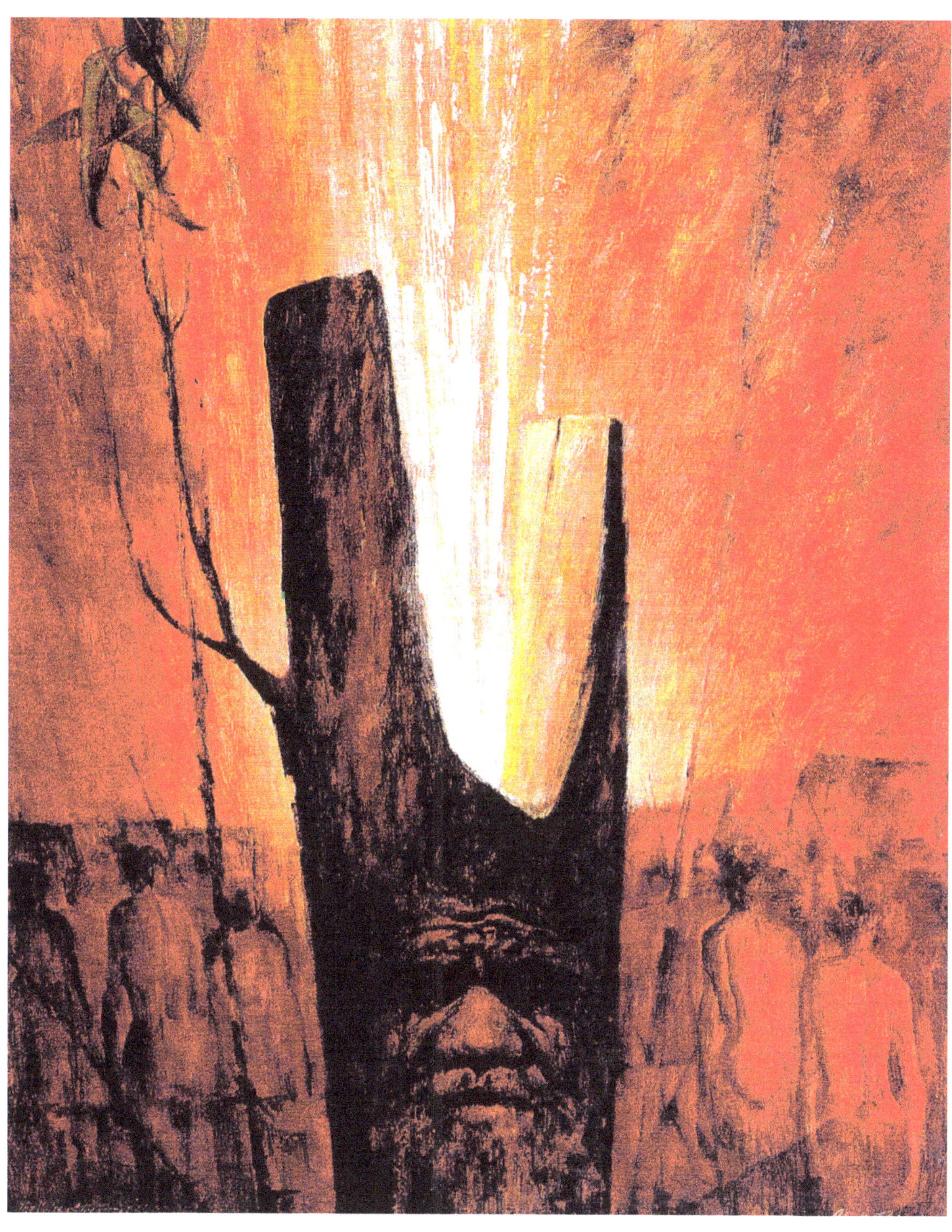

Mr and Mrs R. W. Griffiths.

WUNGALA AND THE EVIL-BIG-EYED-ONE

Wungala was away from the camp with her small son, Bulla, and all morning they had gathered seeds. Afterwards, she sat at her milling stone and ground the seeds into powder, then added water to make it into a thick dough. Bulla ran around, laughing and talking to himself as he gathered sticks to put on their fire.

The sun shone brightly at first, but when some clouds threw a shadow across the earth, Wungala called her son to her and told him to stay close, warning him that he must now remain quiet. When Bulla asked why, his mother explained that with the shadows came the Evil-Big-Eyed-One from his cave in the hills, and should it hear Bulla's chattering, it would seek them out and eat them both up.

Bulla, being very small and forgetful, wandered off again, only to rush back to his mother screaming that he had seen the evil one. Wungala, too, had seen it coming their way, and she said, 'You are wrong, Bulla, nothing is there but the shadows made by some waving bushes.'

She spoke as calmly as she could, knowing that they were safe only if she pretended that the evil-one was not there. If they showed panic, and ran, they would be finished. So she went on talking calmly, making more and more dough, and finally putting it on the hot coals to bake.

Each time the Evil-Big-Eyed-One came closer, and roared at them, Bulla cried out in fear. And, each time, Wungala calmed Bulla by telling him that the noise was only a wallaby, or a cockatoo, or some other creature out there in the bushes.

At this show of indifference, the evil creature was puzzled as to why it should seem to be invisible to the woman. In its curiosity, it crept right up behind her. This was the moment when Wungala carried out her desperate plan. She gathered up the great mass of dough in both hands, swung around, and threw the hot sticky mass in its face.

Quickly picking up her son, Wungala fled back to the camp and the safety of her people, leaving the evil one roaring in agony as it tried to scrape the hot dough from its eye and mouth.

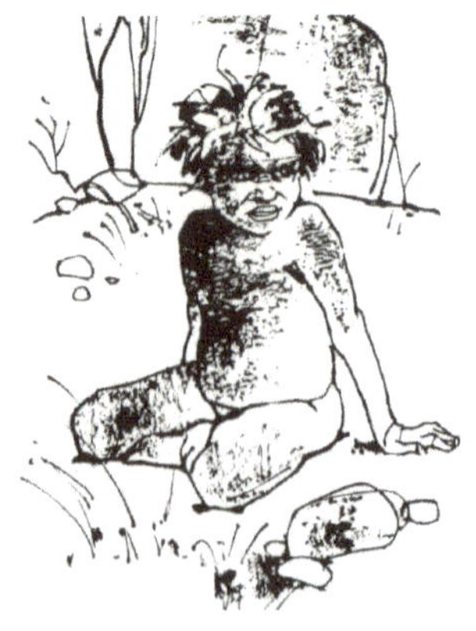

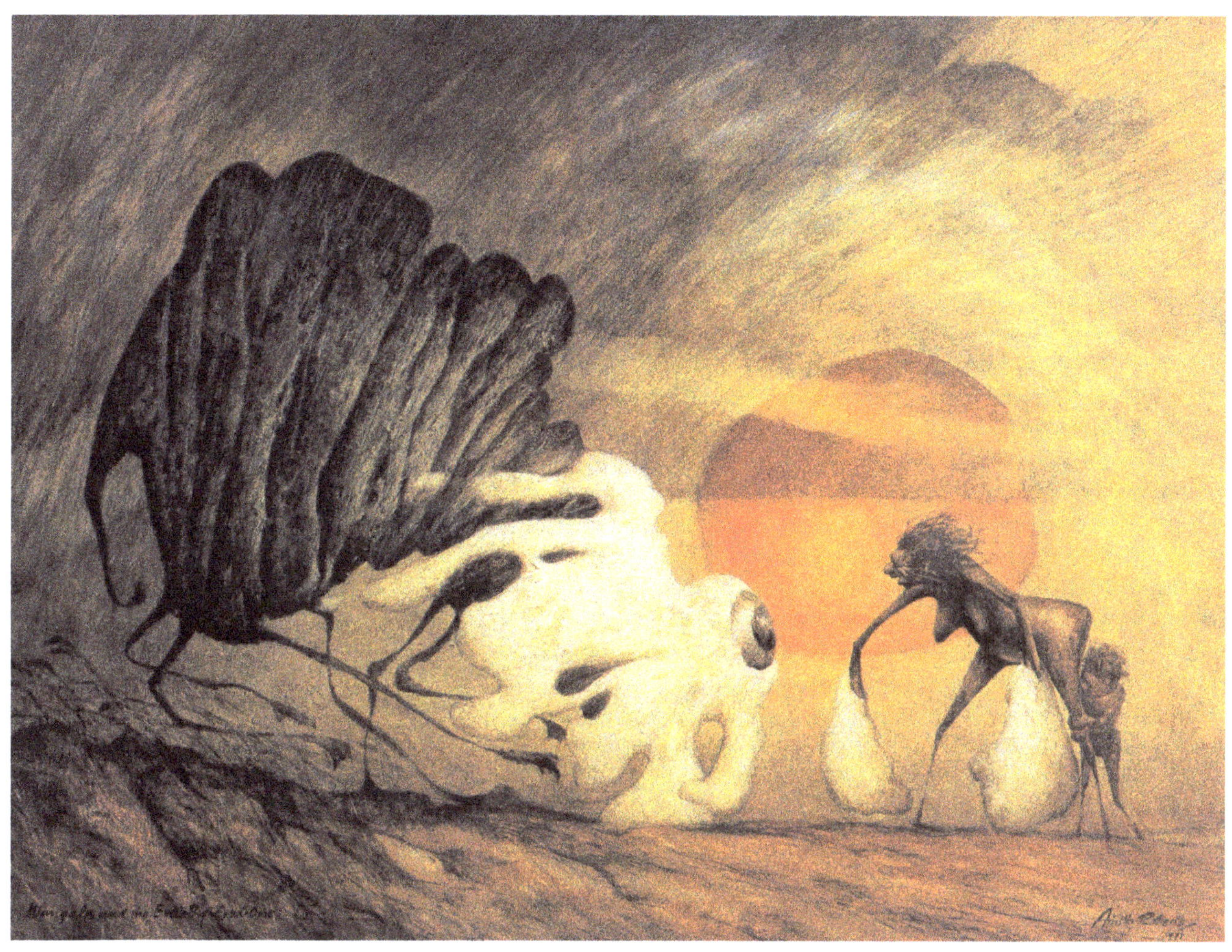

Mr Fraser Hay.

THE WEEPING OPAL

A myth of central Queensland relates that in the days of the Dreamtime, when the world was young and the great creation events were taking place, a giant opal ruled over the destinies of men and women. This Ancestral Being lived in the sky, made the laws under which the tribes should live, and dictated the punishments to be inflicted on lawbreakers.

The creation of this Aboriginal Ancestor came about as a result of a war between two tribes. The fighting had gone on for so long that, at last, the combatants had broken or lost all their weapons. So they began hurling boulders at each other, and a tribesman threw one so hard that it flew upwards and lodged in the sky.

The boulder grew rapidly as the frightened warriors watched, until it burst open and revealed the flashing colours of a huge opal. And as the opal saw the dead and wounded warriors lying on the ground below, it wept in sorrow.

Tears streamed from the opal in such profusion that they became a great rainstorm, and when the sun shone on the opal-coloured tears the Aborigines saw their first rainbow.

From that time on, the Aborigines of that area believed the rainbow was a sign that someone had committed a crime against the tribal laws laid down so long ago, and that the tears of the opal were again falling in sorrow.

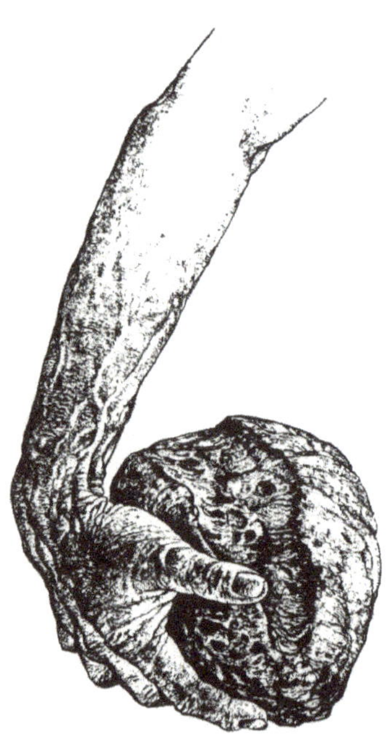

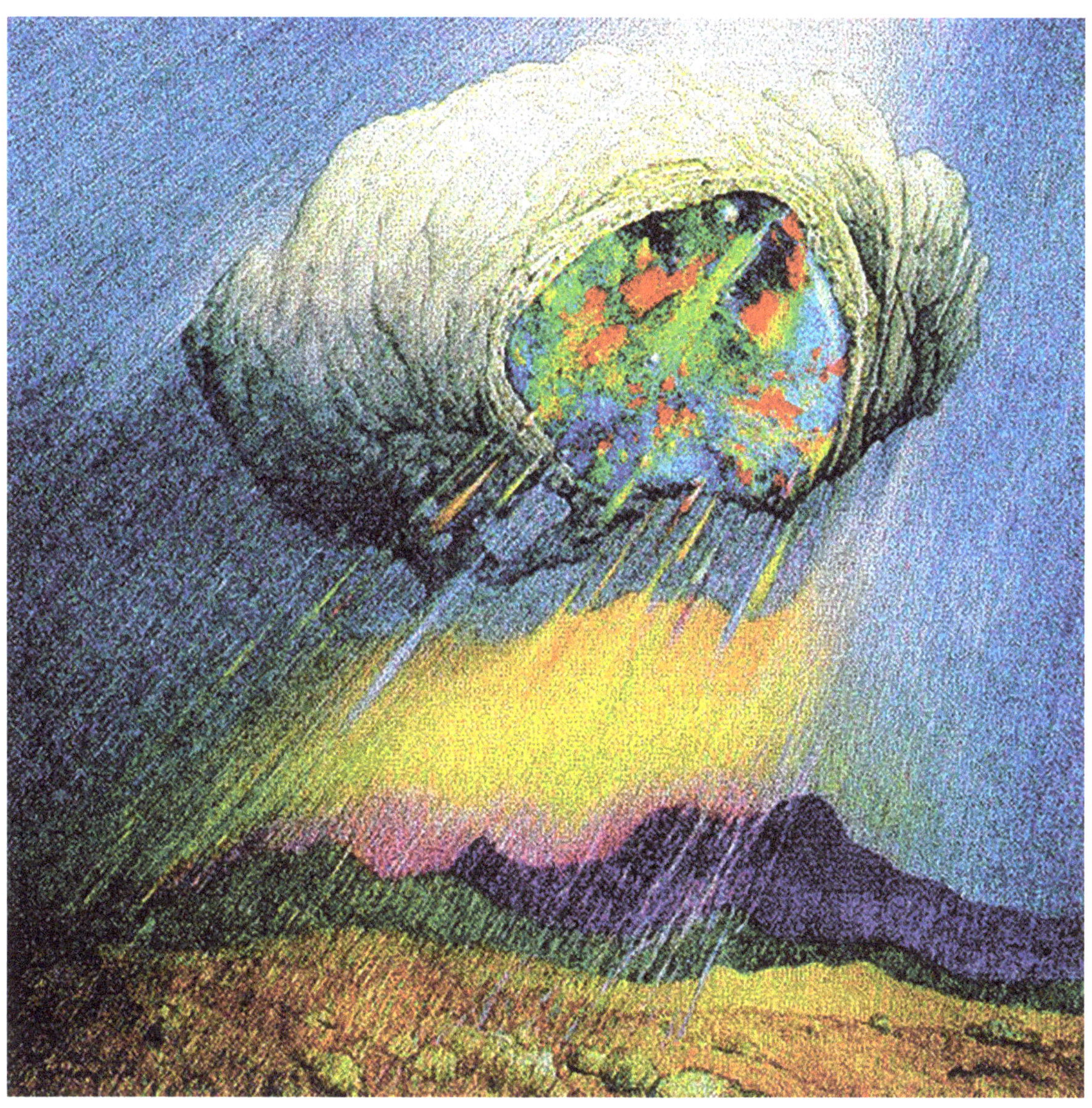

Mr and Mrs Ron Trezise.

YURLUNGUR AND THE WAWALIK SISTERS

This myth is one of the most important in Arnhem Land, its ceremonies taking many weeks to perform. The Aborigines believe that the Wawalik sisters came from a land far away to the east, and as they travelled they named the animals, the reptiles and the plants.

One day the women reached the Mirimina waterhole which, unknown to them, was the home of a dangerous serpent, Yurlungur. Here, the elder sister, knowing that she was about to give birth to a child, asked the younger to prepare a bark hut where she could shelter. The younger sister had just completed the task when a son was born.

Yurlungur, hearing the women moving above him, became angry over their intrusion. Stirring the water into a maelstrom, he rose to the surface and, accompanied by roars of thunder and flashes of lightning, approached the camp of the two sisters. Terrified, they chanted their most powerful songs to frighten Yurlungur away, but were unsuccessful.

In desperation, the women crept into their bark hut and blocked the openings with branches and grass. But the enraged serpent, pushing these obstructions aside without difficulty, swallowed first the younger and then the elder Wawalik sister, and finally her son. Yurlungur then retired to the Mirimina waterhole, where he has lived ever since.

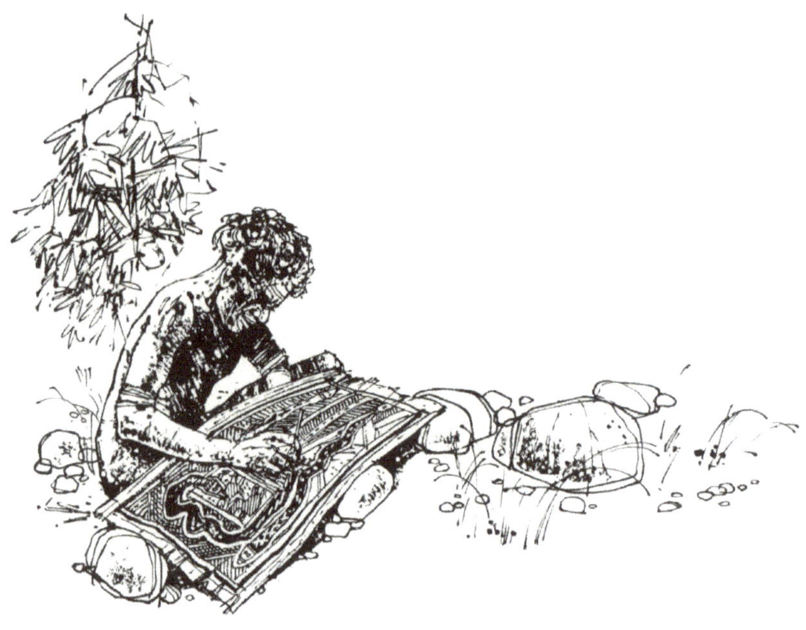

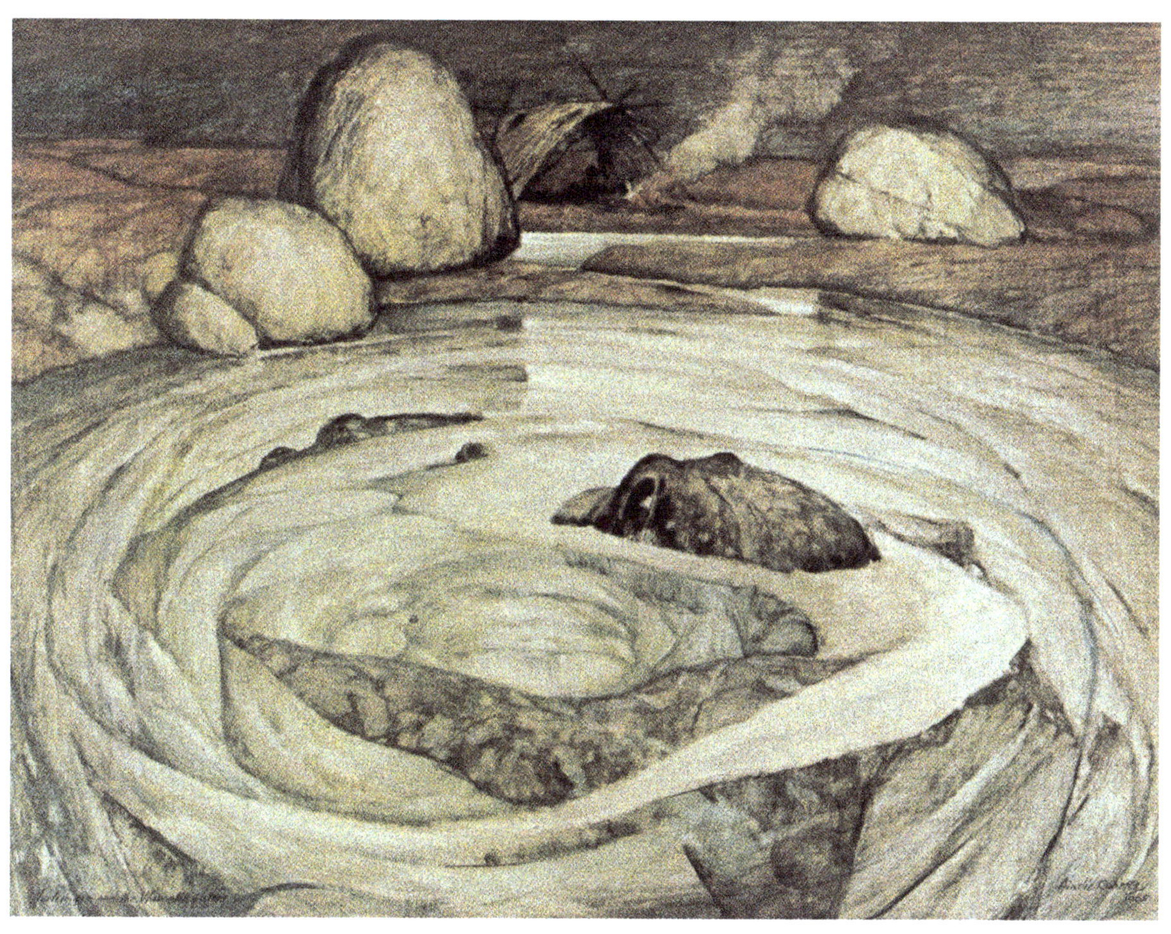

Mr E. J. Barker.

THE LAST HURRICANE

One of the many variations of the origin of fire is the Aboriginal myth which relates that, in the beginning, there was no warmth and the only light was from the stars. This was the way of life for the Aborigines until the day came when a man and his wife, after a heavy thunderstorm, saw a strange glow where a bolt of lightning had struck an old log.

Puzzled by this weird sight, they covered it with bark in an attempt to hide it, but the bark suddenly burst into flame. This frightened them so much that they went to their tribal chief, a noted man of magic, and asked him to destroy the unknown thing they had found.

But when they returned to the now blazing log, and felt the comfort of its warmth, the chief realised that his companions had found something that would give his people light to dispel their darkness, and heat to keep them warm.

He gave a large torch of blazing wood to the woman and a smaller torch to the man, and so that the twin blessings of light and warmth would never be lost he sent them up into the sky to become the sun and moon. He divided the rest of the burning log amongst the tribe, and told them to place a coal in every tree so that the spirit of fire would always be available to everyone.

With fire to cook their food, keep them warm, and light their darkness, life suddenly became so much easier that the Aborigines increased in numbers and gradually spread over their new land. The use of fire not only altered man's way of life, but set him apart from the rest of creation as nothing else could have done.

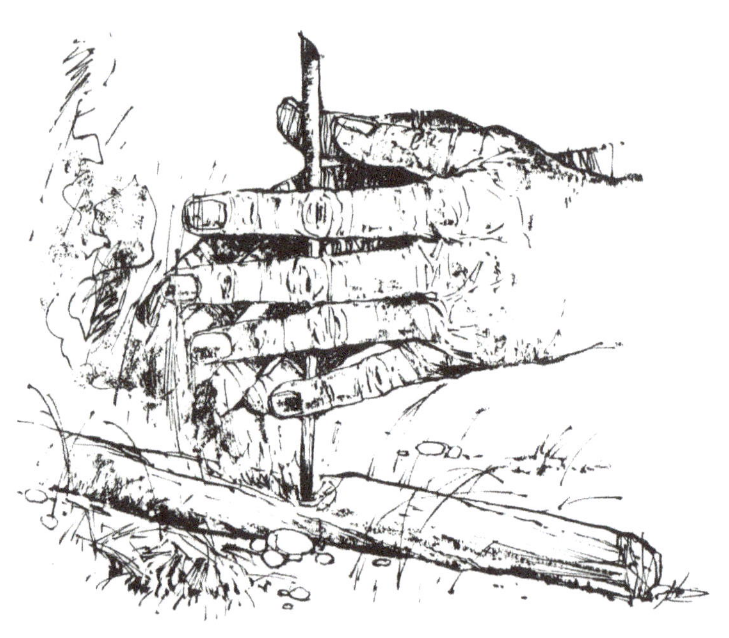

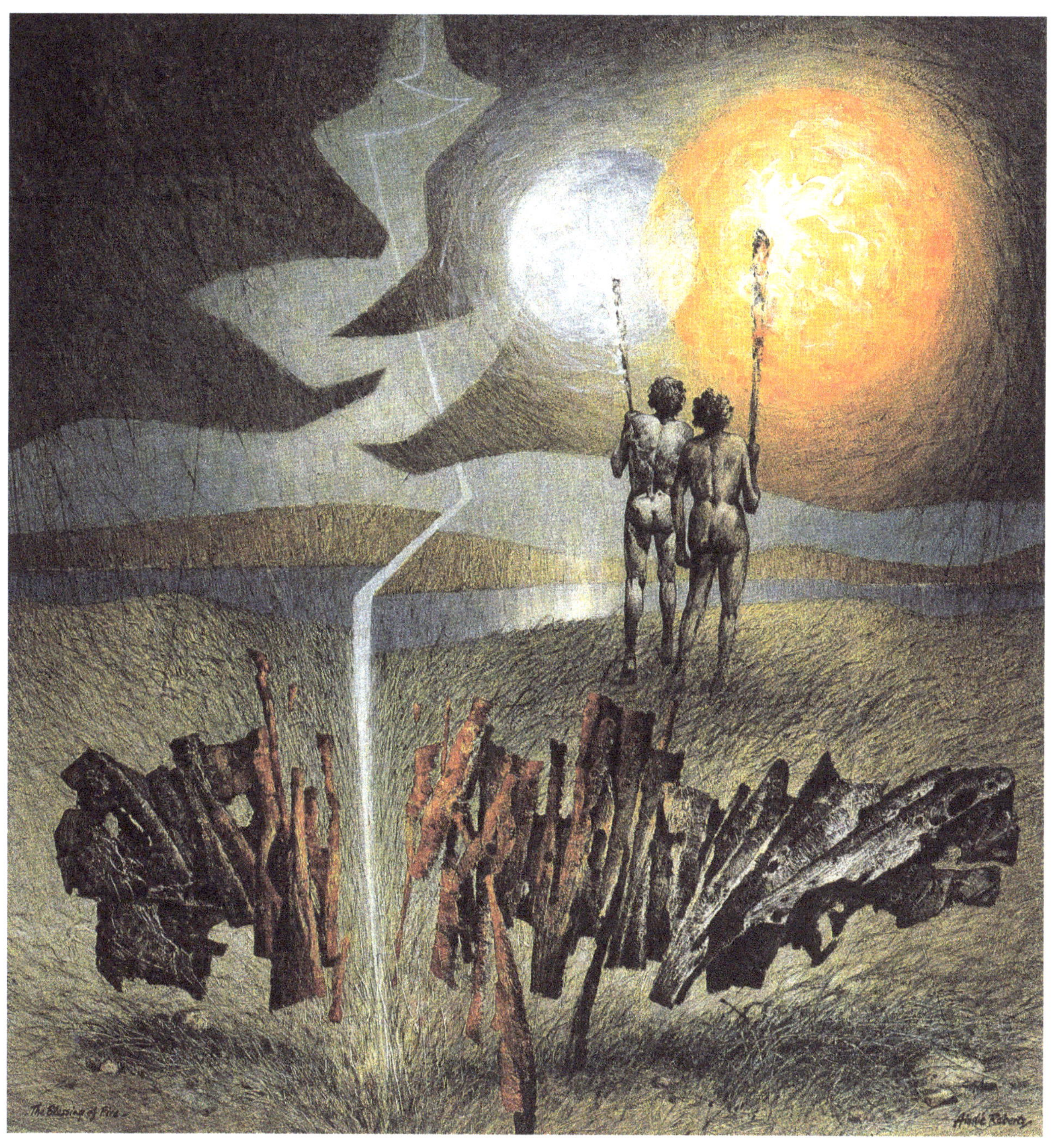

Mrs Melva Roberts.

THE FIGHTING BROTHERS

Long ago, on Victoria's western coast, there lived two brothers who had hunted and fished together since childhood. Pupadi, the elder, was the one who always speared the most game, knew the best fishing spots, and was looked upon as the camp favourite. Gerdang, the younger, secretly resented his secondary role. His jealousy increased when Pupadi took a wife, because she was the woman whom Gerdang most desired.

Gerdang's longing for his brother's wife became so fierce that he begged her to run away with him. When she refused, Gerdang took her by force and carried her far to the east, where a great shelf of rock runs into the sea.

Pupadi returned from hunting, and knew what had taken place because he was aware of Gerdang's envy. In a violent rage he followed their tracks and found them. He attacked Gerdang, and they fought for many hours until the younger brother ran into the scrub and hid. Pupadi climbed a large rock to gain a better view, but Gerdang circled behind him and threw a boomerang with such force that it buried itself deep between his brother's shoulder-blades and knocked him into the bushes at the cliff's edge.

Reckless with triumph, and expecting to find his brother dead, Gerdang leapt into the bushes. But Pupadi, calling on the last of his strength, lay on his stomach with his spear held upwards. Gerdang jumped straight on to it, to die with the barbed point sticking out of his back.

The impact carried them over the cliff, and Pupadi fell into the sea and became the shark. The big fin on his back is his brother's boomerang, still deeply embedded. Gerdang hit a shelf of rock with such force that his body was flattened, and in this form the tide carried it away as the stingray, with Pupadi's spear changed into the barbed sting at the base of the tail. The blow-holes along the cliff top were made by the stamping feet of the fighting brothers.

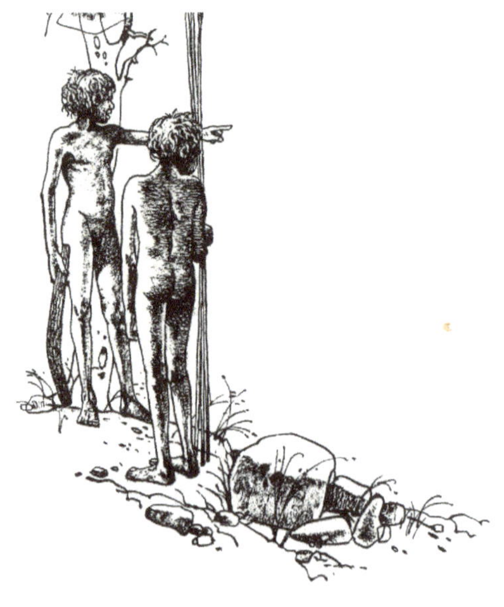

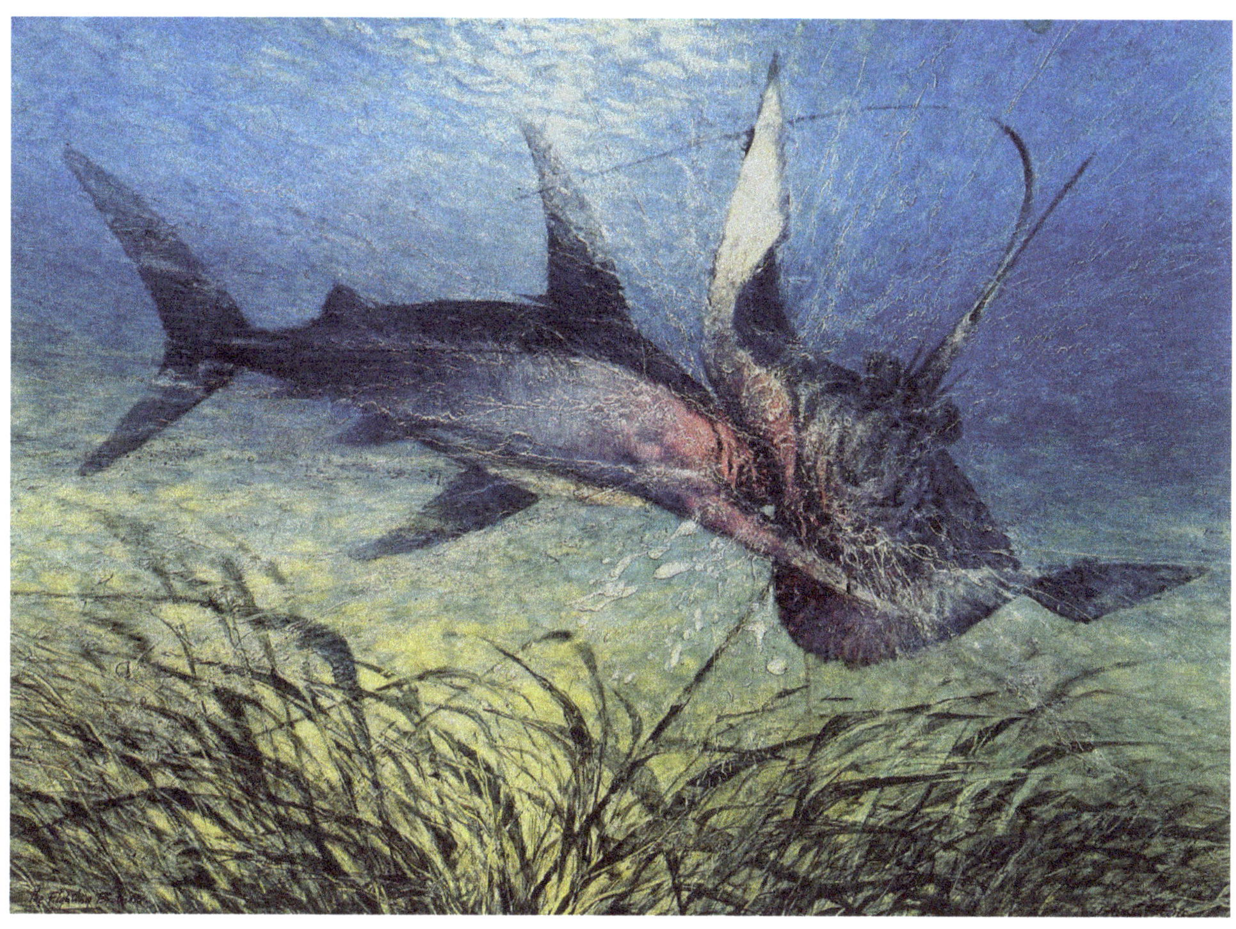

Private Collection.

MANGOWA AND THE ROUND LAKES

Mangowa, the hunter, waiting silently on the edge of the lake to spear some fish, saw a young and beautiful girl, Pirili, paddling her shallow bark canoe toward the distant shore.

The sight of the graceful body of Pirili, and the ease with which she propelled her simple craft, filled Mangowa with an overwhelming desire to possess her. But, although the old men of the tribe agreed that Mangowa could have Pirili as his wife, she refused to agree to the marriage.

To court her favours, Mangowa brought her the best fish he had speared, but she allowed them to rot in the sun; he gave her scarlet feathers for her hair, and the softest of opossum-skin cloaks, but still she remained adamant to his wooing. Overwhelmed with desire, Mangowa pursued Pirili wherever she went, pleading his cause and protesting his affection until one day, in desperation, he seized the girl and carried her to his camp. Pirili, frantic with terror, tore herself from his arms and, flying into the sky, ask ea the women of the Milky Way' to protect her from Mangowa's unwelcome attentions. Furious that the girl had escaped him, Mangowa followed her and, . tearing great handfuls of stars from the Milky Way, threw them at Pirili to drive her back to earth.

But the people of the stars, disgusted over Mangowa's behaviour, banished him to earth, so that Pirili would always be safe in the sparkling constellation of the Seven Sisters. And the stars that Mangowa tore from their homes, falling to earth, made the circular lagoons that fringe the shores of the coastal lakes of South Australia.

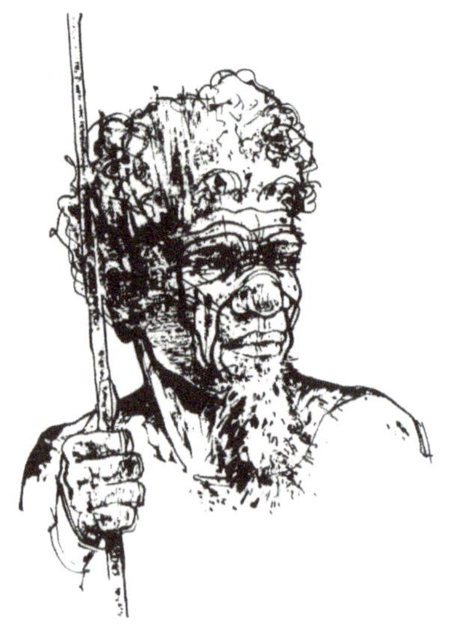

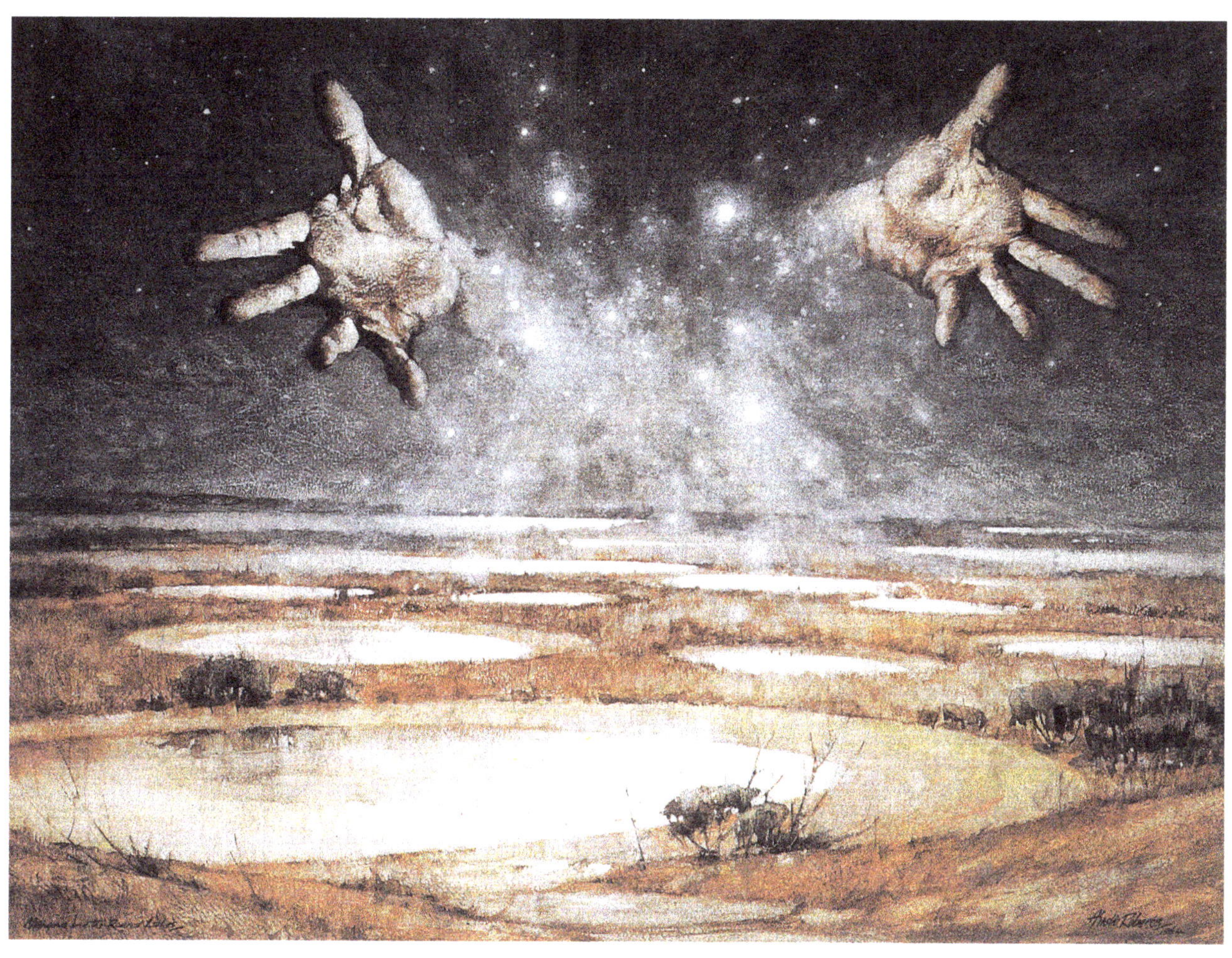

Keith H. Kingsley Estate.

THE CAPTURE OF FIRE

Many different types of terrain and climate may be found within the continent of Australia, and because Aboriginal beliefs were intimately associated with the type of country in which the tribes lived, many myths with a common basis varied according to the locality.

One of the most important factors in Aboriginal life was fire and its benefits. There are many different stories explaining how it was first obtained. Some stories say that a bird brought it to the people, others describe a tribesman's dangerous journey to obtain fire from a burning mountain, and in some myths the gift of fire resulted from lightning which set fire to a tree.

Most fire-myth variations share common themes of greed and reprisal. There is a selfish person who discovers the secret of fire, but keeps it to himself, and there are those who use courage and ingenuity to take it from him so that it can be shared.

A fire-myth from the Murrumbidgee region is typical of this construction. It says that Goodah, a noted magician, captured a piece of lightning as it struck a dead tree during a storm. He imprisoned it as a convenient way to make fire for his own use, and ignored demands that he share this wonderful discovery.

At last the tribe became so enraged with Goodah that a group of elders called up a whirlwind just as Goodah had made a fire with his piece of lightning. The whirlwind picked up the fire and scattered it all over the country, and fire became common property when members of the tribe picked up enough burning wood to make fires for themselves.

To escape the jeers and laughter of the tribe, Goodah fled to the hills to sulk, and to plan revenge.

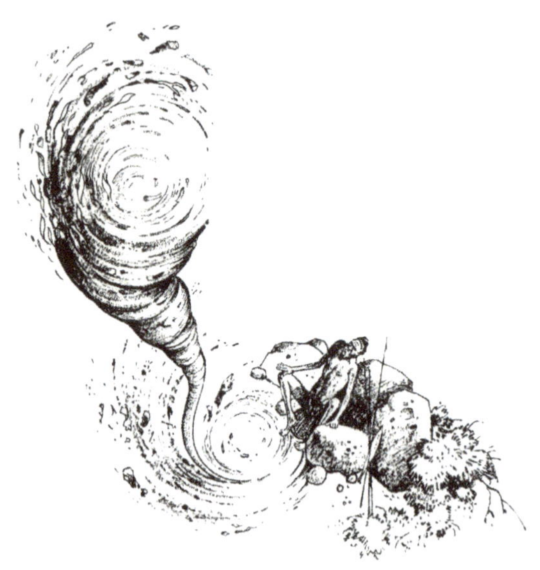

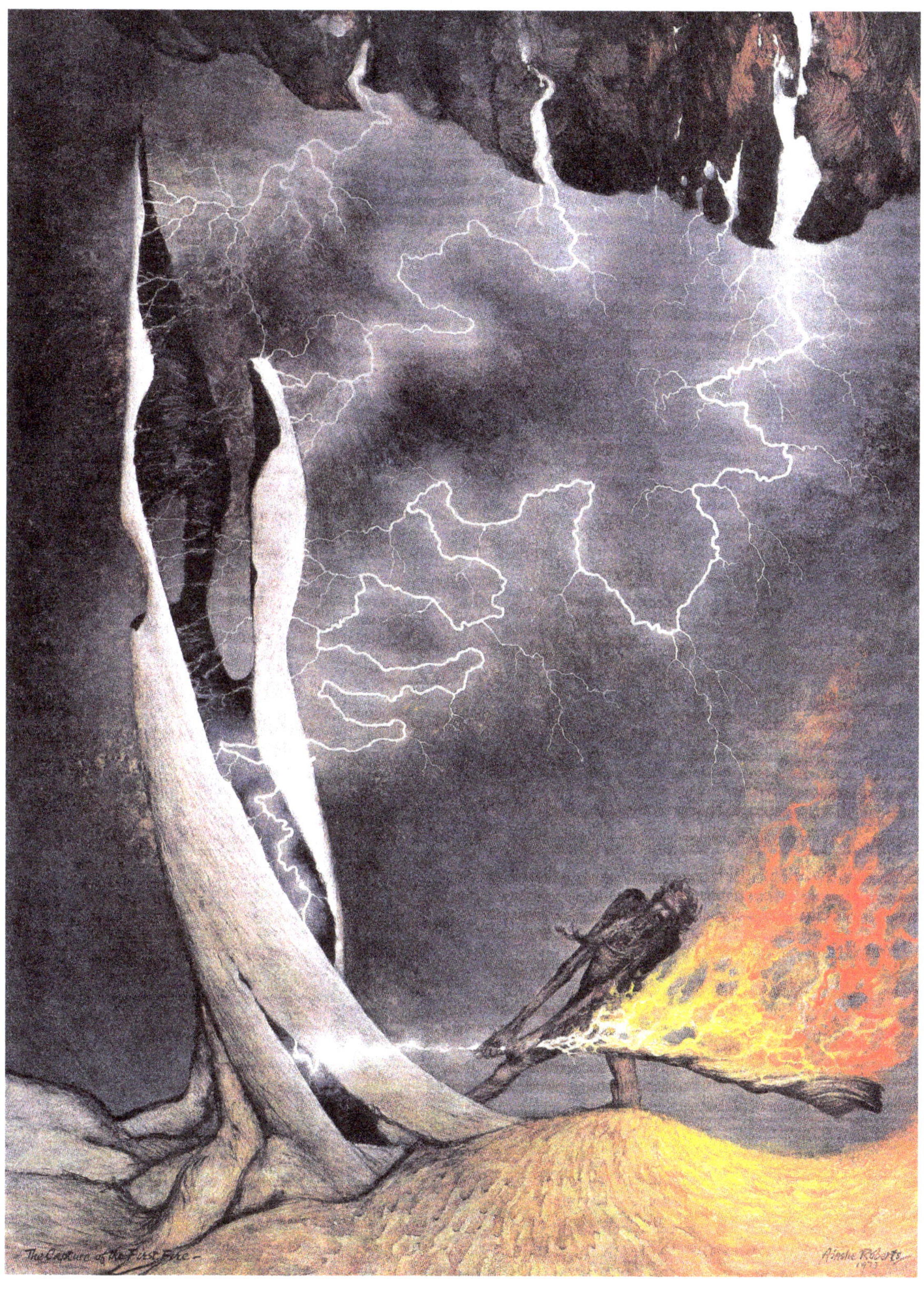

Mr and Mrs P. C. Russell.

THE SAVING OF FIRE

After Goodah lost his precious fire in the whirlwind called up by the tribal elders, the selfish magician soon thought of a way to revenge himself. He was a noted rain maker and he began to conjure up a great storm to extinguish fire for ever.

In the tribal camp, the people were still ecstatic with excitement over the gift of fire. Without thought for the future they feasted and danced for many days, delighted with the fires that cooked their food and kept them warm.

But the wise tribal elders knew that Goodah's revenge would not be long delayed. They changed themselves into bats, and in this form they picked burning coals from the fires and flew with them to the countless trees on hills surrounding the camp. They hid coals in every tree, safe from the rain which was fire's only enemy.

They had barely completed this task before Goodah's great rainstorm came flooding over the hills. It deluged the country and put out all the fires.

Cold and sorrowful, the tribesfolk gazed gloomily at the ashes until bats flittered overhead, chirping the news that the spirit of fire could now be found in every tree.

The people soon discovered this was true. When they rubbed dry wood together, the fire spirit that Goodah had made from a piece of lightning soon came to life again. And for countless centuries since then the Aborigines have made fire in that way.

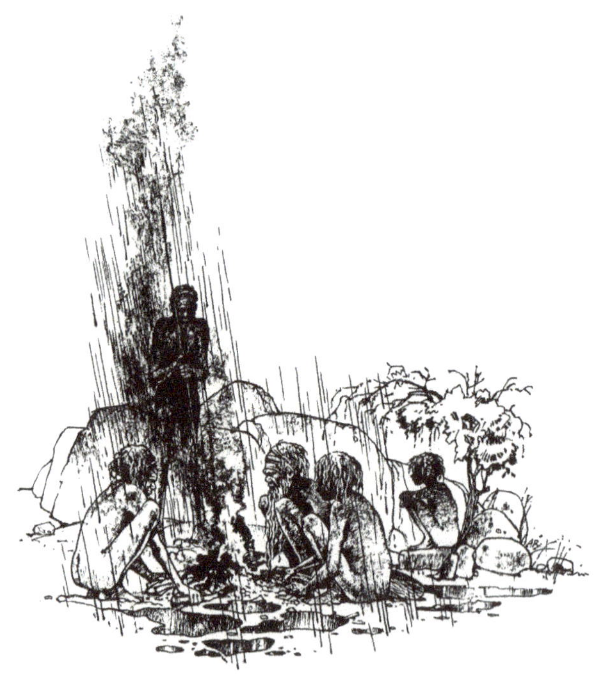

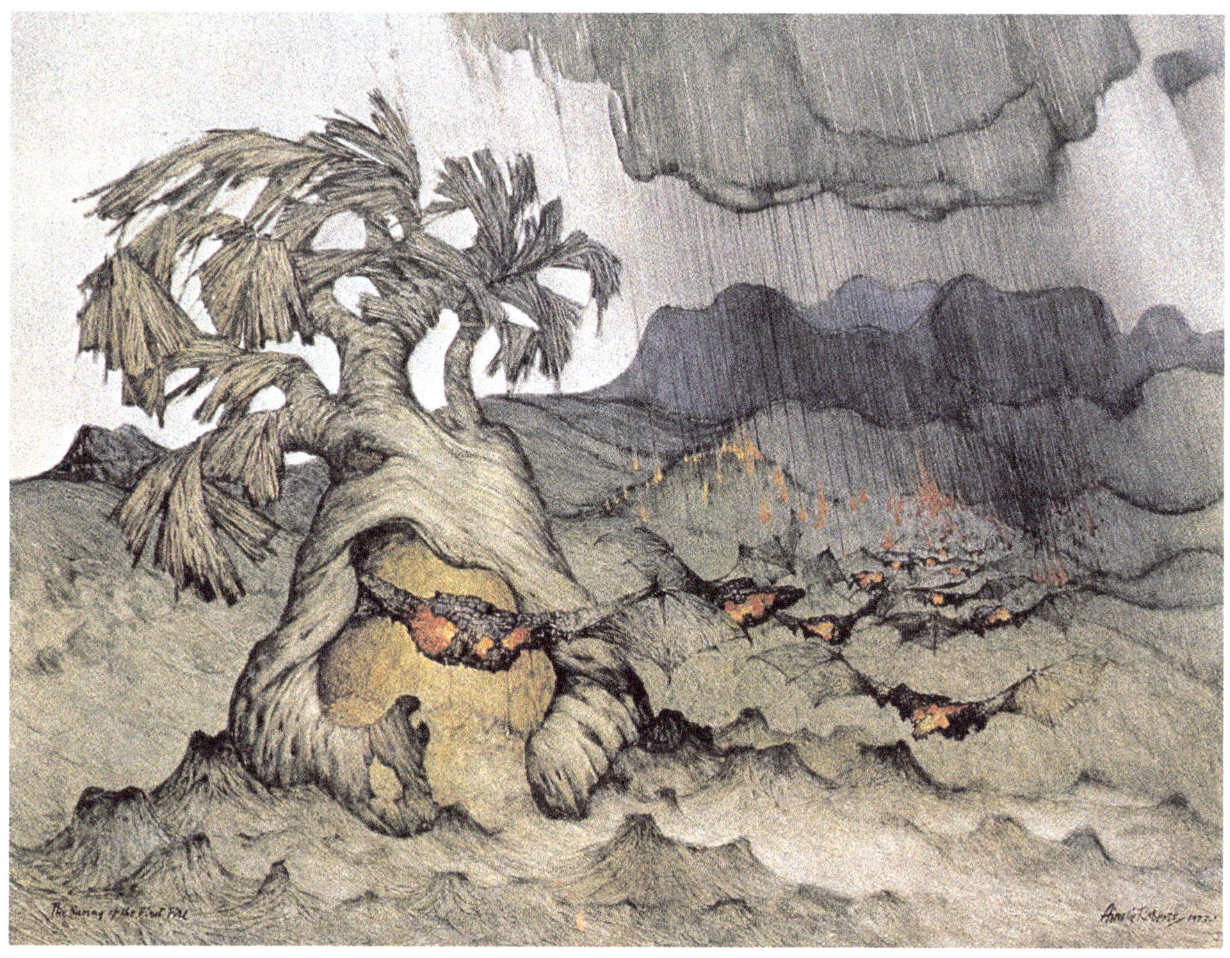

Miss Marcella Reale.

KARKAN AND THE VALLEY OF BLOOD

Karkan was a man of fine build and a great hunter. His tribe admired these qualities but they disliked his vanity and conceit. When Winju, a modest and likeable man, came to stay with the tribe, the friendliness extended to him made Karkan so frenzied with jealousy that he made plans to kill him. So Karkan persuaded Winju to go hunting, and on the night before they set out he sharpened a number of hardwood sticks at both ends. He took these to a place where there were many kangaroo-rats, and pushed them into the earth, points upwards, in the tall grass. Karkan also tied a cord around some of the grass and trailed it to a nearby bush, and then his trap was ready for Winju.

When the two hunters reached the spot, Karkan told Winju that his method of catching the kangaroo-rat was to run to the spot where movement showed in the grass, then jump so that he could land on the animal with both feet. As he said this he twitched the cord so that the grass quivered. The trusting Winju jumped into the grass and drove the sticks deep into his feet and legs. For many days, Winju in his agony thrashed and crawled about until he had made a deep valley, and his blood stained the whole area red.

But because Winju was a good man, his ancestral spirits restored him to health and great strength. Some days later, Karkan had only a brief glimpse of his rival before Winju's spear killed him. The body fell into the camp-fire and sparks flew in all directions. They started a bushfire which swept over most of the country, and from the ashes a brown bird rose to hover above the same spot day after day.

The Aborigines of the Coolgardie area believed that the blood shed by Winju created the precious red ochre, used for body decoration, in the sacred source which they knew as the Valley of Blood. The brown bird is a kestrel, destined to keep watch on the ground forever because it contains the spirit of Karkan, still wary of another attack by Winju.

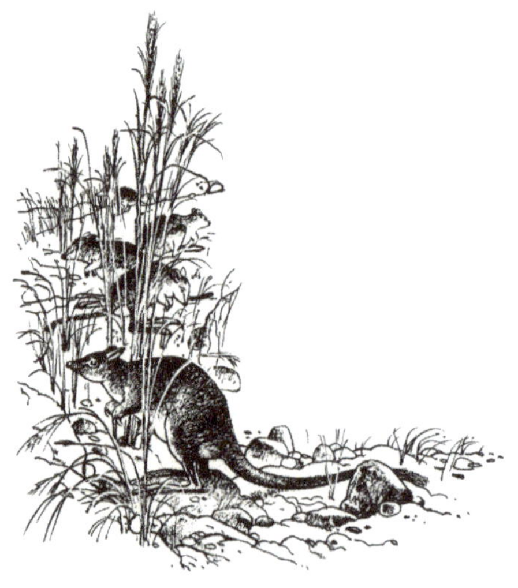

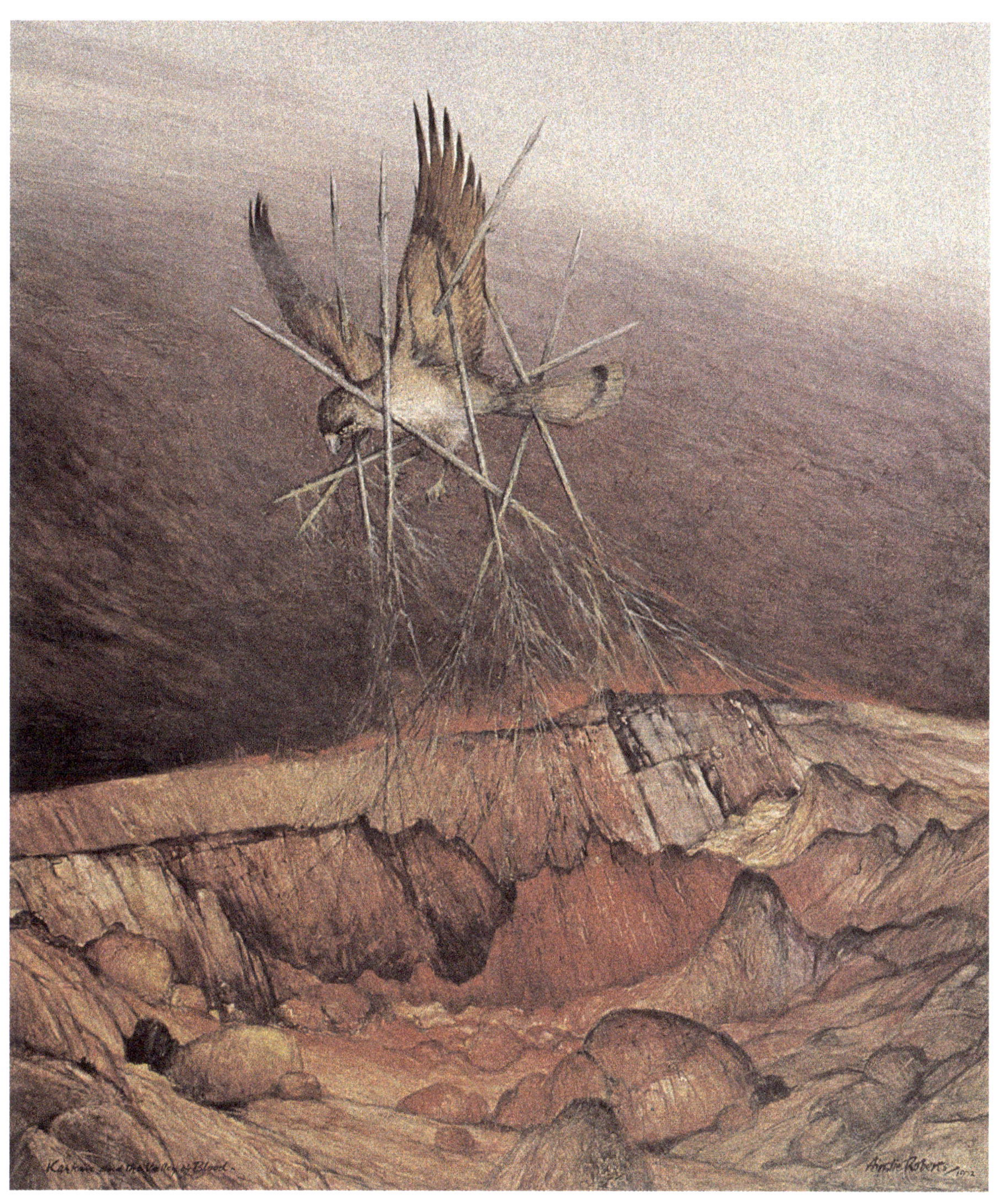

Mr Cameron R. Sands .

THE MAN OF MAGIC

The medicine-man is a person in whom the Aborigines have much faith. Yet he has a family, he hunts with his companions, he takes part in the secular and ceremonial life of his tribe, and is subject both to sickness and to death. But he is a man apart, because the spirits of dead medicine-men, the Wulgis, have admitted him into their world of healing and magic; a world that few Aborigines can enter.

When the Wulgis notice an Aboriginal who shows more than ordinary interest in the psychic life of the tribe, they choose him to become a medicine-man.

The Wulgis wait until the initiate is asleep, take the spirit from his body, and change it into the form of an eagle-hawk. Then they conduct it into the sky, where it is shown many wonders and the secrets of magic and healing which are known only to the medicine men. At dawn, the spirit of the initiate is taken back to his camp, transformed from that of an eagle-hawk to that of an Aboriginal, and returned to his own body. These journeys are repeated many times before the initiate has learnt all the secrets of his profession.

On return to his ordinary life, the newly initiated medicine-man has many new powers; he can heal the sick, find the spirits of children who have lost themselves in the darkness, and hunt the malignant night spirits from the camps.

Occasionally the medicine-man will seek the help of a Wulgi spirit to cure an Aboriginal suffering severe body pains. The Wulgi goes inside the patient and searches until it finds an object such as a stick or stone, which has been placed there by an enemy. The Wulgi gives this to the medicine-man, who shows it as evidence that the cause of the pain has been removed.

It is said that the patient always recovers. No Aboriginal ever doubts the ability of a medicine-man to cure most forms of sickness, or to overcome the effects of evil spirits.

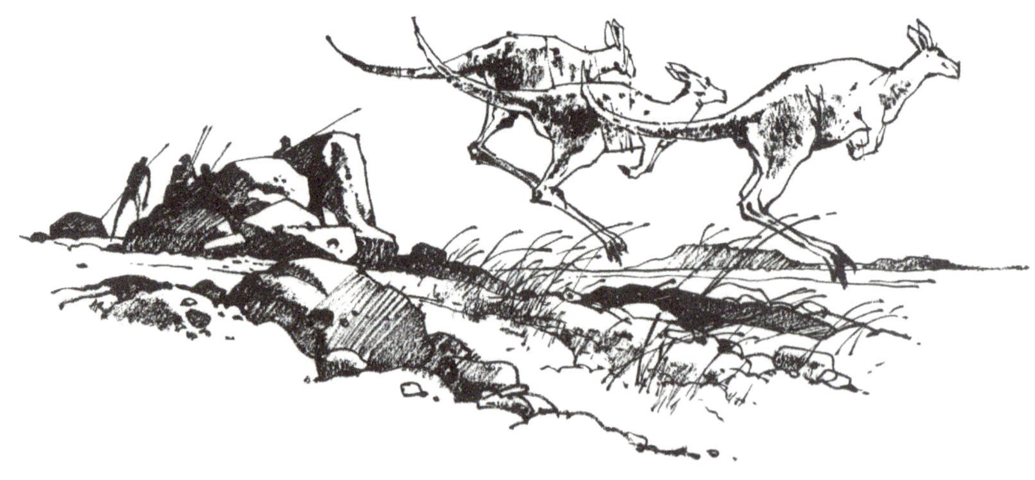

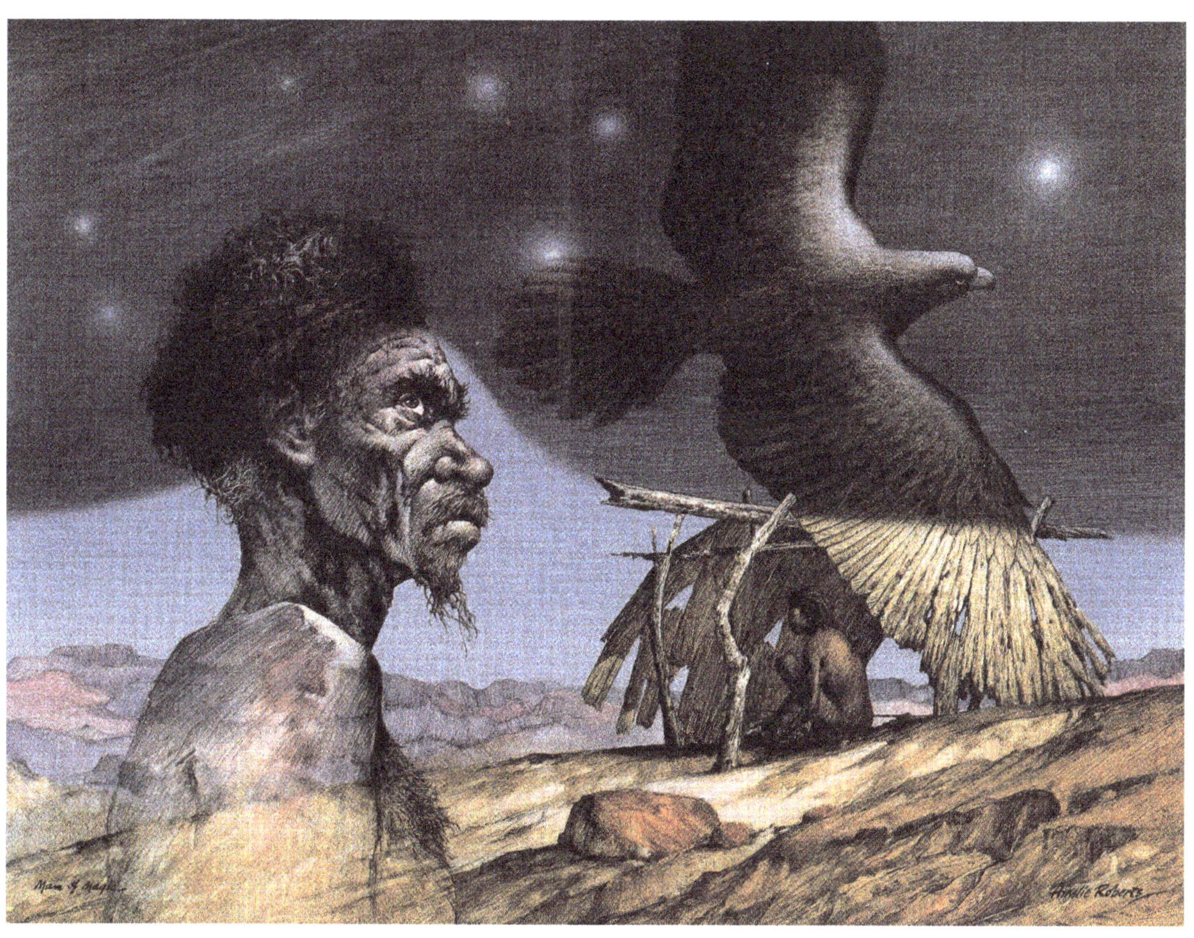

Private Collection..

PUKAMUNI CEREMONIES

The burial ceremonies of the Tiwi Aborigines, of Melville and Bathurst islands, were the most important events in their ceremonial life. The rituals allowed them full expression for their grief and also provided a cultural outlet for their art, music, dancing, and beliefs.

The most important of these events was the Pukamuni, performed only on Melville Island. It was the climax of a lengthy series of corroborees which continued for months after burial of the dead.

The complicated rituals were inspired by fear of the Mopaditis, who were the spirits of the dead, and by the desire of the living to appease them. The heavy body decoration, as shown on the figure of the mourner in the painting, was intended as a disguise, so that a Mopaditi would not recognise the mourner and decide to harm him in some way.

The unique burial poles set the Tiwi ceremonial apart from all other Aboriginal rituals.

They were elaborately carved, and painted with intricate and colourful designs. Many were upwards of five metres in height and they took months to prepare. They were impressive gifts to placate the spirits of the dead.

In the ceremonial, the participants decorated each other with striking facial and body designs and then expressed their grief, their myths, and their talents in vivid tableaux of dance, mime, and song. From the opening rituals, followed by the songs and dances, the payment of the 'workers,' the erection of the burial poles, and the final mourning rituals, the whole Pukamuni ceremony was a dramatic spectacle.

When all was concluded, and the last wailing notes of the *amburu* death song had died away, the grave was deserted and the burial poles were allowed to decay.

The Mopaditi, no longer a menace to the living, was escorted to its new home by the black cockatoos and the camp resumed its normal life.

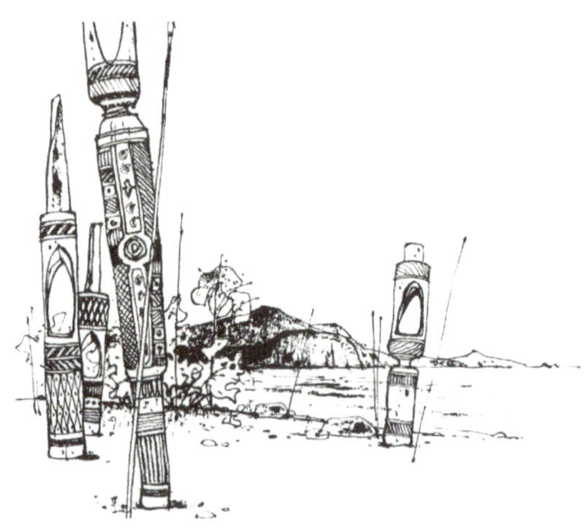

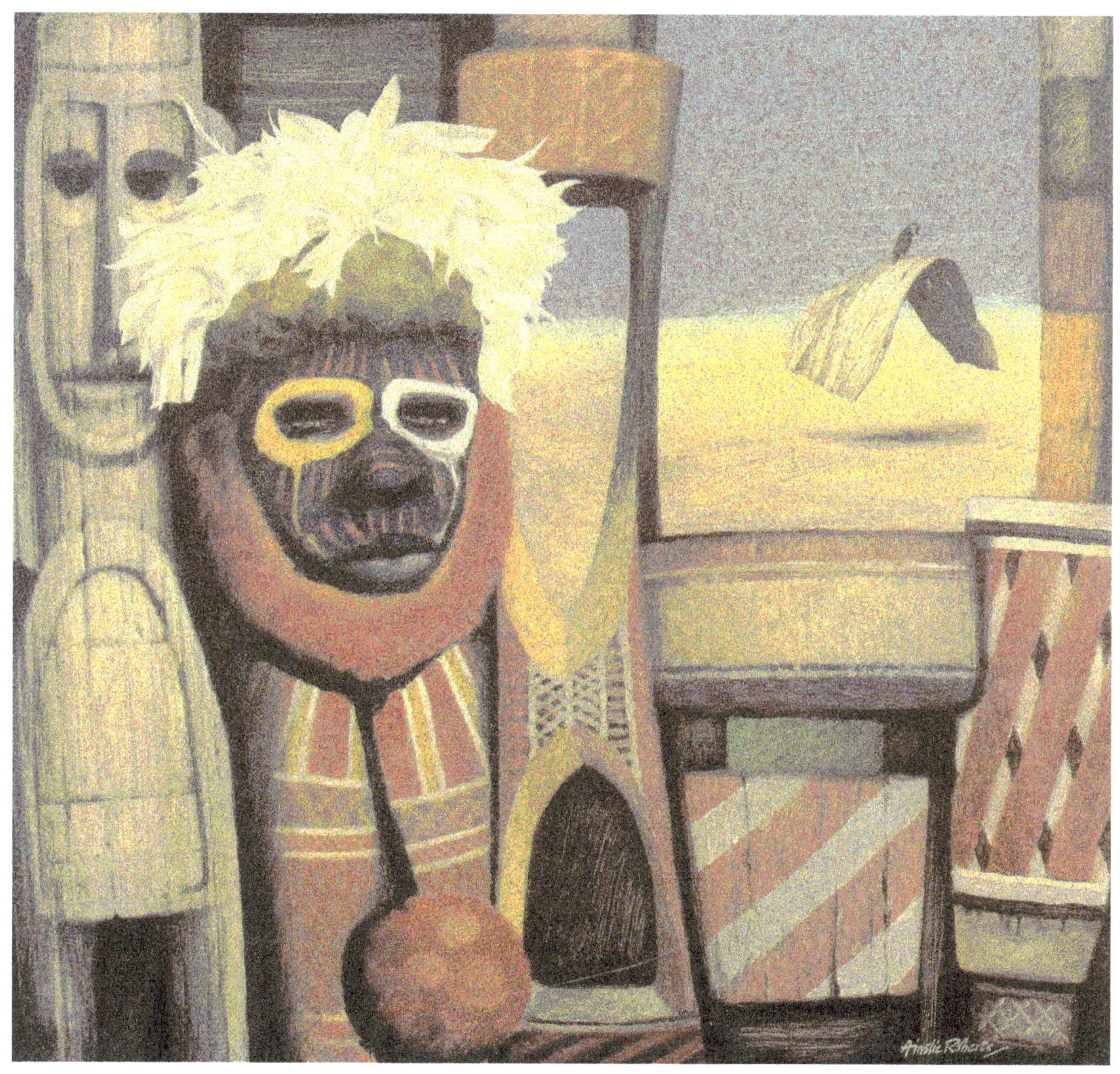

Private Collection.

THE MOPADITIS

The Tiwi people of Melville Island believed that the spirits of the dead, the Mopaditis, lived in self-contained communities. They resembled Aborigines in appearance but their bodies were only wraiths of their former beings.

The Pukamuni burial ceremonies were designed to speed these spirits to their future home. When the ceremony was complete the spirit set out on its long flight, escorted by black cockatoos who warned the inhabitants of the Aboriginal 'heaven' that a new Mopaditi was on its way.

Once safely lodged in its eternal home a Mopaditi normally remained there, but a lonely Mopaditi who awaited the conclusion of the Pukamuni ceremony, or one who had lost its way, was believed to be a great danger to the living. The Aborigines believed that a lonely Mopaditi would steal the spirit of some living person to keep it company, and took every precaution not to be seen or recognised by one of them.

An Aboriginal always knew when a Mopaditi was following closely after him, intent on stealing his spirit. His skin became clammy and his hair stood on end. To protect himself, the victim would carry a torch of flaming bark, shout loudly as he walked through the bush, or even attempt to disguise himself in some way. As a last resort he would attempt to hide. But if all these precautions failed he would surely die, and even the magic of the medicine men was unlikely to save him.

Now and again, a party of Mop ad it is who had recently arrived in their new home would return to a camping place they used on earth, to watch the burial rites of an old friend. When the ceremonies were over, and the living were asleep, the spirit people would repeat the same rituals, until the glow of the sun-woman in the eastern sky warned them that they must hasten back to their new home

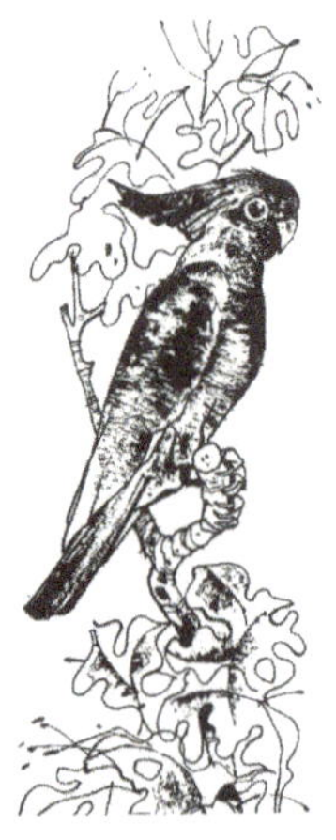

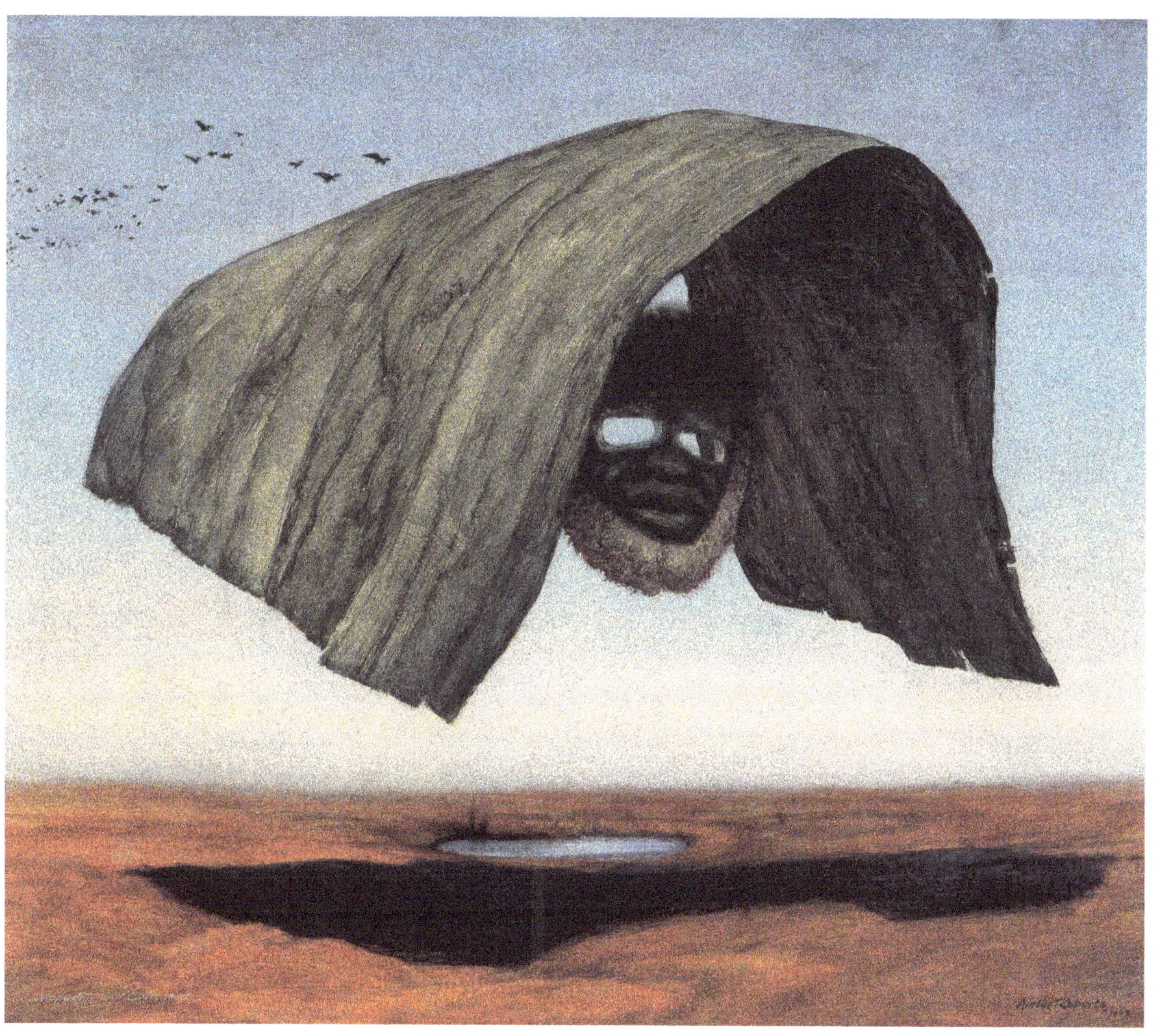

Private Collection.

THE OLD MAN AND HIS SIX SONS

Tonanga, the narrator of this myth, was Albert Namatjira, who related that the Aranda tribe originated in the Creation days when an old man started out on a journey from a cave in Haasts Bluff. He carried a big churinga stone, a spear, and a spear-thrower. Six namatoona (smaller copies of the churinga) were his sons, which he carried in a dilly-bag round his neck.

When the old man wanted his sons to hunt for meat he took the namatoona out of the dilly-bag and rubbed them with goanna fat. This magic caused them to stand up as six men, each with a spear and spear-thrower.

For a long, long time the old man wandered over a large part of central Australia. Each time he met a group of women, the old man instructed them to prepare six camps for he had six sons to give to them in marriage. When the old man decided it was time to move on, he changed his sons back into namatoona stones and put them in his dilly-bag.

Always that old man travelled on, carrying his churinga, his spear and spear-thrower, and his six namatoona. Always he gave his six sons in marriage to the women he met. But at last he became very old and very tired, and died.

He made his last camp and lay down with his dilly-bag beside him. When the old man was dead, the six namatoona wanted to get out. They started to roll about in the dilly-bag, and the dilly-bag rolled round and round in a circle. The old man turned into a stone, and underneath that stone is a big churinga. And close to it is a smaller stone which is the dilly-bag with the six namatoona inside.

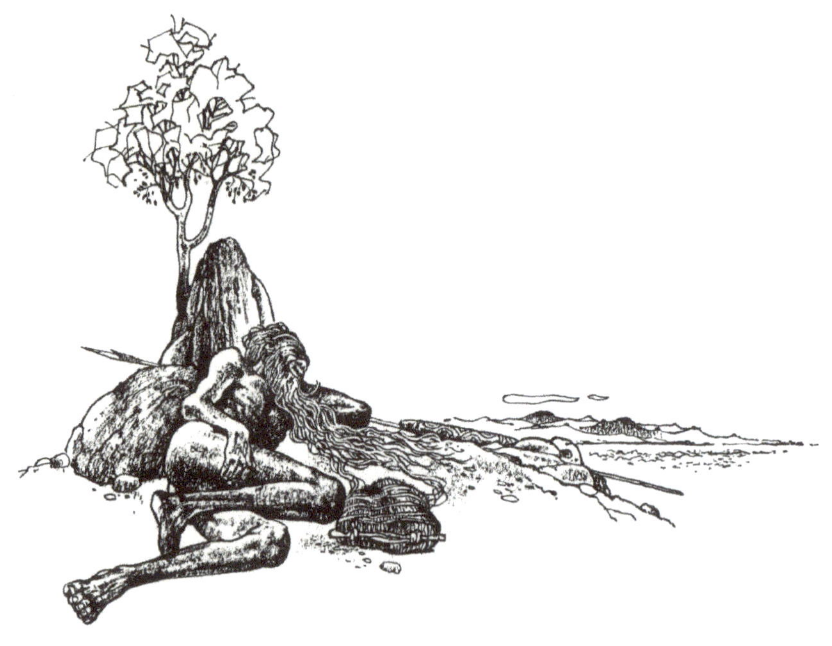

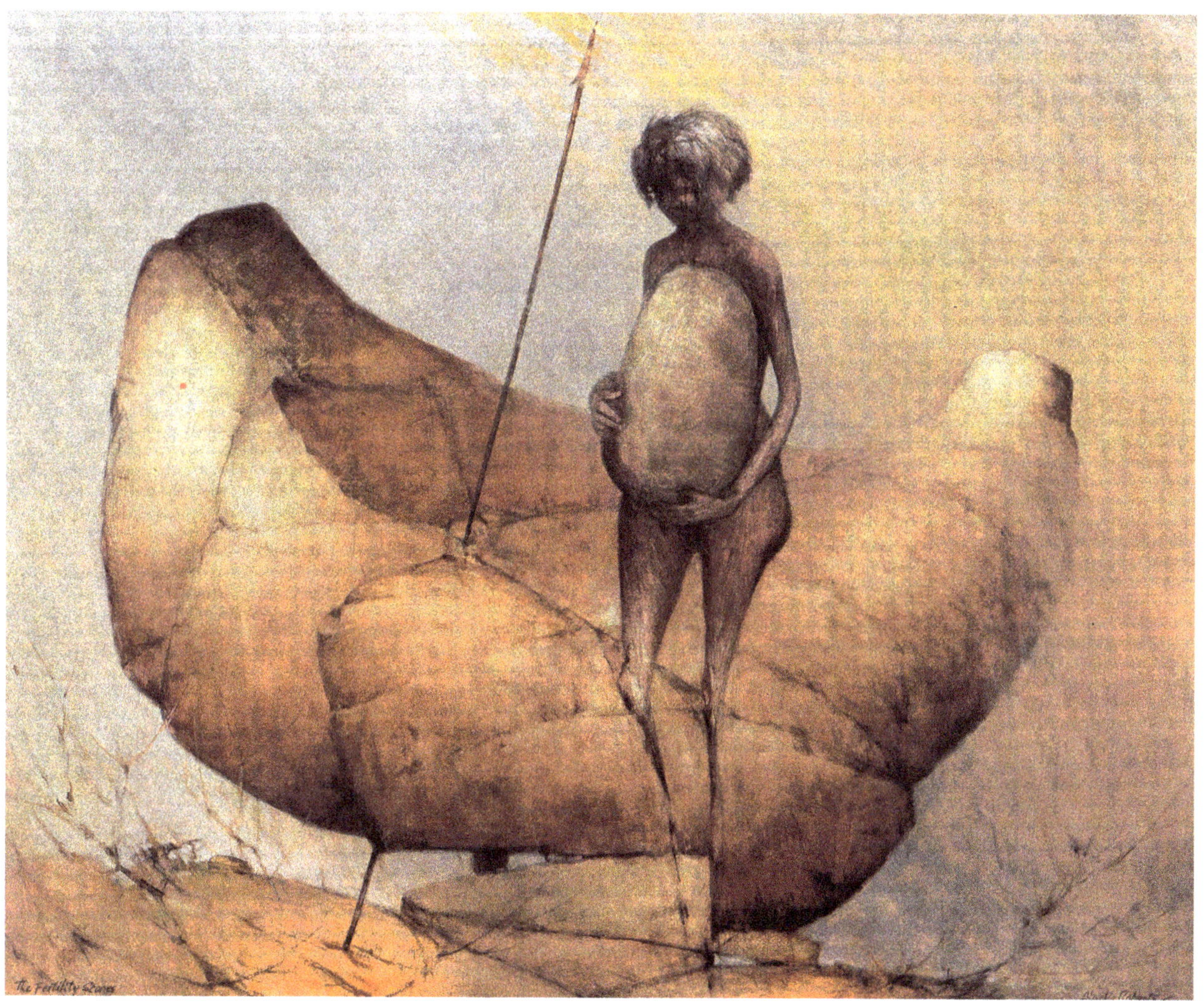

Private Collection.

BIRTH OF THE MOOGOORA

In the Dreamtime of the Encounter Bay tribe of South Australia, an old man called Lime was visited by a friend, Palpangye, who brought him some bream, a river fish not then known in the area. Lime returned the favour by giving Palpangye some sea mullet he had caught that day. As the men sat by the camp-fire after eating the two kinds of fish, Lime told his friend he had enjoyed the bream so much that he wished there were rivers in the neighborhood, so that he might catch bream for himself.

So that night Palpangye, who was a noted man of magic, went into the hills and pulled a huge dead gum tree out of the ground. He turned it upside down, then thrust it into the earth and twisted it round and round. Water and fish flowed up and filled the hole he had made.

Palpangye did this in many places, and the great pools overflowed into each other until the water formed the Moogoora river and reached the sea. He then walked some distance to the east, where he created the Yalladoola river in the same way. These are the rivers known today as the Inman and the Hindmarsh, still favourite breeding waters for bream.

When the time came for the old men to die, Palpangye transformed himself into a bird. Lime became a large rock on the shores of the bay, and the sea in its vicinity has ever since abounded in mullet. The myth records that women and children were never allowed to tread on the rock, but old people, because of their long acquaintance with Lime, were allowed to do so.

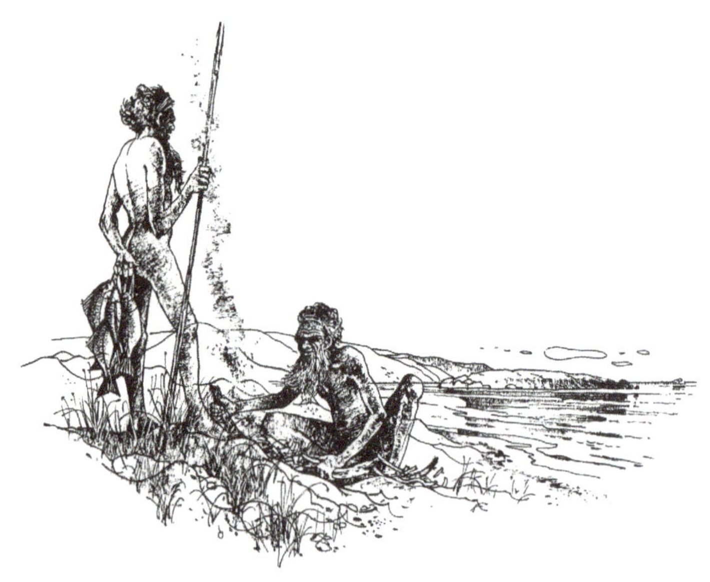

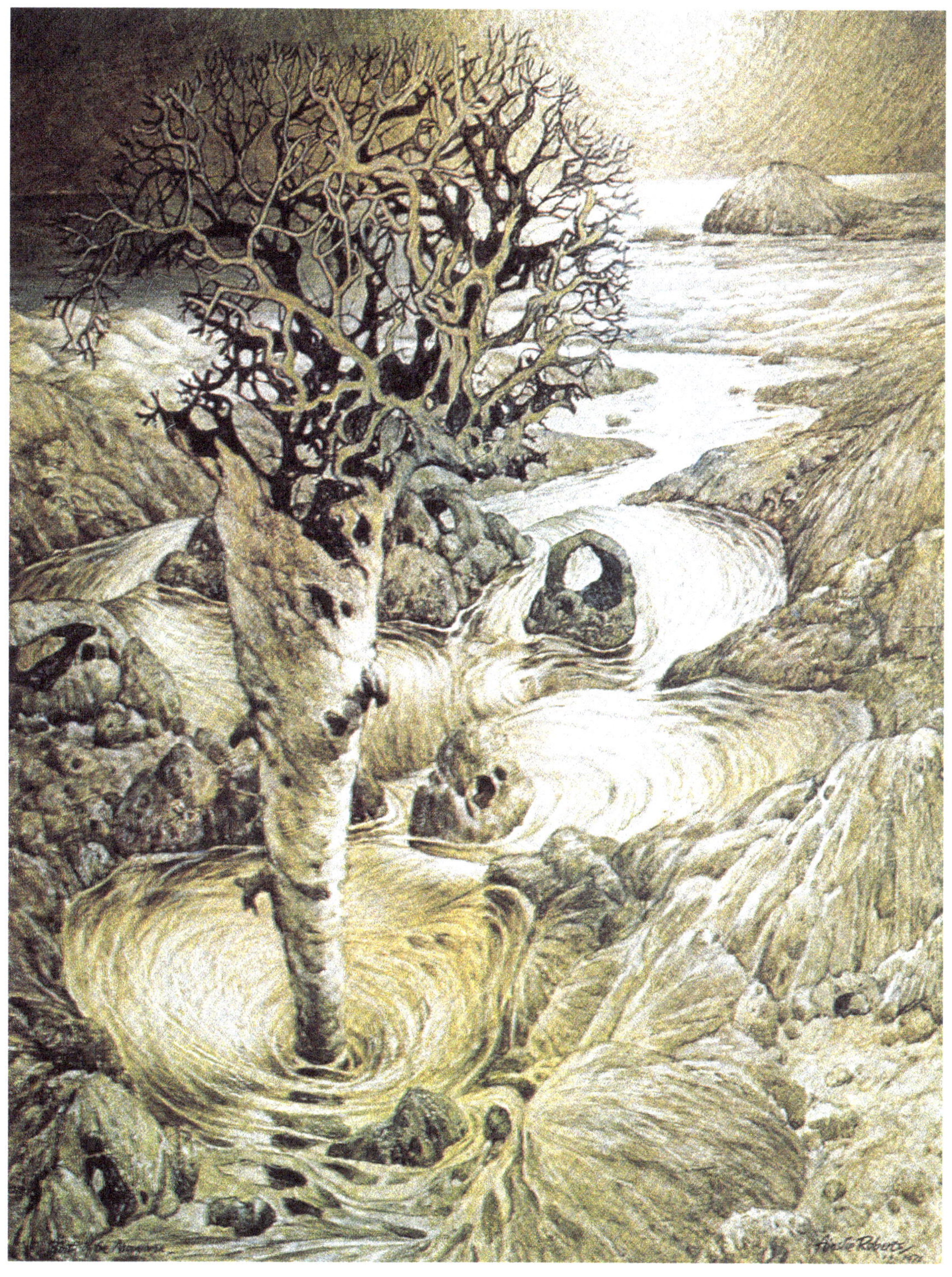

Private Collection.

CONDULA AND BAK-BAK

Long years ago, an old Aboriginal made a cloak from the skin of a red kangaroo for his young daughter Condula. This gift made Condula very happy, for it was more beautiful than any of the cloaks owned by other tribeswomen. As she took the gift, she was told that as soon as her lover Bak-bak had completed his training for tribal manhood, they could be married.

Every evening, when Condula finished her food-gathering, she climbed to the top of an isolated rock to watch for the return of her lover; and every evening the heart of Bak-bak was gladdened by the sight of that red-cloaked figure waiting for him.

But one night Condula was sad, for she heard that Bak-bak, together with other young men of the tribe, had been sent out to fight some enemies who were trespassing on their land. Again she climbed the pillar of stone, this time to watch for the return of the warriors, but Bak-bak was not among them. Visualising her lover lying silent and still on an open plain, she refused to leave her lonely post. Finally, in her grief, she died.

The body of Bak-bak was changed into the rock on which Condula had spent so many happy hours watching for her lover to come back from the hunt, and so many hopeless hours waiting for his return from the battle.

Condula and her red cloak were transformed into a beautiful waratah that grew up beside the rock so that, even in death, the lovers were not separated.

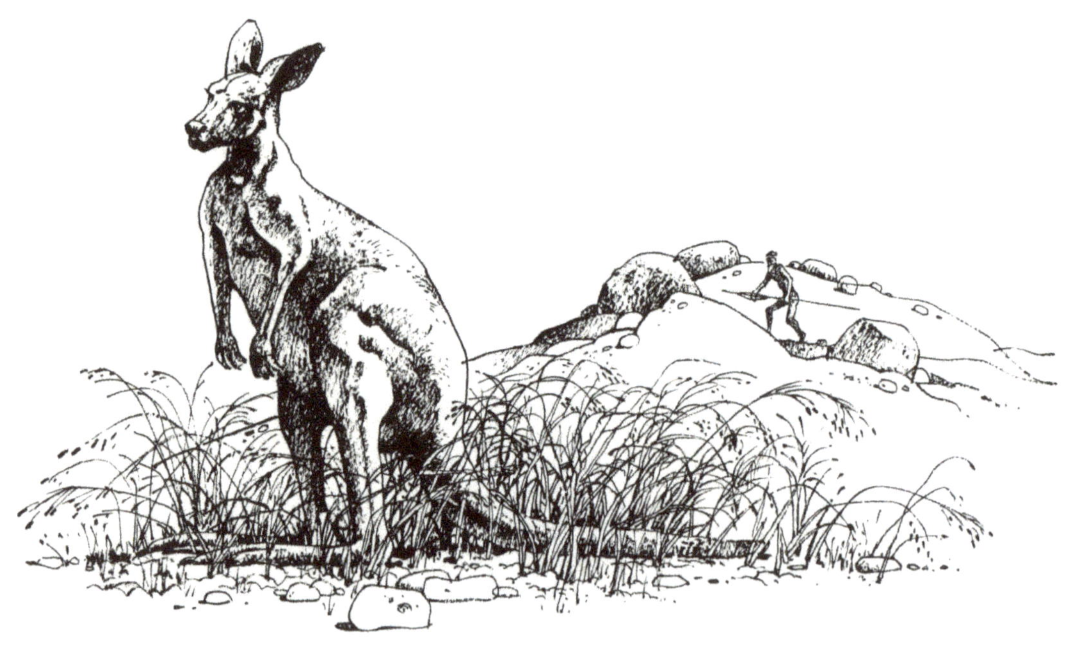

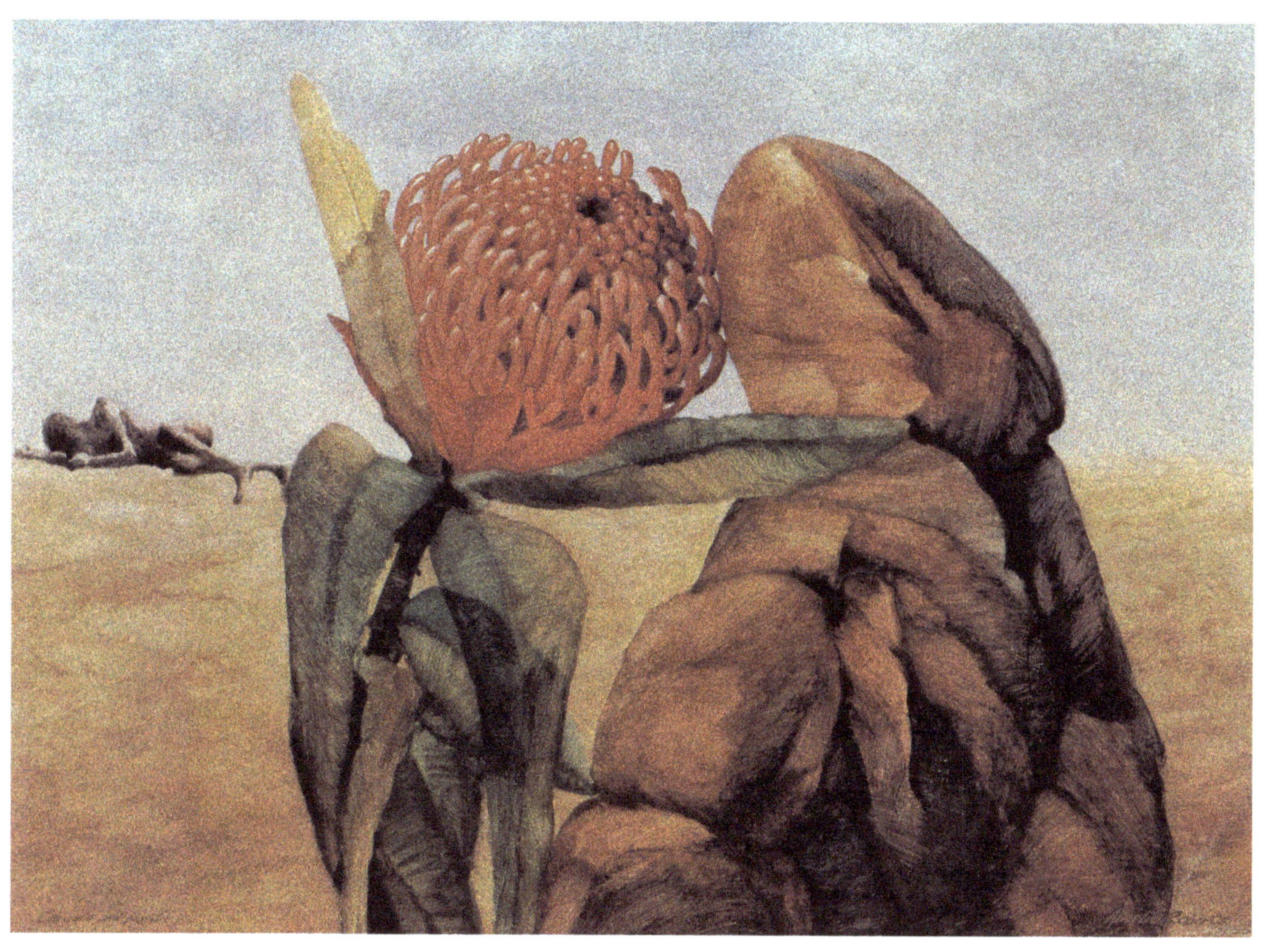

Mrs L M. Moore.

THE BLACK KANGAROO

Once there was an enormous black kangaroo, Kuperee, who left havoc and terror wherever he went. Many brave men had gone out to kill the monster, but he had destroyed them all.

Burdamuk, the leader of one tribe, owned a magical stone axe of great power. Yet, though he was too old to use the weapon against a kangaroo as large as Kuperee, Burdamuk refused to allow the axe out of his sight. For a long time there appeared to be no solution to the desperate situation until Indinya and Pilia, the two elder sons of the old man, finally persuaded their father to lend them the axe.

The brothers then searched for and found the empty camp of Kuperee, surrounded by the bones of his victims. Climbing into the dense foliage of a nearby my all tree, the brothers waited until Kuperee appeared. But when they threw their spears, the weapons, unable to penetrate the thick skin of the kangaroo, fell broken to the ground.

With a roar of fury, Kuperee charged into the trunk of the tree where the brothers were sheltering, hoping to uproot it. He had almost succeeded when Indinya, leaning outwards, struck the kangaroo such a heavy blow with the magical axe that it buried itself in his skull, killing him instantly.

Filled with joy at their success, Indinya and Pilia returned to tell their father and his people that they now could hunt without fear, or camp in peace beside the billabongs.

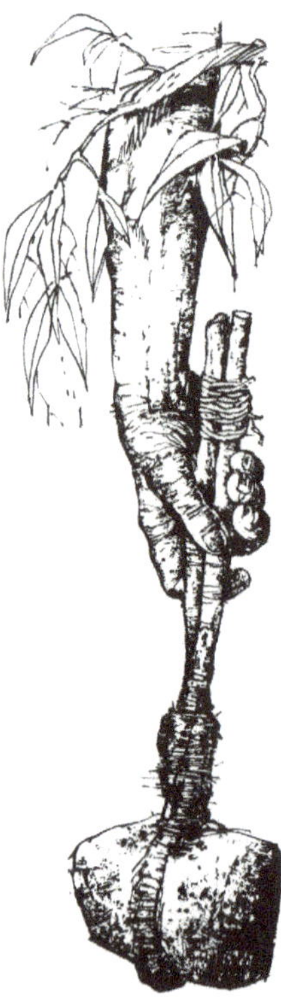

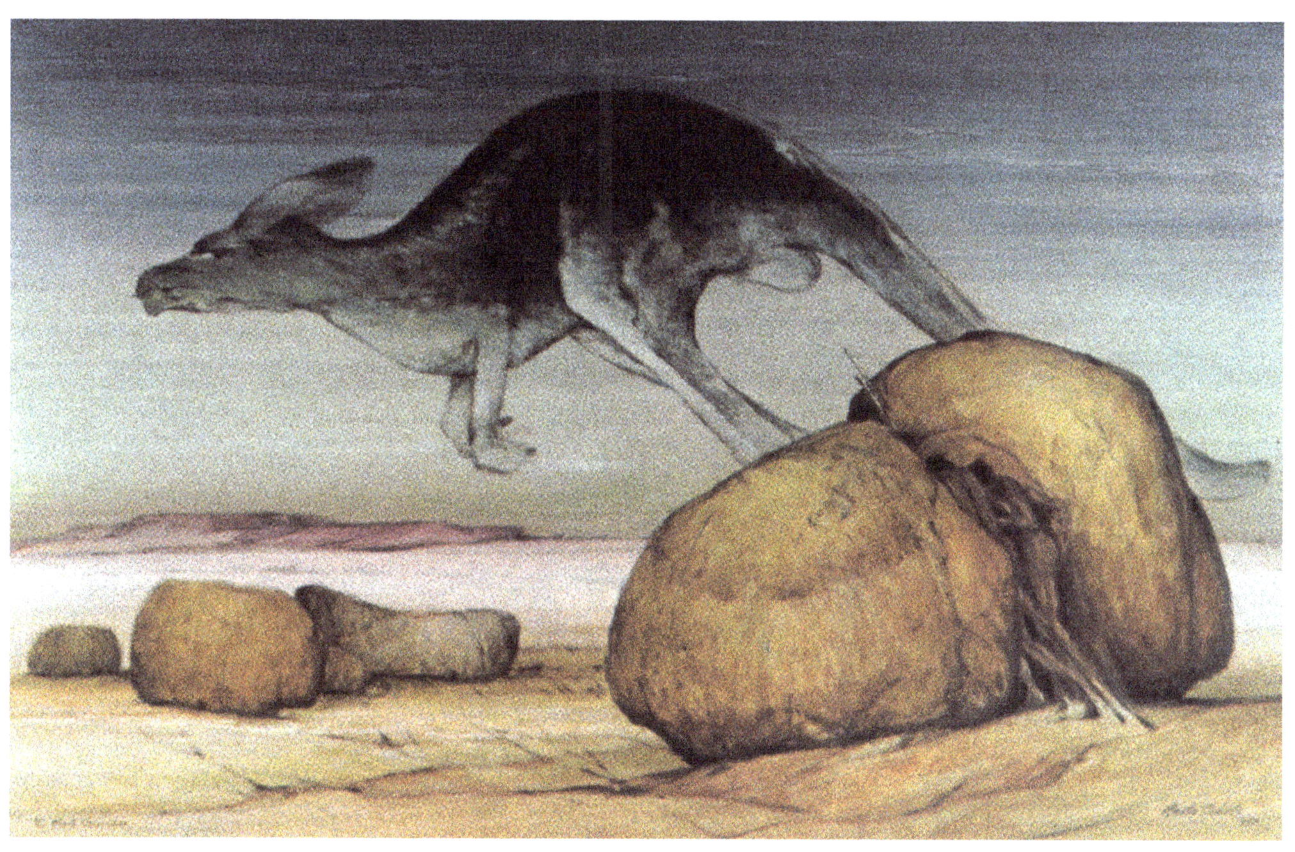

Mitsubishi Motors Australia Ltd.

LINGA OF AYERS ROCK

This myth, handed down by the Pitjandjara tribe, relates how Linga, a little lizard-man, lived by himself near the place where Ayers Rock (Uluru) now stands. Linga had spent many days making a boomerang, and when it was finished he threw it to test its balance. The boomerang flew higher and higher into the air and spun across the desert until it buried itself in the soft sand of the great red sandhill from which Ayers Rock was later created.

Greatly distressed at the loss of such a fine weapon, Linga hurried to the spot and dug everywhere with his bare hands to find it. Today, many of the spectacular features of Ayers Rock are the result of Ling a's frantic digging. The deep holes and gutters, which he made in the sand, have since been transformed into large pot-holes and vertical chasms in the steep face of the huge monolith.

Linga, forever associated with the sand in which he lost his boomerang, became the little sand-lizard. And, if you are quiet enough, and quick enough, you may surprise him alongside a small hole in some red sandhill.

If, in awe, you wonder how he survives in such an arid region, your curiosity is a tribute to the Aborigines of the desert. For countless thousands of years, and with only five simple tools, they gained an adequate living in an environment so harsh that no white man could live there unless he carried his own food and water.

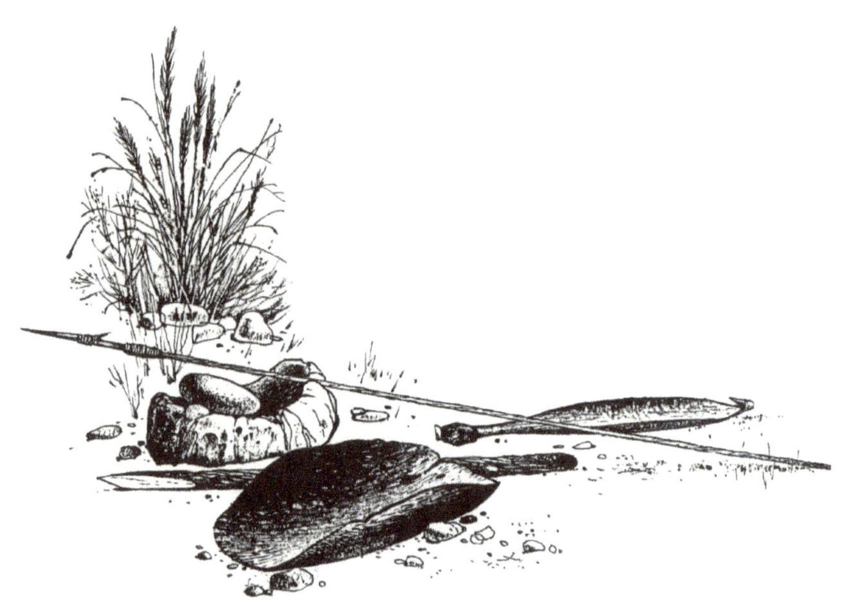

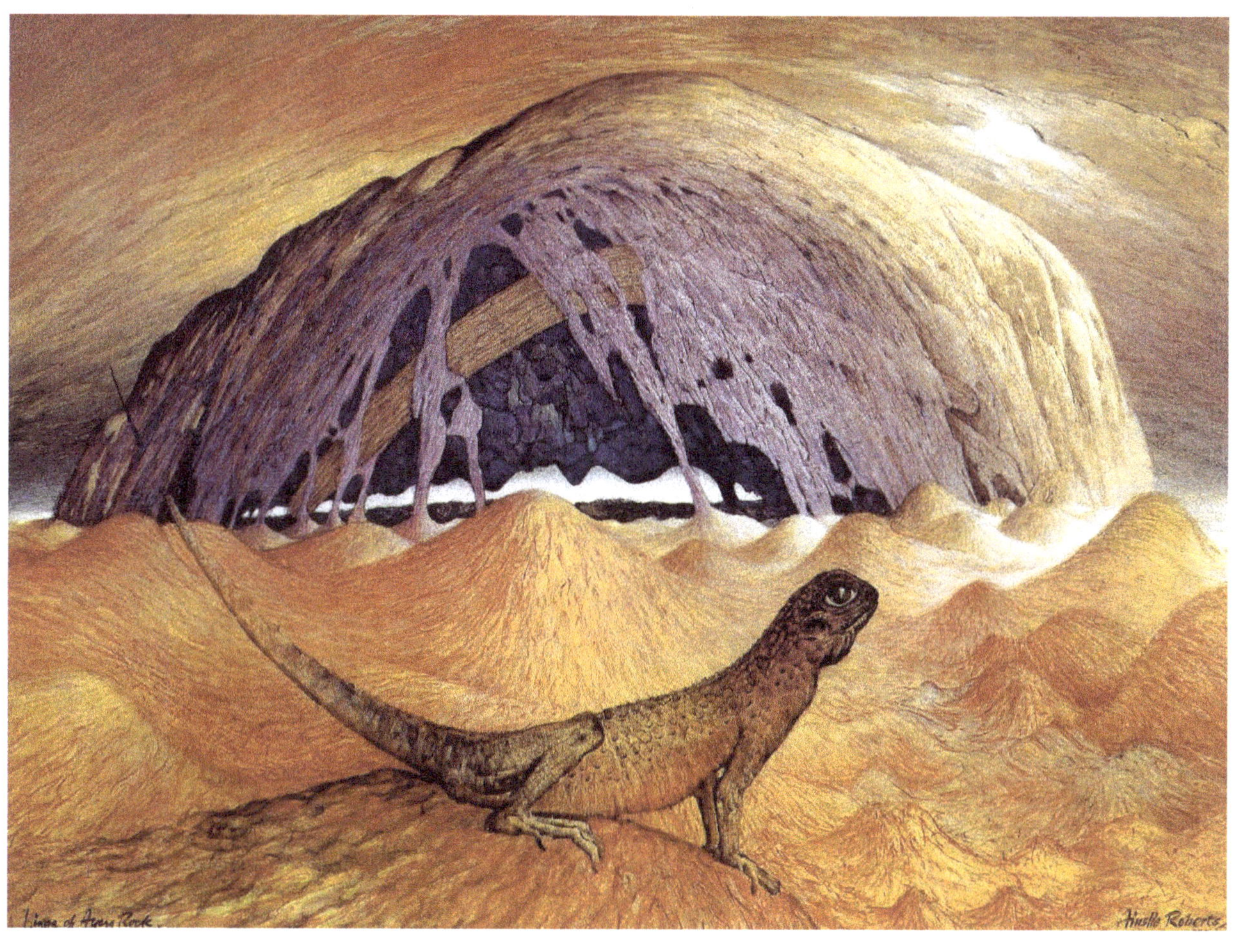

Private Collection.

THE NATIVE CAT, THE OWL, AND THE EAGLE

The mythical people of the Dreamtime were both evil and good, just as men are today. Of all the evil people" the native-cat man, Kinigar, was most feared, for he killed for the sheer joy of taking life.

When Kinigar was about, the women and children stayed in their camps, while the men, if forced to travel, always carried their spears and spearthrowers. Yet in spite of these precautions the haunts of the native-cat man were strewn with the lifeless bodies of men, women, and children.

This slaughter became so serious that the tribal elders agreed that, at all costs, Kinigar must die. After rejecting many schemes, the men decided to block the openings of all springs but one; thus forcing Kinigar to drink at the remaining water-hole, where the best spear-men would be hidden.

The owl-man, Mopoke, and the eagle-man, Wildu, who had been chosen for this task, went to the spring before dawn and prepared an ambush. Here they waited patiently throughout a long hot day until, in the late afternoon, they heard Kinigar coming. The native-cat man, after carefully searching the surrounding bush to make sure there were no enemies about, had just bent down to drink when the waiting men speared him in so many places that he died.

That evening the Aborigines saw a red star rise slowly into the sky from the spring where the native-cat man had been killed. A few days later an unknown cat-like creature, covered with white spots, was seen running about in the grass.

The red star of Betelgeus in the constellation of Orion is the spirit of Kinigar: the little creature that still lives in the bush is his transformed body, the white spots on his coat being the scars from the spear wounds that killed him.

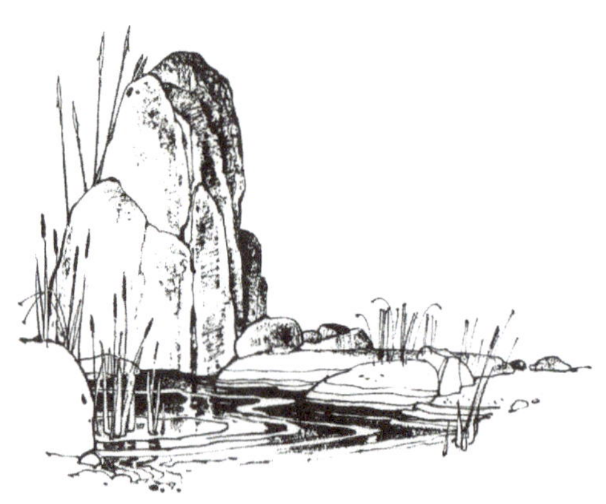

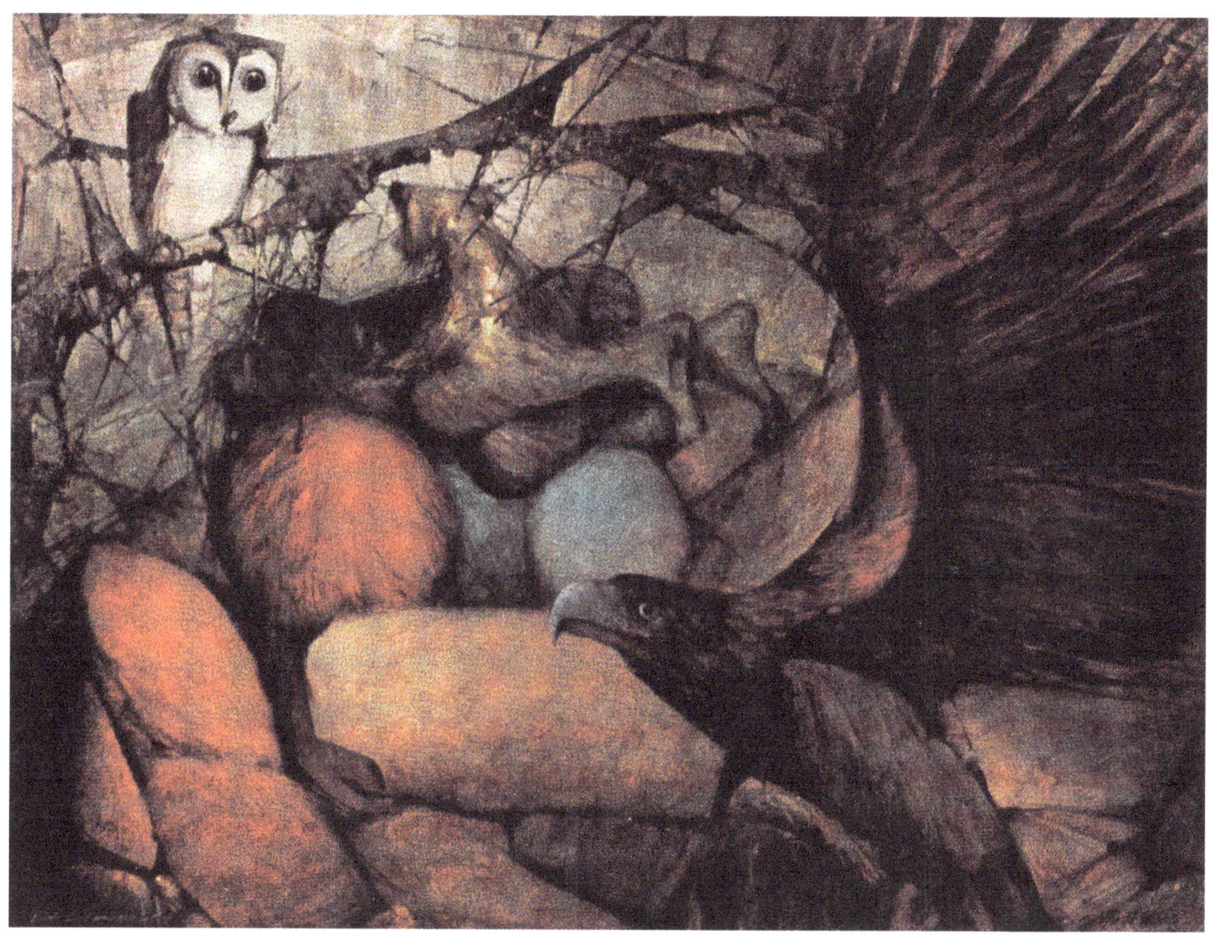

Mr Robert H. Irwin.

THE STORYTELLER

Since the dawn of time, Aboriginal elders have been the storytellers who have handed down the Dreamtime myths. The creation myths say that, in the beginning, no life existed in the world. It was void: without form and in darkness.

Then the Great Creators appeared. Each creation myth describes the journey of a Creator through the Dreamtime world. As he travelled, he gave topographic features to the world, created natural forces, and created life in all its forms, including the Aboriginal people. A number of myths relate the way in which a Creator made mankind in his own image.

The Creators also established the tribal laws which govern the conduct of Aboriginal society, so that its members would live in harmony. They decreed that everyone should partake of food caught by the hunters, and that a hunter should always take a lesser share. His reward was to be the satisfaction of achievement. The laws also stressed the importance of the family group and gave all members of the tribe an equal responsibility for the care of the aged.

When the Dreamtime creation figures had completed their work on earth, many of them made their homes in the sky and became the sun, moon, and stars.

The Dreamtime mythology does not attribute all power to a single God, nor does it tell of a Son who came in human form, but throughout the pattern of the myths passed on by Aboriginal storytellers are woven many threads which resemble the Christian commandments and beliefs.

If we are prepared to study these myths with an open mind, we will find that the apparent gulf between the two cultures is not as wide and impassable as it may seem

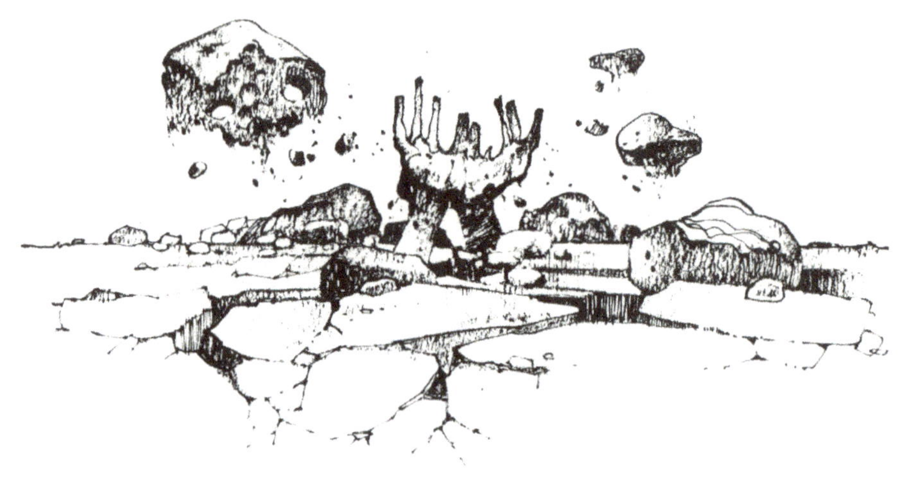

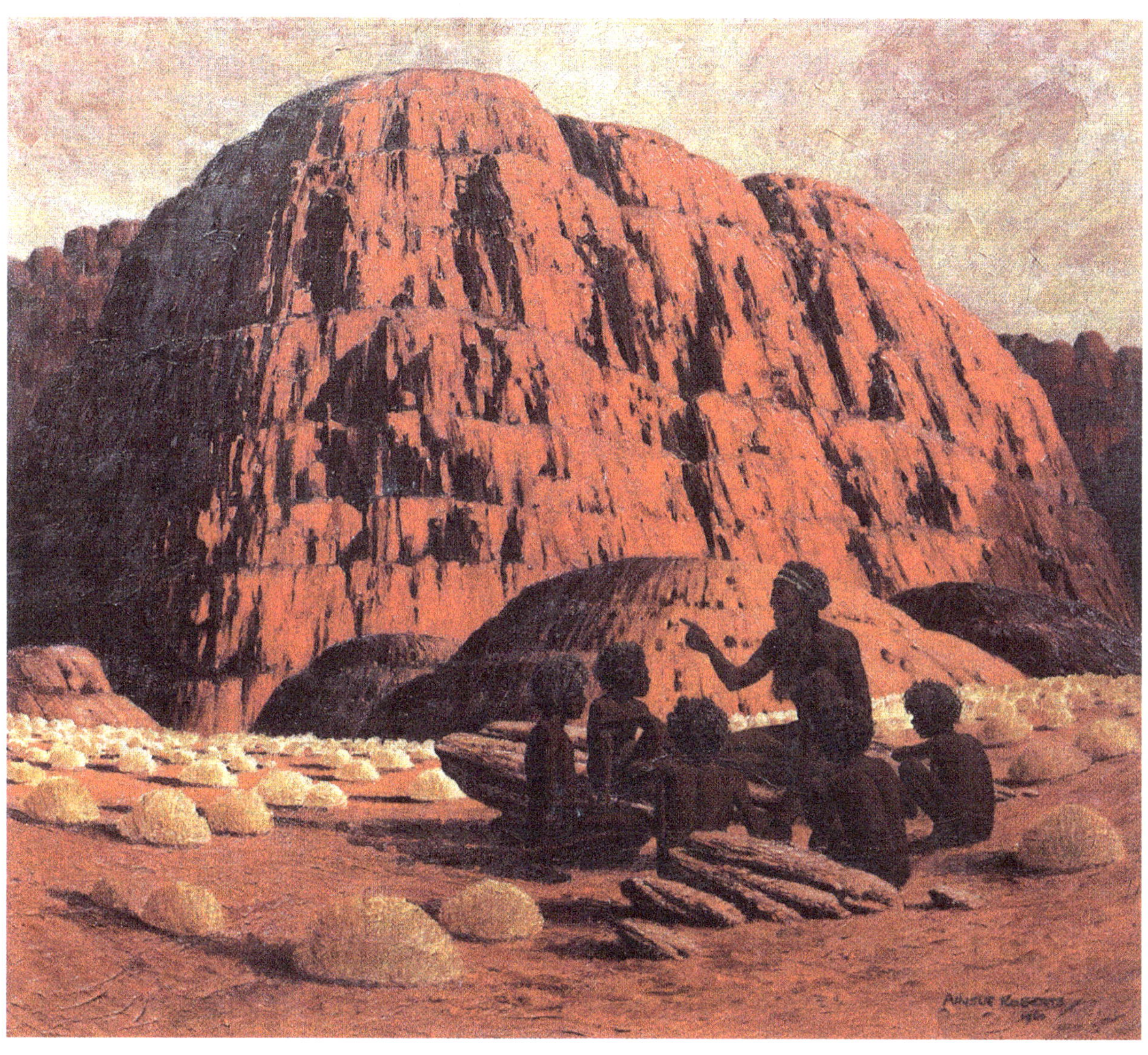

Mrs B. I. Griffiths.

THE REBIRTH OF WIRA

It was once the duty of a lazy and bad-tempered moon-man, Wira, to train his two nephews in the ways of the tribe. When they became efficient hunters, and skilled in the magic which he taught them, he spent most of his time resting, and in ordering them to feed him.

Eventually the two brothers became so angry at this behaviour that they worked out a plan to free themselves from his domination.

They knew that his favourite food was the wood-grubs that live high in the gum trees, but tribal law forbade young men to take the grubs from the trees. Whenever they found them, they had to tell Wira and he would go greedily to eat them all for himself.

One day they ran to him and said that they had found a tree rich with the grubs, and in great excitement Wira followed them to the tree which they indicated. He climbed up it as they watched from below, and when he was high in the branches they used the magic he had taught them to make the tree grow higher.

It grew so high, and so fast, that Wira soon found to his astonishment that he was raised high enough to touch the sky. Curiously, he hooked his fingers into the sky to discover what it felt like, and the nephews instantly brought the tree down to its normal size. Wira was left hanging by his fingers from the sky.

The nephews called up to him, 'We've put you up there to punish you for your laziness and bad temper. And each month you will become sick and thin, and come down into the mountains to die. Then, after three days, you will be reborn and go up into the sky again to grow large and fat, then come down to die again. And that will happen to you for ever and ever.'

But the triumph of the nephews was short-lived, because the moon-man called up his own powerful magic to change them into two stars and rise up into the sky. For ever afterwards they have had to live there, still close to their lazy uncle.

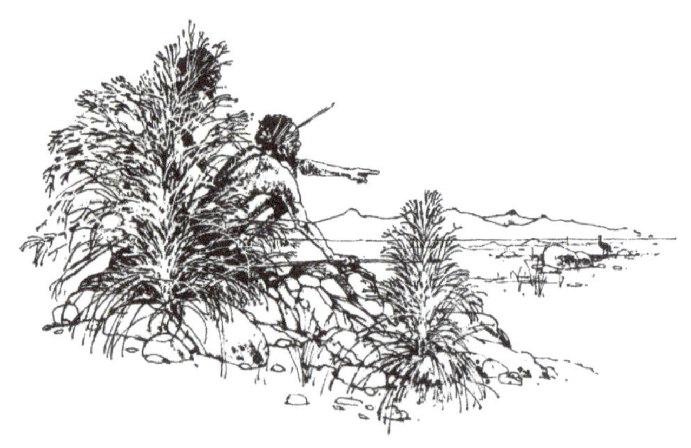

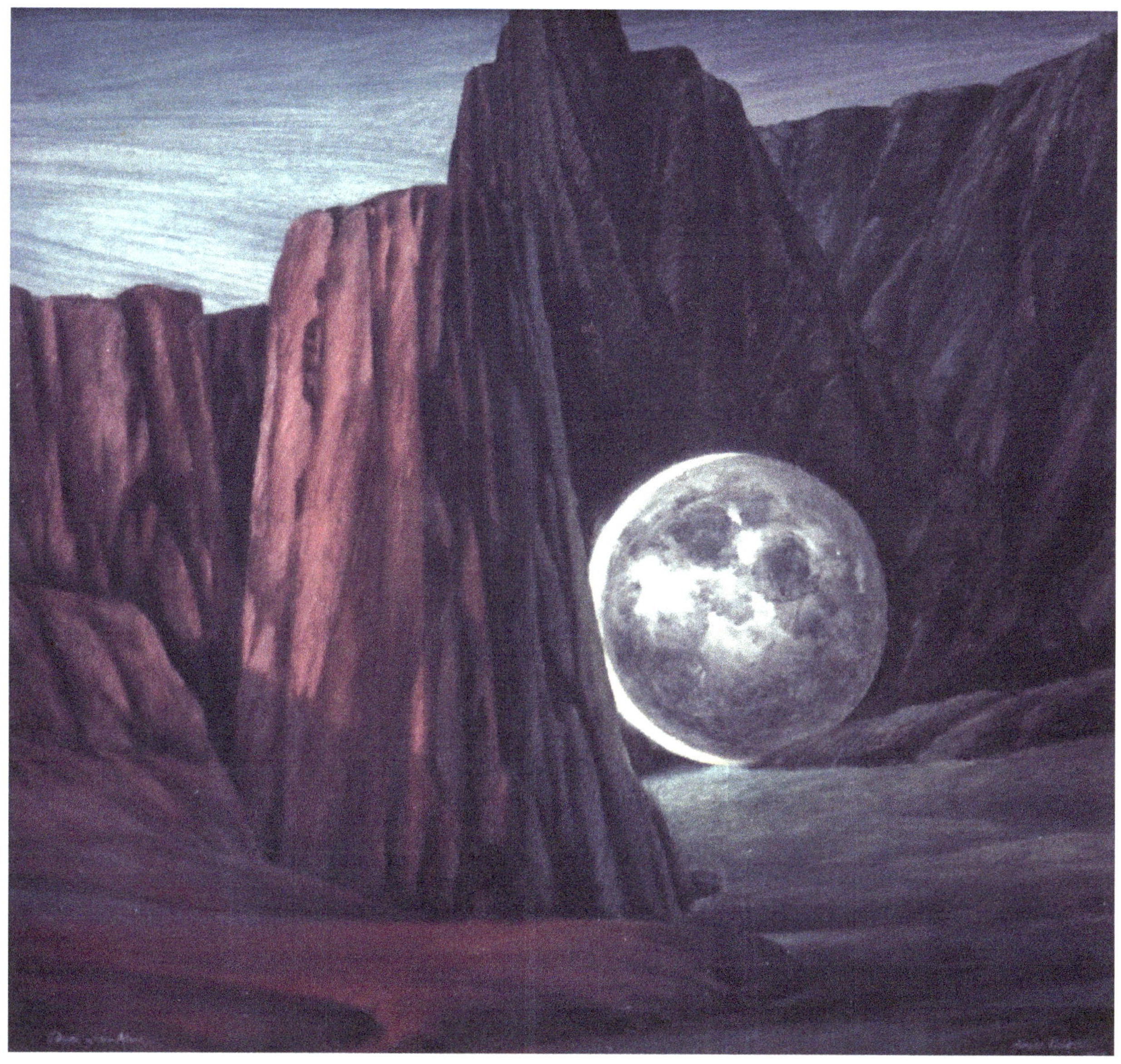

Private Collection.

ULAMINA THE STARFISH

Lying off the northern coasts of Australia was an island, rich in fruit and game, which the bandicoot-men could not visit because the only canoe in the country was owned by a selfish starfish-man, Ulamina, who refused to lend it to anyone.

One bandicoot-man, Banguruk, who was determined to steal the canoe, set out to make friends with the starfish-man. If Ulamina needed help, Banguruk was always ready to assist, and should the bandicoot-man spear a kangaroo he always gave half to the starfish man, until the latter began to trust him.

One day, Banguruk was overjoyed to receive an invitation from Ulamina to go out in his canoe on a turtle-hunt. The bandicoot-man caught a large turtle, and, being much stronger than his companion, pulled the canoe up on the beach, put the turtle on his shoulder, and carried it over the ridge of the sandhill, out of sight of the sea and the canoe.

When the other bandicoot-men saw the smoke from the fire on which the turtle was being cooked, they sneaked along the beach, launched the canoe, and paddled out to sea.

After a while, the starfish-man became suspicious, looked over the sandhill, and saw the other bandicoot-men paddling his canoe to the distant island.

Ulamina rushed into the sea after his canoe, but, realizing that he was outwitted, he changed himself into a starfish, and made his home on the sea-bottom. Even to this day, he waves his arms about, hoping one day to recapture the canoe stolen from him by the bandicoot-men.

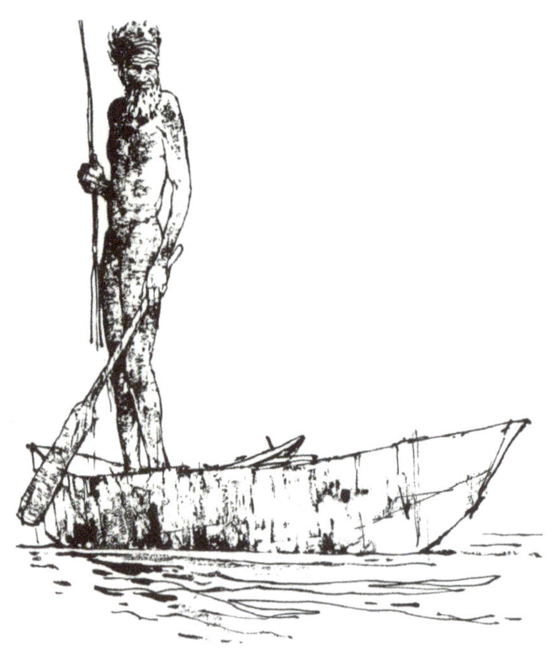

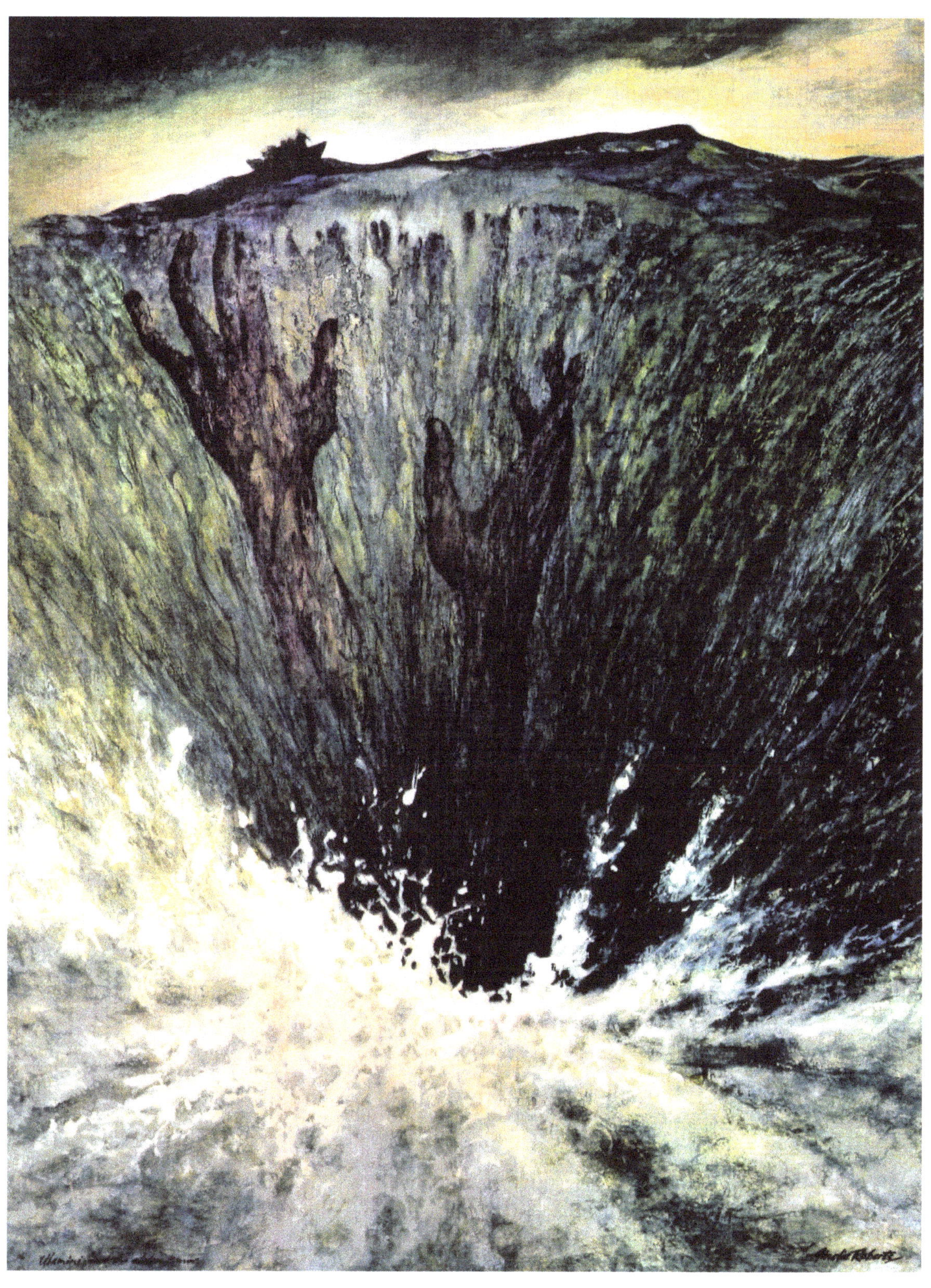

Mr and Mrs Harry S. Hanks.

THE DEATH OF KULTA

In the beginning of the world, Kulta was a man. He was a huge Aboriginal, selfish and ill-tempered, who lived in his own camp well away from the tribe. He was a good hunter, and seemed to know better than anyone else where the best game would be found. The Aborigines of his tribe thought that this was the reason why Kulta always appeared to be well fed. But the truth was that Kulta lived on human flesh, for which he had a craving. He knew that other hunters would follow him into the bush, hoping that he would lead them to plenty of game, and by clever bushcraft he would outflank and ambush one of them. Such unfortunate hunters were the meat on which he waxed fat.

At last, the tribe realised that the disappearance of so many of their hunters was no coincidence. They suspected Kulta, and after two more hunters had disappeared they raided his camp. To their horror, they discovered the truth.

They speared Kulta to death, and buried him in the bank of a creek near his camp. That night, the creek came down in flood, and washed the body out of the earth and into the lagoon. There, Kulta's body turned into an enormous snake, which lived in the depths of the lagoon and still possessed his craving for human flesh. In search of it, Kulta the snake travelled great distances from the lagoon by digging channels and letting the water flow along with him, because he could not live out of the 'water. He moved so fast that no Aboriginal could escape him.

But Kulta had to die a second time. One very hot day, he went too far from the lagoon, and the water in his channel dried up before he could return. The Aborigines now say that the dry channels radiating from the lagoon, which fill with water only in the wet season, are those which were dug by Kulta.

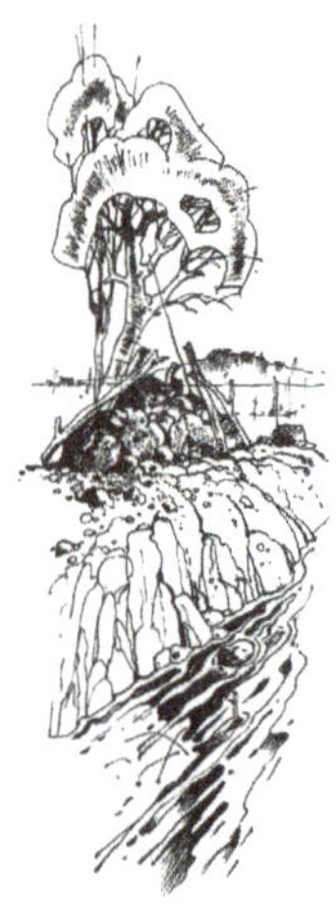

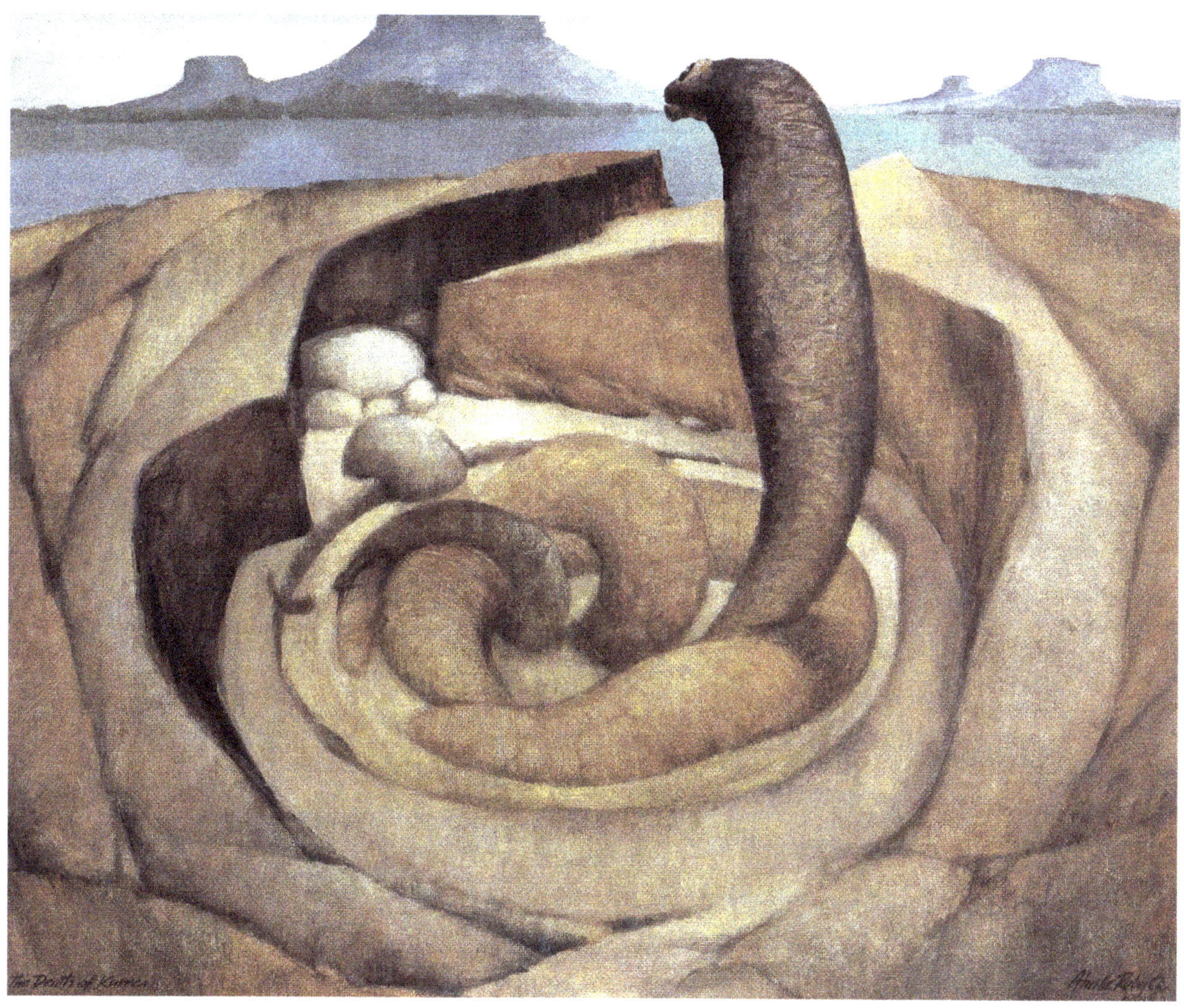

Private Collection.

CREATION OF THE COORONG BIRDS

During the Dreamtime, when all the birds were still Aborigines, they had a favourite fishing spot near the Murray mouth. When they used their nets they worked as a team, and the only man who was a misfit was the magpie-man. He was lazy and disliked the water. It was his duty to carry the firesticks so that a fire could be made to cook the fish.

One cold day, after the men in the water had made a good catch, they called out to the magpie-man to build a fire, so that they could warm themselves and cook the fish. But the lazy magpie-man, being away from the water and not feeling cold, said there was not enough wood to build a fire and urged the others to go on fishing.

This happened again and again, until the disgusted fishermen waded ashore and made their own fire. When all the cod, mulloway, and perch had been shared, the only fish left were bony bream. These are so bony that they were seldom eaten, and so the fishermen gave them to the magpie-man as a punishment.

This so angered the magpie-man that he took a bream in each hand and attacked the rest of the party. In the commotion that followed the men turned themselves into birds, and many of them were splashed white with flying scales.

The pelican, his previously black body now partly white, jumped into the water, and the net he once carried was changed into the large pouch under his bill. The cormorants and ducks dived under water to escape harm, and the coots ran into the reeds. The magpie, his black body also marked with the silvery scales, flew to the top of a cliff. To this day he keeps away from the water and the fishing birds with whom he once quarrelled.

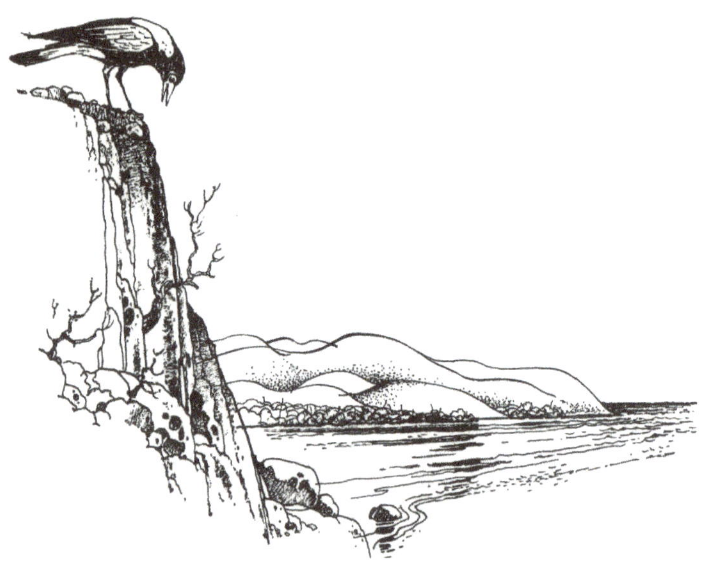

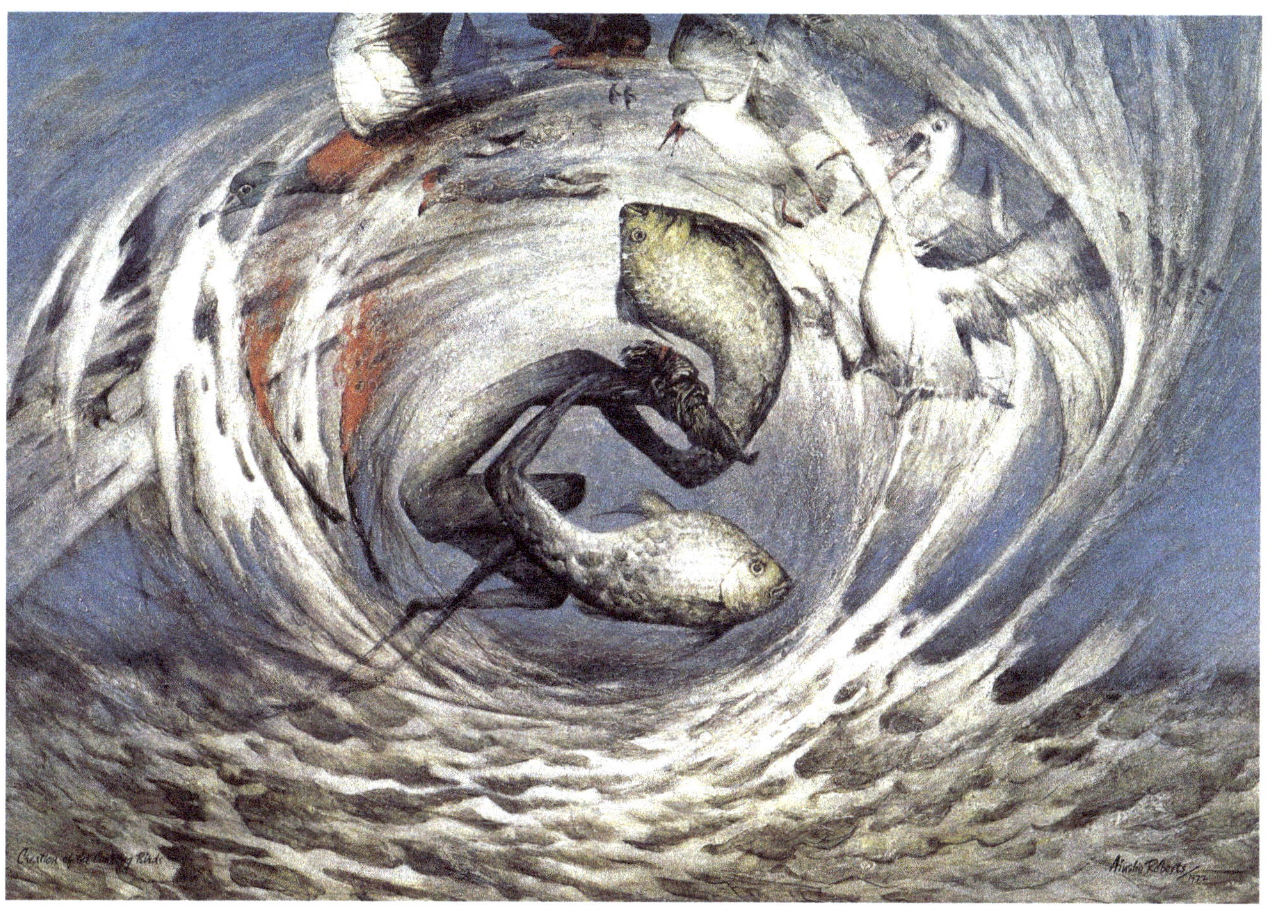

Private Collection.

THE BUNYIP

When the white men first came to Australia the Aborigines warned them about the bunyip, a strange creature which lived in a deep waterhole and destroyed everyone who camped nearby. Many early settlers believed the story. They never pitched their tents near a bunyip hole and they took care not to disturb the waters too much when they were filling their billy-cans.

As time went by, and the bunyip never appeared, the settlers forgot these precautions, but some of them thought that this persistent and widespread Aboriginal myth might contain some elements of truth. They tried to gain more knowledge about the legendary creature and discovered that it was described differently in various parts of the country.

The tribes of central Australia claim that the wanambi, which is another form of the bunyip, is an immense highly¬coloured snake, often hundreds of metres long. It has a mane and a beard, lives in all permanent waterholes, and attacks any creature that lives near its home.

The Aborigines of the Coorong, in South Australia, believed the bunyip to be a huge man-eating creature endowed with a bellowing call that could be heard for miles around. It had a long neck, a head like a bird, and an elongated fur-covered body that was part animal and part human. This bunyip laid enormous eggs and always lived near water.

Perhaps the legendary bunyip is really a kind of racial memory of the great dinosaurs and other prehistoric creatures whose bones have been found in Australia. It is certain that a true bunyip has never been seen.

In the absence of any other evidence, the concept of the Coorong bunyip shown in the painting is based on the humorous overtones of the artist's imagination. It is as likely to be correct as any other interpretation.

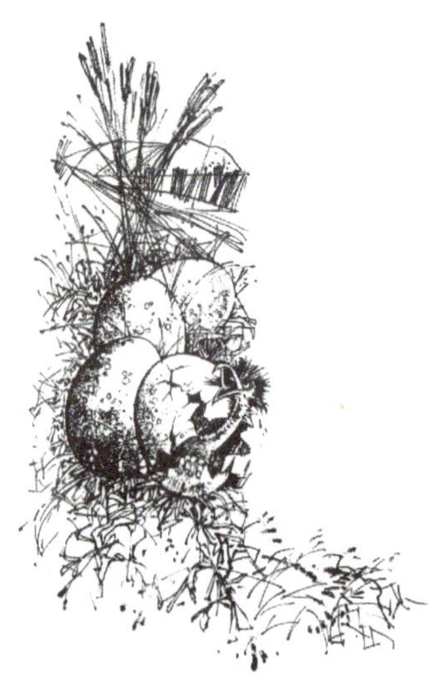

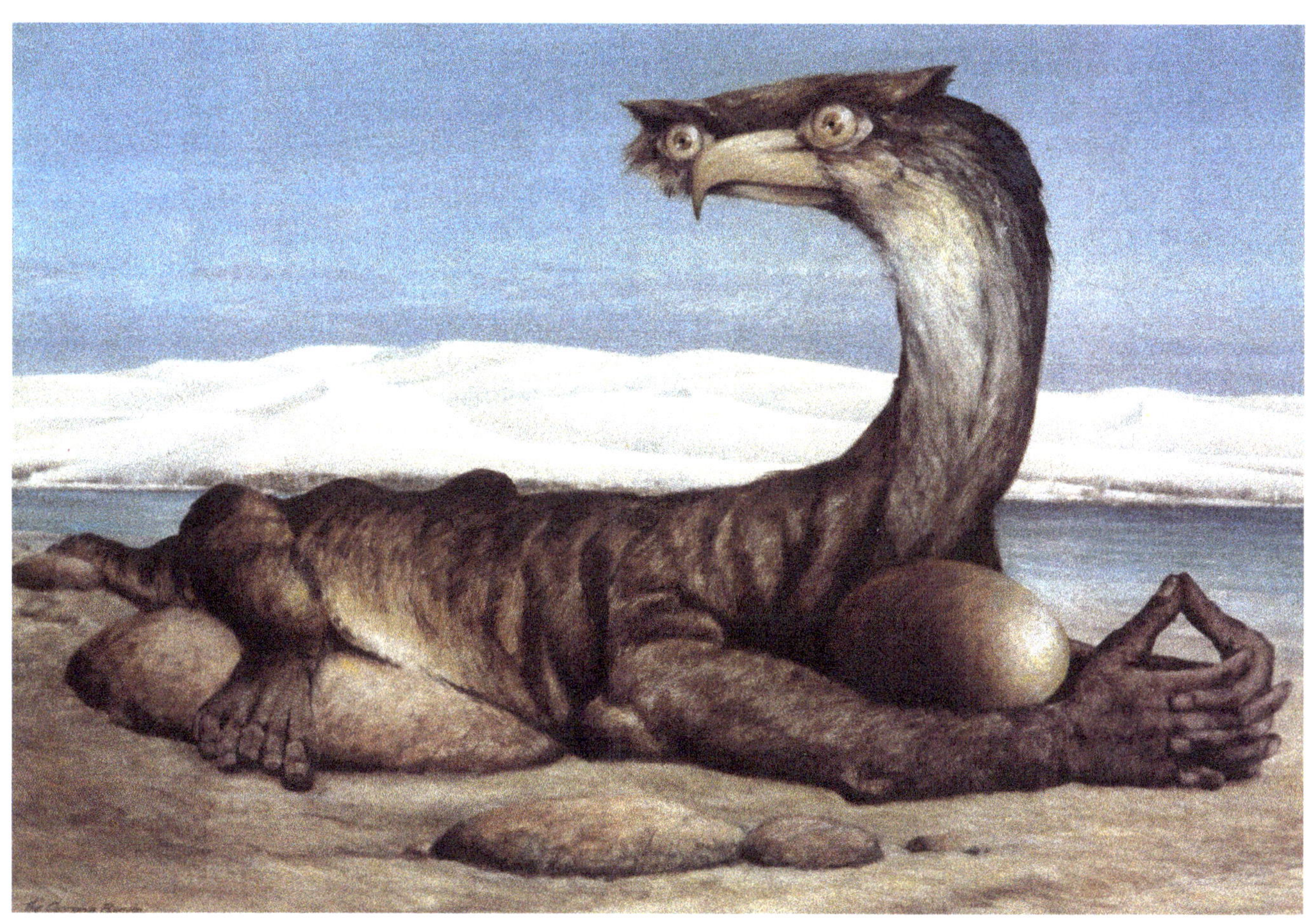

Colonel Aubrey Gibson.

THE RAINBOW-SERPENT

In the mythology of the Australian Aborigines, the most widespread of their beliefs was in the existence of a huge serpent which lived in waterholes, swamps, and lakes. In most myths it was associated with the rainbow. Rainbow-serpent myths were Australia-wide, but the greatest variety came from northern Australia, where the thunder-clouds and violent rains of the monsoonal season provided the ideal environment.

The Rainbow-serpent myths vary widely in their telling, and in the names given to the serpent, but the creatures had many characteristics in common.

Most myths describe a huge snake that spent the dry season resting in a deep waterhole. In the wet season, it went up into the sky as a rainbow. It was of immense size, brilliant in colouring, and often had a mane and a beard. Usually it was an object of fear to the Aborigines, especially when resting in its waterhole, and the greatest care was taken not to annoy or offend the mighty snake. Should anyone disturb its rest, the Rainbow-serpent would inevitably create some disaster, from simply eating the offender to making the waterhole overflow and thus drowning everyone in the world.

In some myths, Rainbow-serpents appear as Ancestral Creators. Their bodies contained not only the first Aborigines, but all the natural features of the land which in that remote time was flat and featureless. In others, the appearance of a rainbow meant that the serpent was travelling from one waterhole to another. Sometimes it was linked with the rainbow colours of quartz crystals, which the medicine-men of many tribes used as objects of magic. But whatever its shape or name or habits, the Rainbow-serpent was an awesome creature of power and importance.

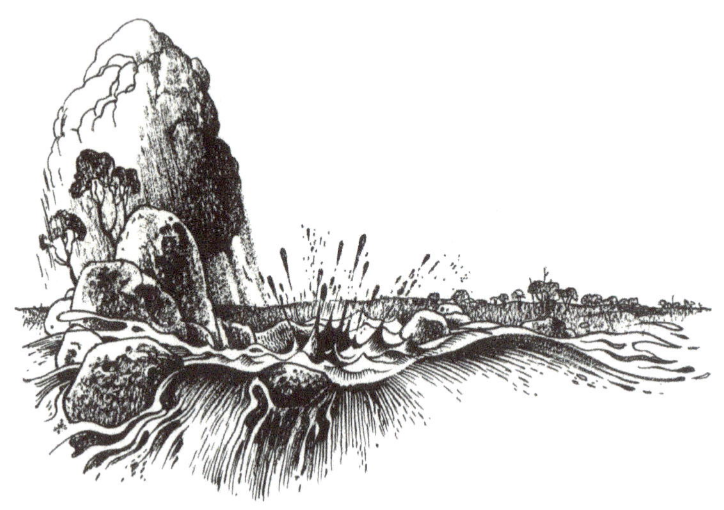

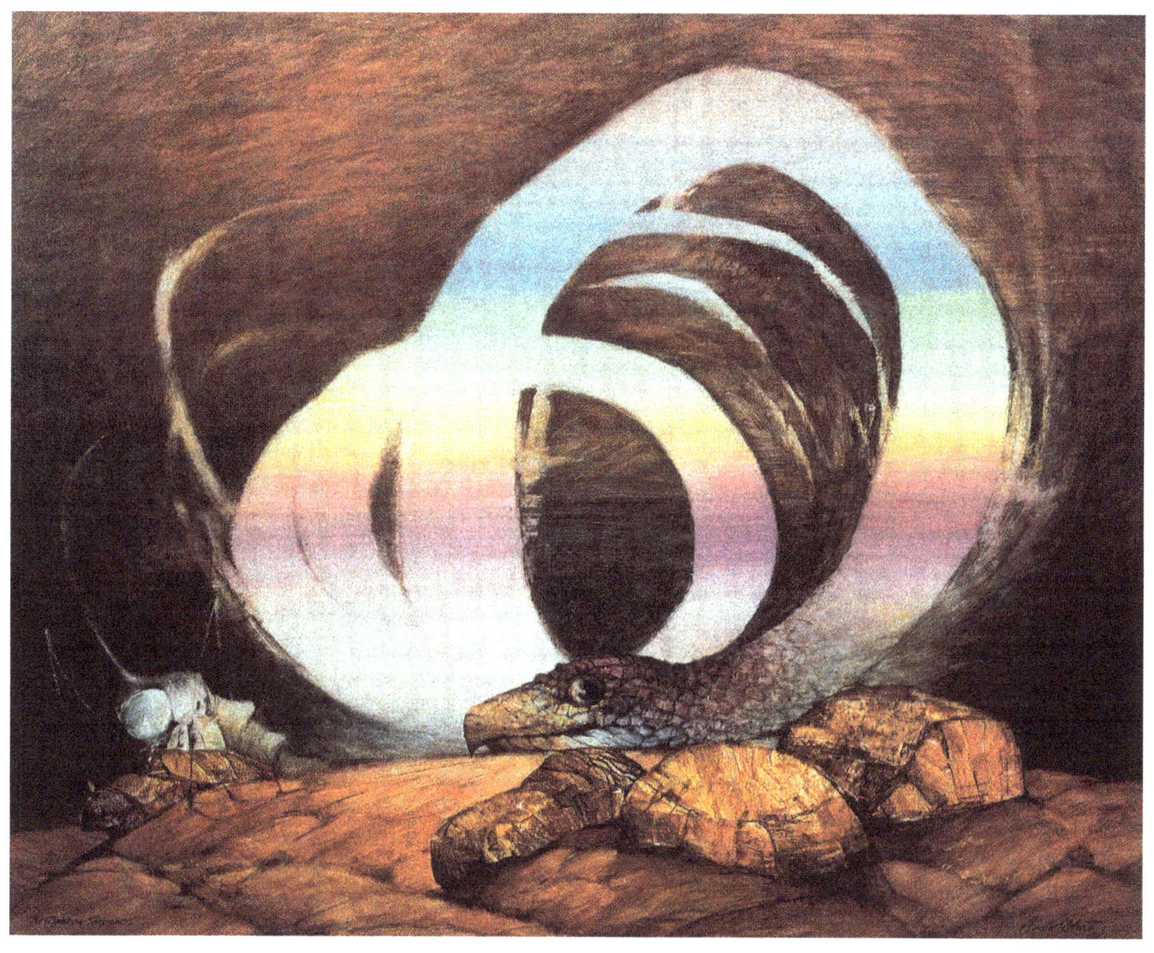

Mr and Mrs R. W. Griffiths.

THE ABDUCTION OF BROLGA

Brolga was the favourite of everyone in the tribe, for she was not only the merriest among them, but also their best dancer. The other women were content to beat the ground while the men danced, but Brolga must dance; the dances of her own creation as well as those she had seen. Her fame spread and many came to see her. Some also desired her in marriage.

An evil magician, Nonega, was most persistent in his attention, until the old men of the tribe told him that, because of his tribal relationship and his unpleasant personality, they would never allow Brolga to become his wife. 'If I can't have her,' snarled Nonega, 'she'll never belong to anyone else.' For already he had planned to change her from a girl into some creature.

One day, when Brolga was dancing by herself on an open plain near her camp, Nonega, chanting incantations from the centre of a whirlwind in which he was travelling, enveloped the girl in a dense cloud of dust. There was no sign of Brolga after the whirlwind had passed, but standing in her place was a tall, graceful bird, moving its wings in the same manner as the young dancer had moved her arms. When they saw the resemblance everyone called out 'Brolga! Brolga!' The bird seemed to understand and, moving towards them, bowed and performed even more intricate dances than before.

From that time onward the Aborigines have called that bird Brolga, and they tell their children how the beautiful girl was transformed into the equally beautiful grey bird which still dances on the flood plains of northern Australia.

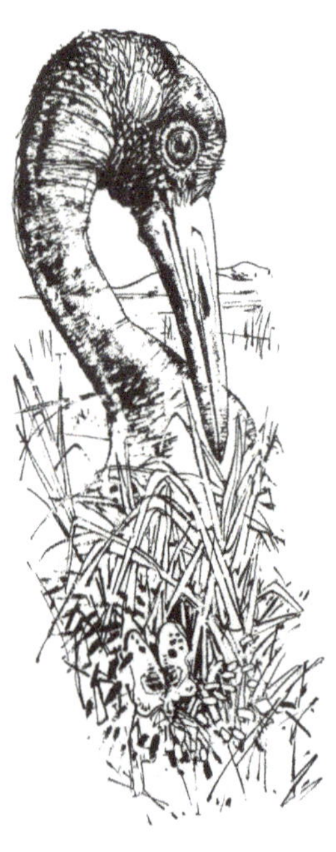

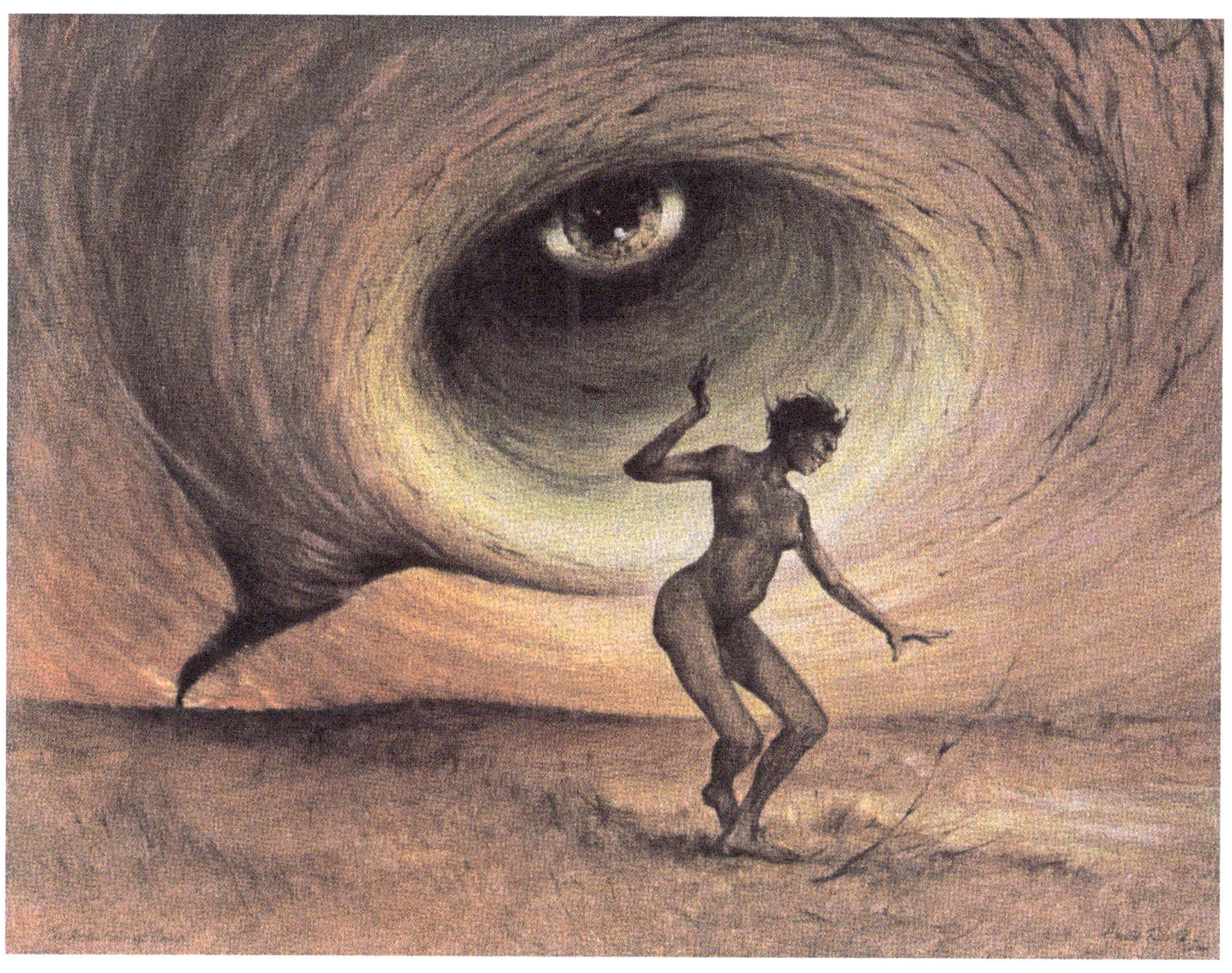

Keith H. Kingsley Estate.

THE CREATION OF THE JENOLAN CAVES

The Aborigines of New South Wales believed that, in the Dreamtime, Mirragan the hunter tried to spear Gurangatch, a huge half-fish, half-reptile which lived in a deep waterhole in the Wollondilly River. After failing many times, Mirragan tried to poison the water with hickory bark. But Gurangatch escaped by tearing up the ground along a near-by valley, so that the water in the river flowed along after him.

Mirragan was relentless in his ambition to capture such a large creature, and he caught up with Gurangatch many times. Each time they fought fiercely, but each time Gurangatch escaped. Finally he burrowed into the mountains and created a huge cave.

The determined Mirragan then climbed to the top of the range, and drove his spear into the ground to frighten Gurangatch out of the cave. He drove his spear down in many places, and each time Gurangatch dug further into the mountains until he had created a labyrinth of caves. At last he broke out on the other side and disappeared into the J oolundoo waterhole. Mirragan returned with the tribe's best divers, but none of them could dislodge the creature from this deepest of all waterholes.

The encounter between Mirragan and Gurangatch resulted in the formation of the Wollondilly and the Cox rivers, the Jenolan and Whambeyan caves, the blowholes on top of the Blue Mountains and, in the places where they fought, the many deep water holes in the two rivers.

The Aborigines always avoided these waterholes, believing that they were inhabited by the descendants of Gurangatch

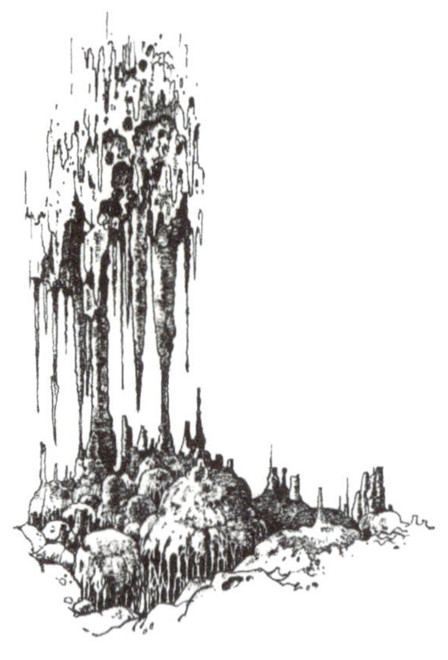

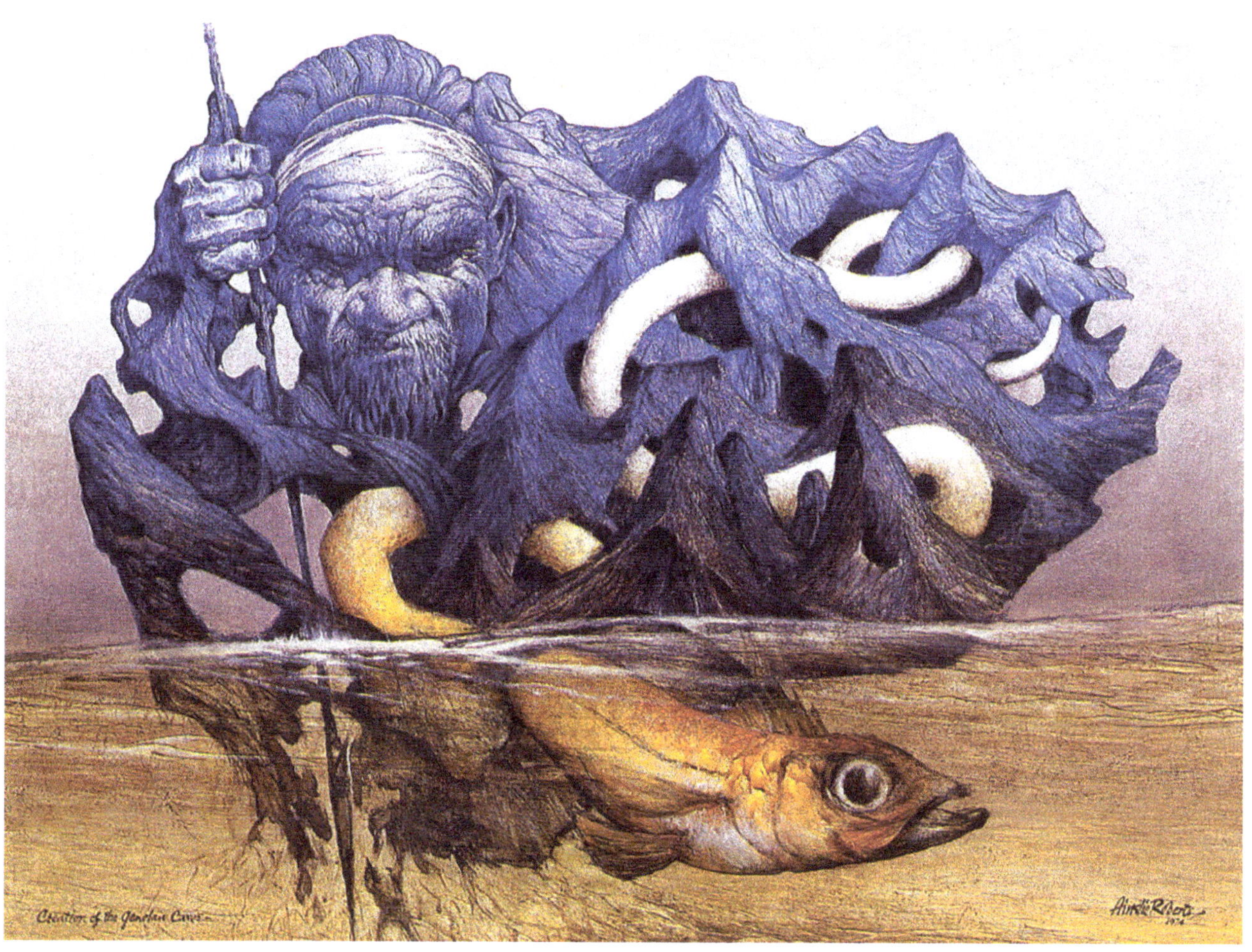

Private Collection.

THE FIRE SPREADERS

Australian Aboriginal mythology has recorded many beliefs which explain how fire was first obtained, how fire-making was perfected, and how it was used for cooking, for warmth, for lighting night ceremonies, and for many other purposes. Fire, and its benefits, was possibly the richest Dreamtime heritage of all. One of its most spectacular uses was as an aid to hunting.

At the time of the year when speargrass, spinifex, and other grasses were dry, the Aborigines set fire to them and waited for the rush of goannas, snakes, kangaroos, and wallabies escaping from the blaze. In this way they could kill game more quickly, and in larger quantities, than by any other method.

But the Aborigines were not the only ones to gain their food out of the flames. The fork-tailed kites also benefit from fires, and they have added some refinements of their own. They gather in their thousands above a grass-fire, to feed on the wing on insects rising in the thermal currents created by the heat, and to swoop on small rodents fleeing from the fire.

The Aborigines regarded these birds as masters of cunning comparable only with dingoes, for they have seen fork-tailed kites deliberately start fresh fires by picking up smouldering sticks in their claws and dropping them in distant patches of dry grass. Having used this 'tool of fire', they climb and await the wild exodus of scared and half-blind insects, rodents, and reptiles that soon appears.

There is nothing in Aboriginal mythology that records whether the Aborigines or the birds first discovered how to use fire in this way, but today the fork-tailed kites still carry on a tradition that was born in the Dreamtime of the Aborigines

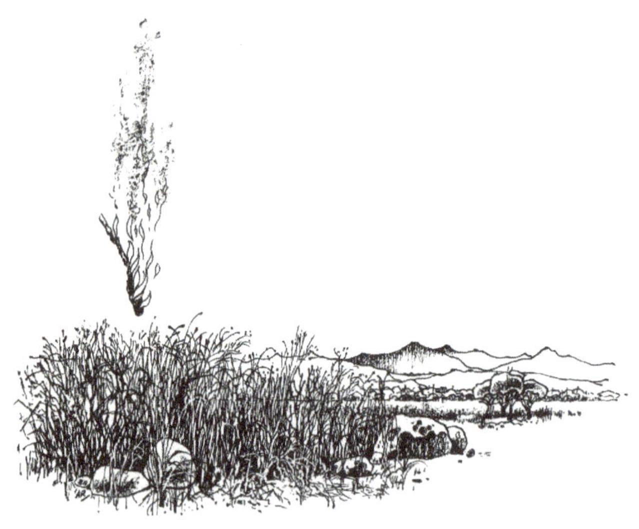

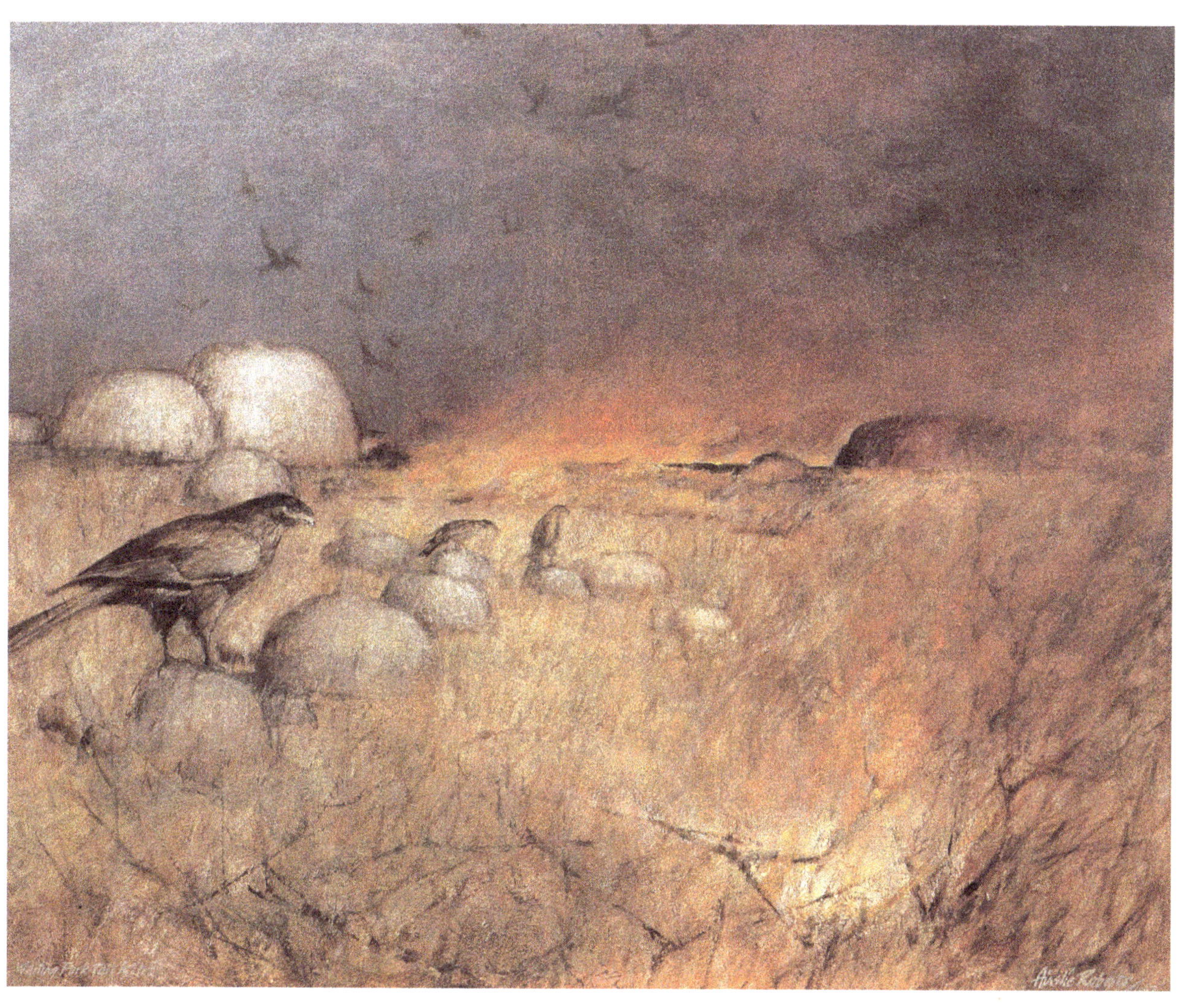

Mr and Mrs B. Glowrey.

JITTA-JITTA AND KUBIRI

In a mountainous area of Western Australia there are many caves. One of them was the home of a giant man-eating dingo, and another of a huge snake. Every morning these creatures emerged to roam the country and raid the camps of the Aborigines in search of victims.

The only large waterhole in the area was close to the caves. The tribes lost so many of their people, who tried to collect water from the hole, that they had to depend on what little water they could collect after rains. They dared not light fires to cook their meat, or to warm themselves, lest the snake and dingo follow the scent of cooking to its source. As a result of these hardships, more and more of the people were becoming weak, ill, and dejected.

But a willy-wagtail man, Jitta-jitta, and a robin-man, Kubiri, both resourceful hunters, determined to end the tragic position. They made and abandoned many desperate plans, until one evening when the hot winds were blowing strongly from the north, Kubiri said to Jitta-jitta, 'Tomorrow, at dawn, we will light a big fire outside the cave of the dingo. This wind will fill the cave with smoke. It might blind the dingo long enough for us to kill it when it runs out.'

So Jitta-jitta followed their plan, and it worked. One lucky blow from his club killed the blundering dingo instantly, but Jitta-jitta had had to do it all alone. Kubiri had made a brave speech the previous evening, but when the time came he climbed a nearby tree. He sat in the topmost branches shivering with fright and feeling thoroughly ashamed of himself.

During that day, however, poor Kubiri's courage returned. He set out alone on the following morning, to use the same trick to destroy the great snake. In this he was successful, and when the Dreamtime ended, and the two men were transformed into birds, tribal laws decreed that neither Jitta-jitta the willy wagtail nor Kubiri the robin shall ever be killed, or molested in any way.

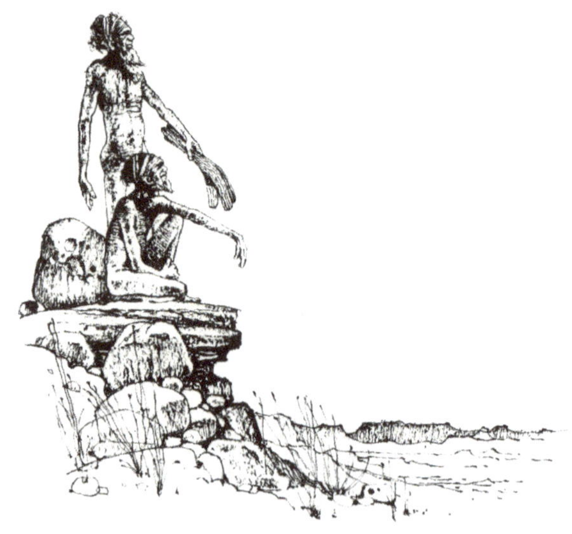

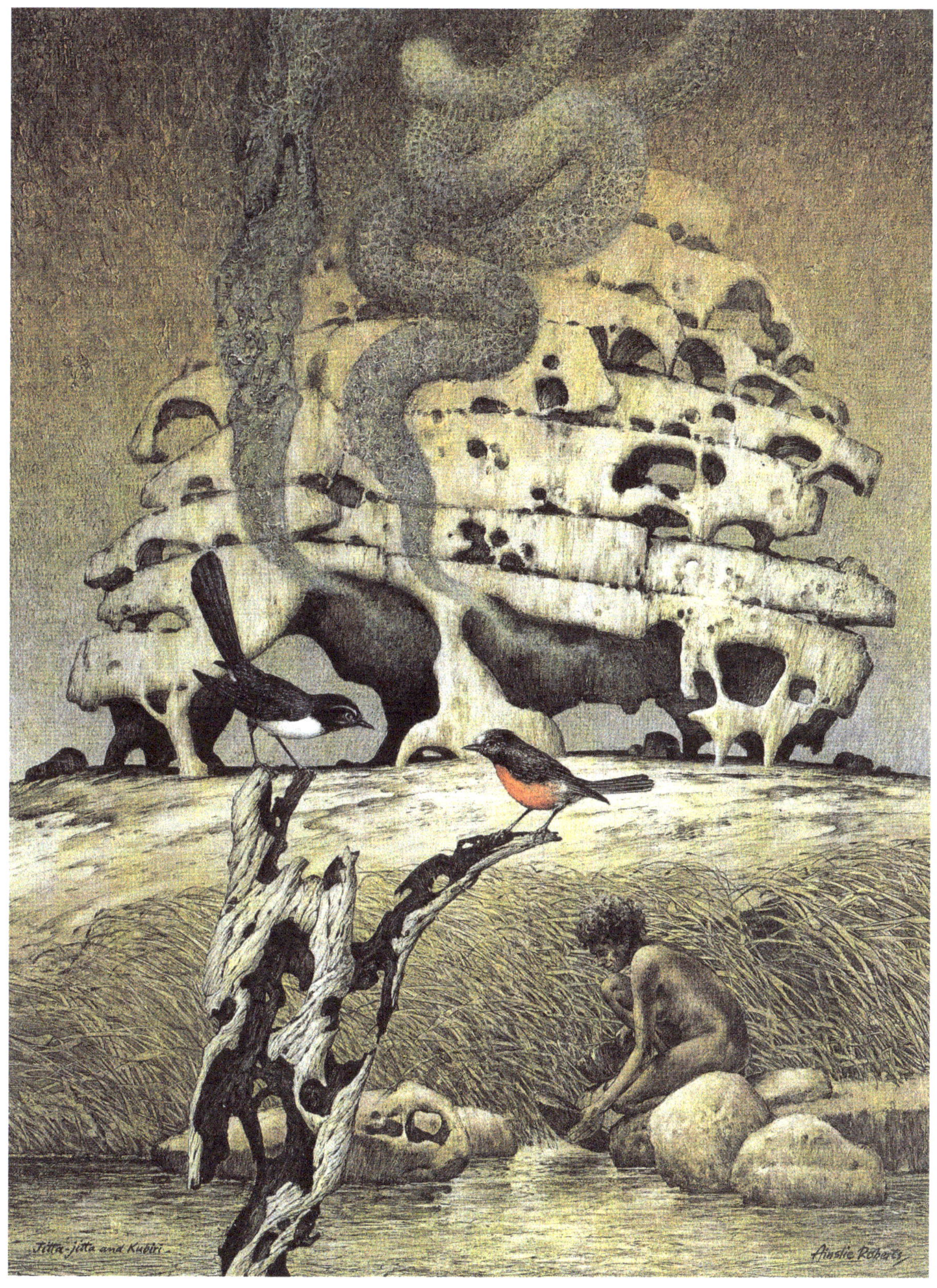

Private Collection.

THE FIRST DAWN

The Aborigines of the Dieyerie tribe, in the far north of South Australia, believed that all living creatures were created by Pirra, the moon. This task was carried out under the direction of the Mooramoora, the great spirit who made all things. Pirra created man by first making two small black lizards. He then divided their feet into toes and fingers and, with a forefinger, formed the noses, eyes, ears, and mouths. Pirra placed the creatures in a standing position, which they could not retain, and so he cut off their tails and the lizards walked erect. They were then made male and female, to perpetuate the race.

But when these first men and women began to move about the land, guided only by the moon's light, they found it dark and bitterly cold because the sun had not been created. Hunting weapons had not been developed, and the small animals they caught for food had to be run down on foot.

The biggest creature in that far-off Dreamtime was the emu. It was many times larger than it is now, and the hunters knew that the flesh of an emu, could they but capture one, would provide food for the tribe for a long time. They made many attempts to capture the big bird, but it was so fast, and the world so dark and cold; that they never succeeded. The emu always vanished into the darkness.

So the hunters held a great gathering, performed many ceremonies, and pleaded with Mooramoora to make their world warmer and lighter so that they could capture the emu. And Mooramoora listened to their troubles and made the sun, thus creating day and night.

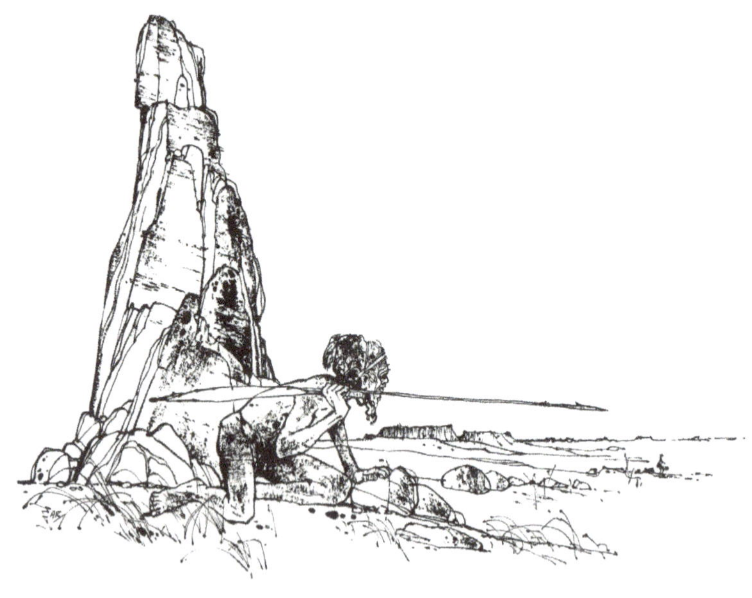

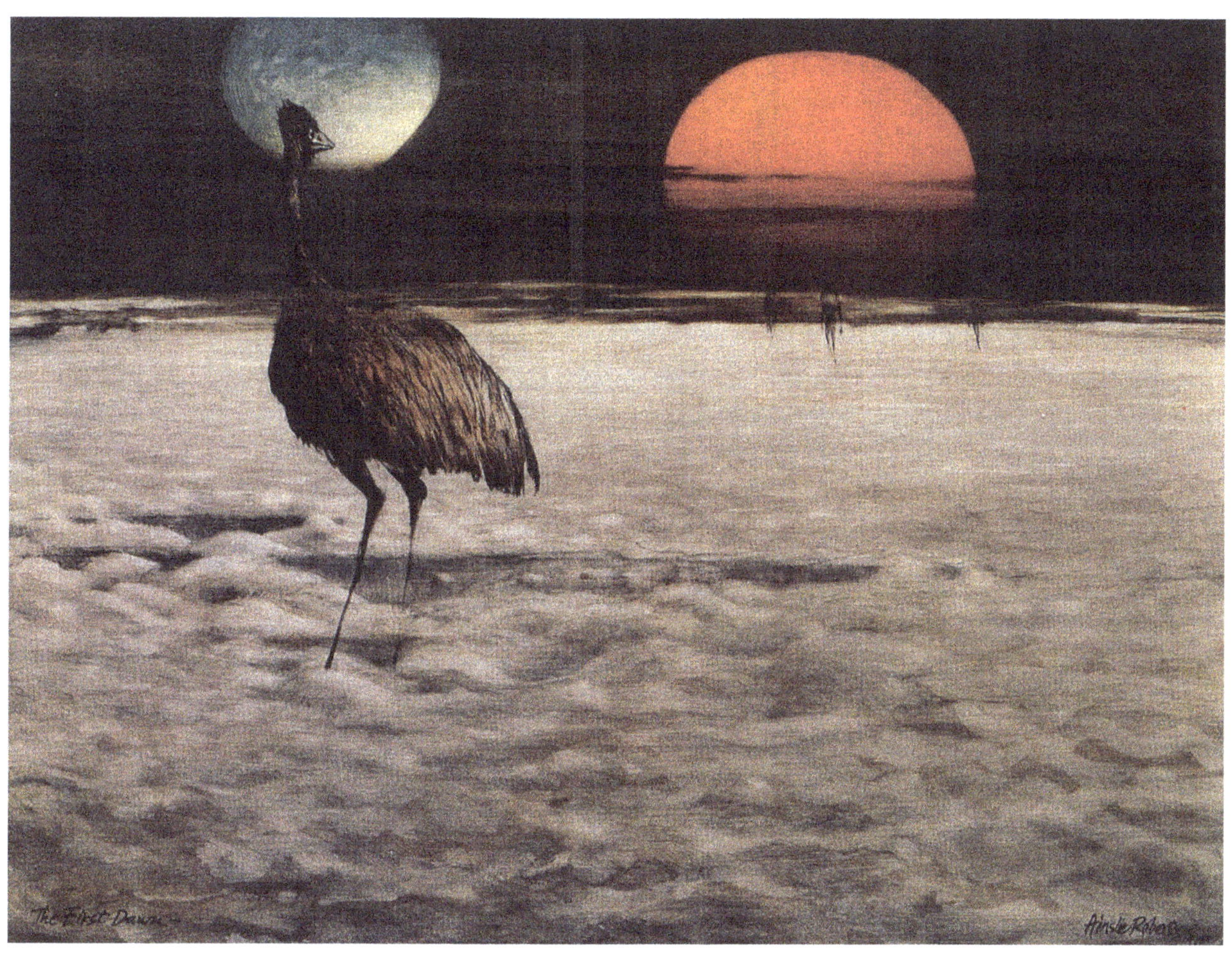

Mr and Mrs Charles E. Hulley.

ULDANAMI, THE LITTLE MOTHER

The Aborigines of northern Australia believed that the curlew originated as a result of the wrongdoings of Bima, which caused the death of her son. The Aborigines of the Flinders Ranges, in South Australia, have a totally different myth related to the curlew.

It was that of Uldanami, the little mother, who heard that a bush-fire had driven her two sons into the sky, where they became the Pointers of the Southern Cross. All of her other relatives having been dead for many years, her sons were the last on whom she could lavish her affection.

Lonely for human companionship, and unable to believe that her children were not on earth, Uldanami searched everywhere for them, her plaintive calls echoing and re-echoing among the rocky hills and steep gorges.

The spirits have now changed the little mother into the curlew, who still wanders at night, calling for her loved ones.

When, sitting beside their camp-fires, the Aborigines hear that strange wailing call, they are reminded of the grief of Uldanami. It is then that the parents, pointing out the two bright stars in the southern sky, tell their children the story of how those stars were once the sons of the little mother, Uldanami.

Still mourning her loss, Uldanami believes that, if she calls loud enough and long enough, they will in time answer her call and return.

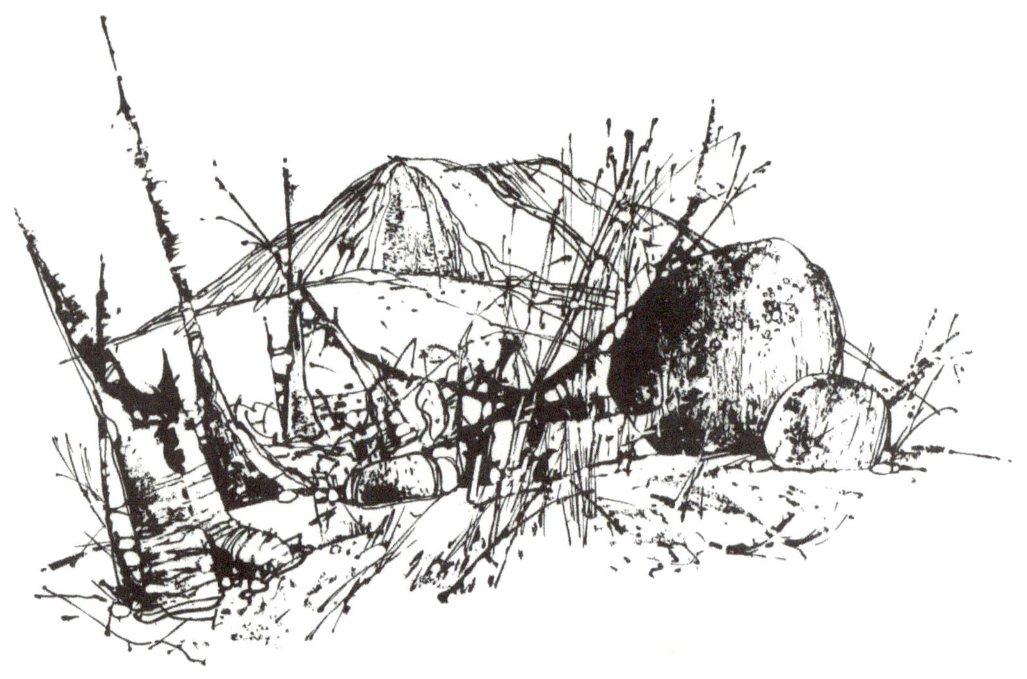

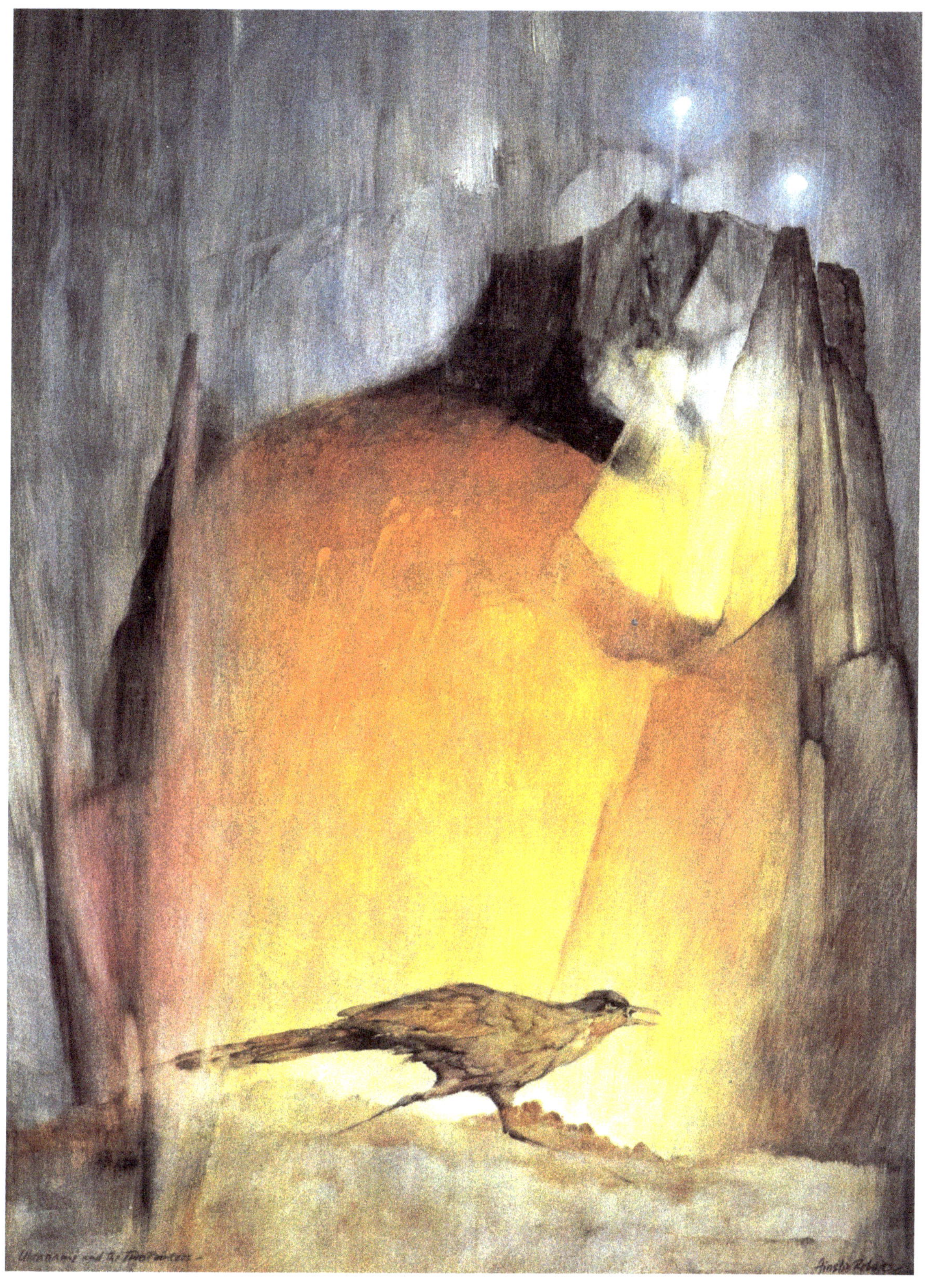

Mrs Pat Trabilsie.

BIRTH OF THE BUTTERFLIES

When the world was young, the birds and animals had a common language and there was no death. No creature had any experience of its mystery, until one day a young cockatoo fell from a tree and broke its neck. The birds and animals could not wake it, and a meeting of the wise ones decided that the spirits had taken back the bird to change it into another form.

Everyone thought this a reasonable explanation, but to prove the theory the leaders called for volunteers who would imitate the dead cockatoo by going up into the sky for a whole winter. During this time, they would not be allowed to see, hear, smell, or taste anything. In the spring they were to return to earth to relate their experiences to the others. The caterpillars offered to try this experiment, and went up in the sky into a huge cloud.

On the first warm day of spring a pair of excited dragonflies told the gathering that the caterpillars were returning with new bodies. Soon the dragonflies led back into the camp a great pageant of white, yellow, red, blue, and green creatures - the first butterflies, and proof that the spirits had changed the caterpillars' bodies into another form.

They clustered in large groups on the trees and bushes, and everything looked so gay and colourful that the wise ones decided this was a good and happy thing that had happened, and decreed it must always be so. Since then caterpillars always spend winter hidden in cocoons, preparing for their dramatic change into one of spring's most beautiful symbols.

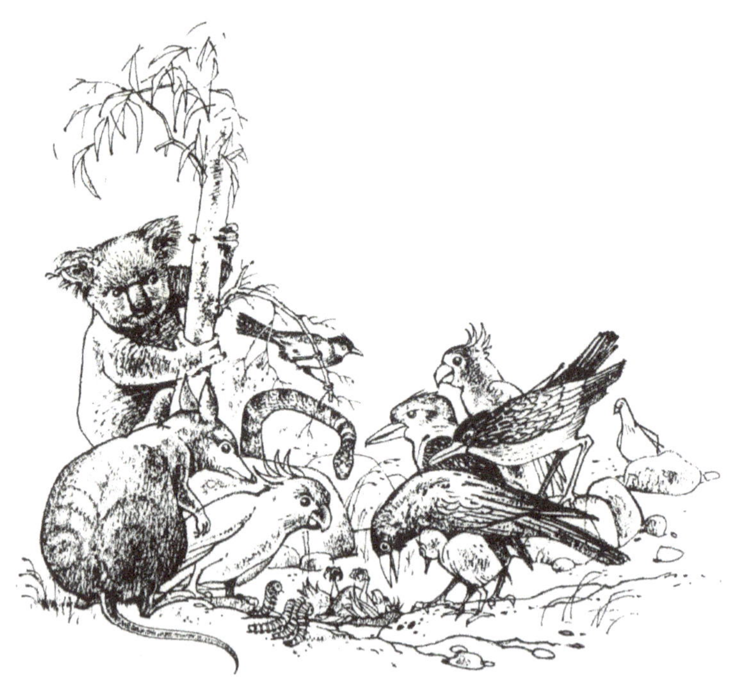

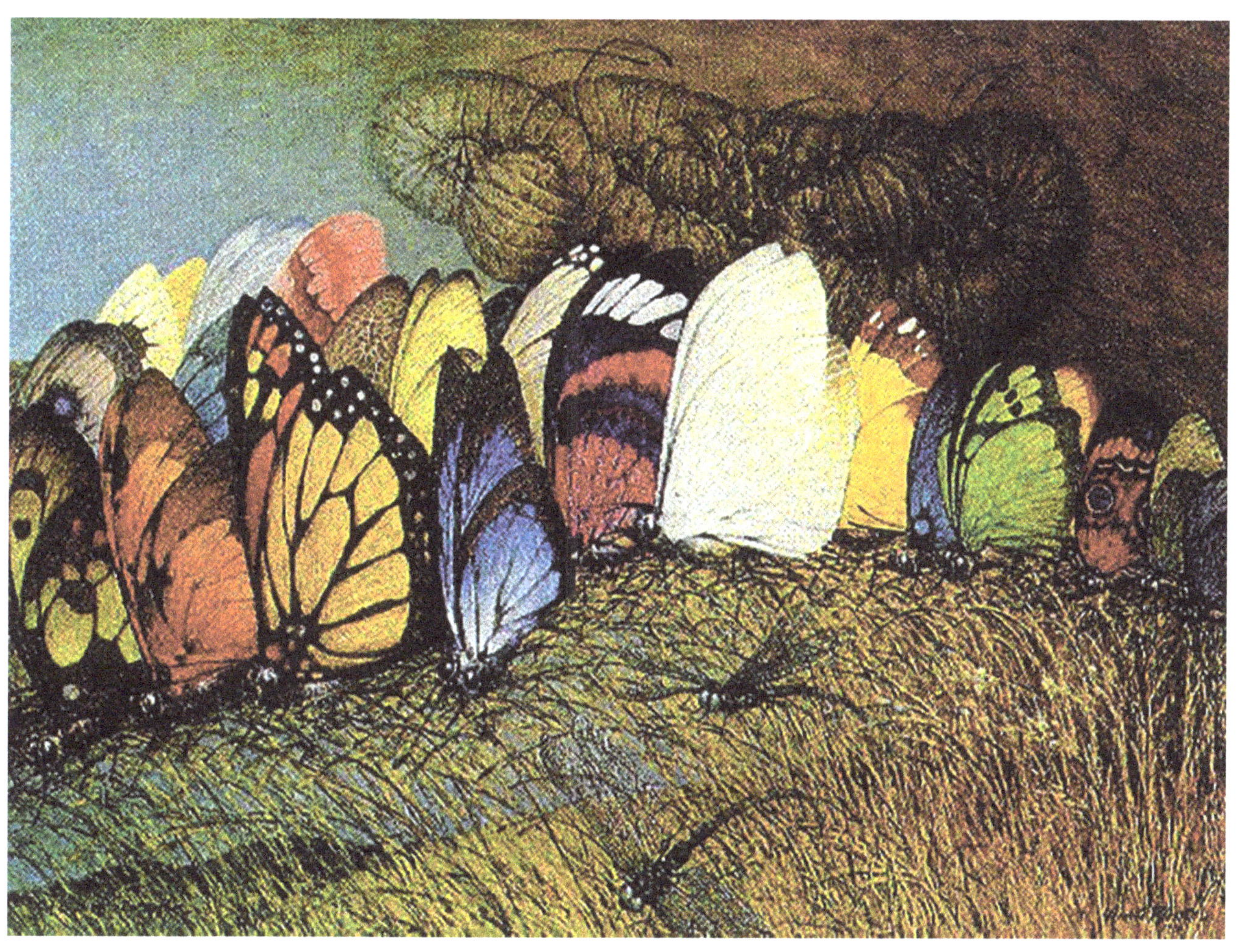

Sir Robert Helpmann.

THE IRON INTRUDER

The sea, which for so many centuries protected the Aborigines against invasion from the world outside their land of the Dreamtime, at last betrayed them when it provided a highway for the invaders. They arrived only in small numbers at first, and existed in scattered and isolated settlements, but as their colonies increased so the portents of their coming went before them.

In the accompanying painting, the old iron mooring buoy symbolises the long shadow cast by the invaders. It could have broken adrift from any of the new seaports around the coast, and drifted with the currents until at last the surf cast it ashore to rest among the seawreck, on some beach as yet untrodden by the white man.

There, an Aboriginal would have found it as he walked along the beach on his daily foraging expedition. He would have regarded it warily and with some wonder, unable to realise that this iron intruder forecast the destruction of a lifestyle ordained by his spirit ancestors.

And perhaps he carried it back to his people in their sandhill camp, where they abandoned it when they wandered off again to roam their ancient territory. It lay there for a century or more until a white man discovered it again and captured its symbolism in paint.

In the meantime, the changes forecast by this innocent symbol had overwhelmed the people of the Dreamtime. A tidal wave of upheaval and bewilderment, a jarring conflict between the old and the new, had spread into every corner of the vast continent.

The iron intruder is now no more than a piece of rusty trivia, of no significance in a world where great events continuously forge the destiny of every nation into new patterns, regardless of the skin colour of its inhabitants.

The question of how the Aborigines will fit into the patterns of the future is still without an answer. We can only hope that the magic and mystery of their ancient culture will in some way be reborn and cherished.

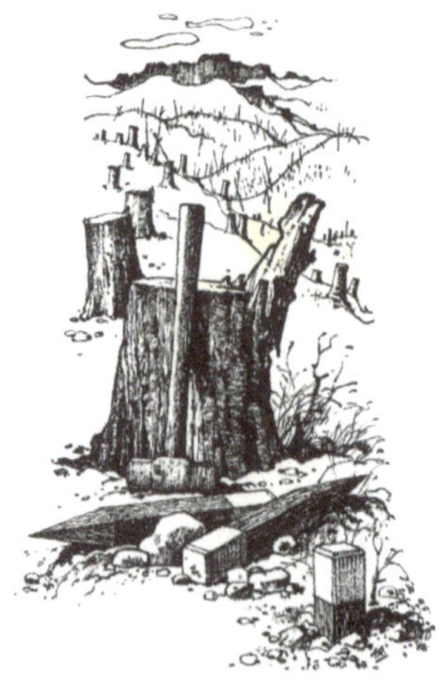

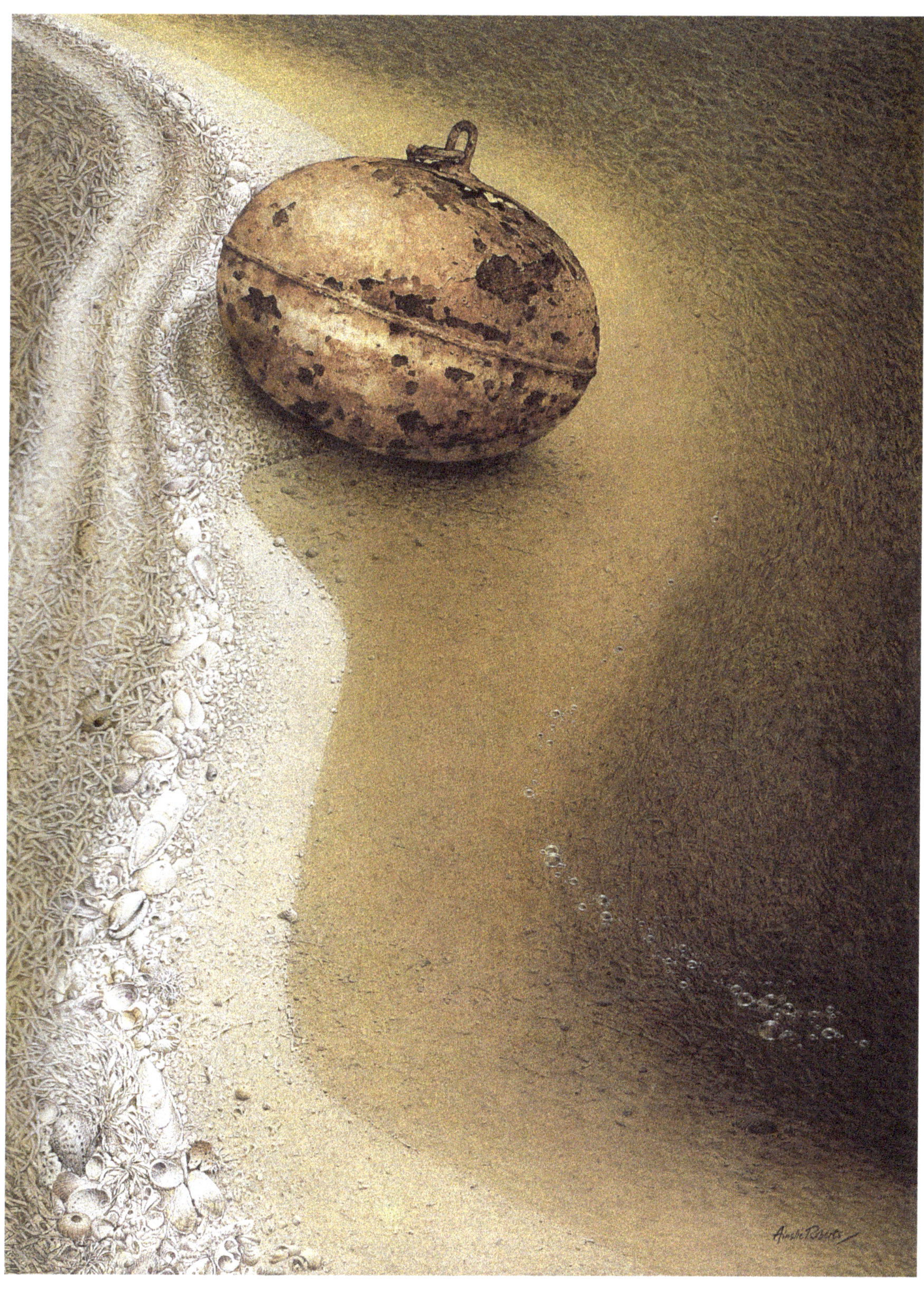

Private Collection.

ACKNOWLEDGEMENTS

A number of the myths in this volume are printed for the first time. Others have appeared in numerous versions over the past 140 years and every effort has been made to discover their origins. The fact that different tribes used variations of some basic myths, and that early European writers interpreted these in many different styles and ways, has made it difficult to ascertain the dates and authors of the first versions to be published in English. The sources listed are the earliest that can be traced, and we thank those who have granted permission to use such sources as reference. In some cases it has not been possible to trace either the author or the publisher of the original material. The debt to the Australian Aborigines, who originated and perpetuated these myths of their Dreamtime, is most gratefully acknowledged.

SOURCES

Australian Inland Mission Frontier Services. *The Storyteller.* 1976. Brewster, Mrs Edna. Adelaide, 1974.

Harney, W.E. *Tales from the Aborigines.* Robert Hale, London, 1959.

Lockwood, Douglas. *Northern Territory Sketchbook.* Rigby, Adelaide, 1968.

Looser, Hans. The Mountain oJ Death. Privately printed, Cooktown, n.d

McKeown, Keith C. *Land of the Byamee.* Randle House, Sydney, 1938.

Mathews, R.H. *Mythology of the Gundungurra.* Folk-Lore Society, London, 1909.

Peck, C.W. *Australian Legends.* Stafford & Co., Sydney, 1925.

Poole, G.G. *Leigh Creek.* Adelaide, 1946.

Robinson, Roland. *Aboriginal Myths and Legends.* Sun Books, Sydney, 1966.

Smith, W. Ramsay. *Myths and Legends of the Australian Aboriginals.* George G. Harrap, London, 1930.

Spencer, B. and Gillen, F.J. *The Northern Tribes of Central Australia.* Macmillan & Co. Ltd, London, 1904.

Taplin, Rev. George. *South Australian Aboriginal Folklore.* Adelaide, 1879·

Turner, R. *Australian Jungle Stories.* Northwood Press, Camperdown, Victoria, 1936.

Woods, J.D. (ed.). *The Native Tribes of South Australia.* E.S. Wigg & Son, Adelaide, 1879.

Dr CHARLES P. MOUNTFORD,
OBE, MA, D.Litt.(Adel.), Dip.Anthropol.(Cantab.), Hon.D.Litt.(Melb.).

The authors wish to record their appreciation to the memory of Dr Mountford, good friend and fellow wanderer, for his encouragement and patience; through his eyes the authors caught their own first glimpse of the magic and mystery of the age-old culture of the Australian Aborigines. The authors extend their thanks to Mrs Bessie Mountford, for her ready permission to use myth interpretations by her late husband, which appear on pages 20, 48, 50, 52, 58, 62, 74, 82,96,98, 100, 112, 120, 128, 134, 138.

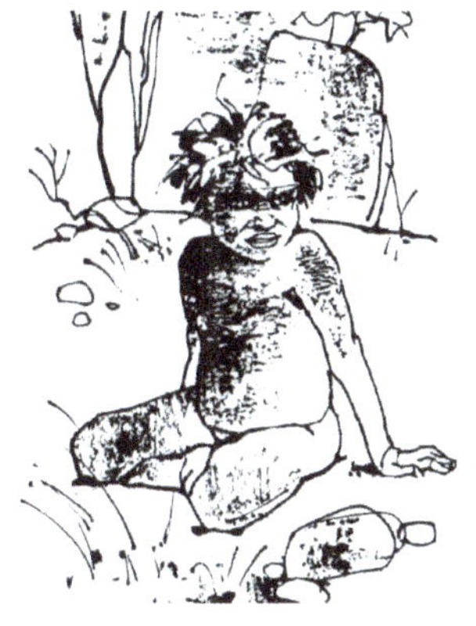